Dedicated to the memory of

Catherine Locks

A loving mother, devoted teacher and everlasting friend.
The world has grown colder without you.

I love you mama, and I always will.

BEHIND MY EYES

First edition. July 2, 2024.

Copyright © 2024 B. D. Lockwood.

ISBN: 979-8227907080

Written by B. D. Lockwood.

Behind My Eyes

B. D. Lockwood

Forward:

A friend of mine once said to me that, he thought I had all the makings of a great American author – and when I asked him why, he said:

"Because you're *depressed*, you're *Southern*, and you're an *alcoholic*."

I'm still not entirely sure if that was a compliment or not, but I liked it all the same.

This work is the natural byproduct of my own depression, and was penned roughly over the course of a year between the autumn and winters of 2022 and 2023 respectively.

Inside of these pages I will talk about myself and how life has affected me – how it has affected friends of mine – and how I have seen it affecting the people around me. I will discuss a wide variety of topics, ranging from issues of faith and anxiety to economics and politics. Some chapters will be presented from my own personal perspective, and others from a much broader one. Some will be very emotional, while others will be very statistical. It really just depends on the given chapter and how I felt when writing it.

I have never taken a creative writing course in my life, and in fact I've never even had a formal typestry lesson. I do not pretend to be a professional by any stretch of the imagination – only a man who is willing to speak his mind.

This book has been written less like a manual, guide or biography – and more like a conversation than anything else. Most of it is simply me... talking. Talking as if we were sitting in the same room together. There are some sections which are written quite flowery, if I'm honest – and there are others which use harsh language when I feel it is appropriate – but at no point is this book ever presented as being politically correct.

My goal, if I must have a goal, is to weave the thread of interrelation between the things being done in our society, and the consequences of those actions which are playing out across the world.

While I am, myself, both Christian and Conservative – this book has not necessarily been written with Conservatives and Christians in mind. Obviously my personal views are going to be reflected throughout this written work, and I make no bones about the fact that this book is adamantly anti-Liberal – but the real motivation for writing it did not come from a place of pure political interest.

It came from a human one.

The message that I am trying to convey is not one of "I am right and you are wrong," but rather it is to directly address the fact that every time I turn on the TV, or go watch a video on the internet, or listen to a broadcast on the radio – I hear Left-wing politicians telling me that everything in life is going just "fine." That we have nothing short of beautiful, perfect "progress" and that everyone is happy, healthy and better off for it.

The purpose of this book – the purpose of my message – is to ask the simple quest of: "Who the hell are you referring to?" Because unlike the social elite, I live in the real world – and life in the real world is pretty damn ugly these days.

I've taken the time to speak with so many people – not just from here in Georgia, or even the United States as a whole – but also from Canada, England, France, Germany, Australia and New Zealand – even some folks who are all the way over in Japan. I've spoken to friends and strangers alike – and while not all of us share the same beliefs, there is more often than not a running theme of mutual unhappiness.

An ability to agree that life today does not function the way we are being told that it does.

A lot of them have said that they feel as though they cannot talk about these issues openly – either because they feel uncomfortable voicing their feelings of discontent, or because they feel as though they lack the ability to articulate their concerns.

Those are the people that this book is for.

Maybe you will read my chapter on faith and relate to similar feelings that you have had or have witnessed in others. Maybe you will read my chapter on fear – which I suppose touches on anxiety and depression – and notices similarities with yourself or possibly someone close to you. Maybe you will relate in some small way to most of the frustrations and concerns that I express throughout this book. Maybe you will know somebody else who might relate to them as well.

If that is the case, this book is for you.

If you have ever felt voiceless, or powerless, or irrelevant – then this book is for you. If you have ever felt overburdened or weighed down or suffocated by life today – this book is for you.

And on behalf of my future critics, of which I'm sure there will be many, allow me to say that with this book being the first literary work I have ever created – there are going to be many things for you to critique. From layout and formatting, to general structure and grammatical errors, I'm sure you can have a field day.

But if you are going to read this work and willingly take my words out of context, or intentionally turn a blind eye to the problems I present herein – then *you* are part of the problem – and as far as I am concerned, will have invalidated yourself in the process.

Index:

Section I: Introduction

Introduction

Chapter I: Midnight

I'm not really sure what to write if I'm being honest. I have no idea where to begin or even how to get started.

I suppose I could write about the histories of the world, or the legends of Gods and men.

I could write about the utterly repugnant nature of current world politics – or the decaying state of civilization in the West.

Maybe I could write about the fact that there are still people – in the year 2022 – who genuinely believe that the Earth is actually flat.

I could write about anything. I could write about everything, but I can't.

Sitting here, alone, surrounded by the woodland symphonies of a midnight hour – with nothing to keep me company but a pack of cigarettes and an old worn out typewriter – I have the freedom to say whatever I want, and yet I cannot find the words to do so.

It's taken me well over two hours just to work up the courage to get this far – and I have absolutely no idea what I should say.

I guess the obvious answer is to talk about myself, but in that regard I think that it would be infinitely more entertaining to just describe the various stages of drying paint.

I suppose I feel as if I'm lost. As if life itself has somehow conspired against me.

I exist in a world where my value – the value of my entire life – has been reduced down to nothing more than the number of papers that carry my name on them.

Whether it's a High School Diploma or a G.E.D. – Certifications and College Degrees – paper upon paper that say I'm worth something instead of looking into my eyes and seeing for yourself.

It sickens me. It disgusts me – and what's worse is that it makes me feel disgusted with myself – because after hearing the same thing for so long, you start to believe it. It becomes this deeply internalized belief that you really are worthless and have no true value in life.

It's heartbreaking.

I grew up with the sort of principles and values that say a firm handshake and an honest word should be enough to get your foot in the door almost anywhere, but nowadays it seems like you can't even see the door without jumping through hoops – and I am not an acrobat.

At the time of writing this, I'm working three different jobs in order to make ends meet – but I can't hardly find a decent one – despite the fact that everybody keeps saying that they're desperate for employees, because I don't have that piece of paper.

I'm a good worker. A hard worker, but nobody cares. Nobody wants to give me the time of day – not for anything substantial.

Ironically, it would seem, that while paper is my problem – parchment is my only friend.

I don't really know what good this will do – or if it will do any good at all – but it's not exactly as if I have a whole lot of options left to me at this point so, I may as well just say what's on my mind. I may as well just go ahead and talk about all those things I said before – and more – but from my own perspective.

Whatever that may be.

I suppose if that's what I'm going to do, then I should start by pointing out that a frustration which I often experience is people telling me that I have no right to hold an opinion on the world, and on occasion, even the general goings-on in it.

I could not possibly begin to tally the countless number of times that I've been told that I am too young and have not lived enough or seen enough of the world to have a voice worth hearing. To have a concern worth addressing or even just a question worth answering.

So I guess the real question is, what exactly is it that I need to do or achieve in life for the world to finally find some value in me?

I am not even thirty yet, and so far in my life I have lived through the horrors of 9/11 and the subsequent War on Terror in both Iraq and Afghanistan. I have been alive to witness natural disasters such as hurricanes Katrina and Sandy, and experience their devastating impact on the country. I was here during the AIDS resurgence in the mid-2000s. I have seen the Internet grow from a relatively niche and novel concept – reserved only for the most technologically inclined individuals – into a global normality that can be found in even the most remote places around the world.

I have been alive for four distinct Presidencies of the United States of America – as well as three separate Popes in the Vatican.

In my lifetime the world has witnessed the deaths of famous and notable figures such as Ronald Reagan and Elizabeth Taylor, David Bowie and Muhammad Ali – as well as infamous and notorious ones such as Osama bin Laden and Saddam Hussein. Fidel Castro and Kim Jon-il.

I've been around to see the death of Queen Elizabeth the 2nd and the coronation of King Charles the 3rd.

I have lived through the nightmarishly vapid "pandemic" of COVID-19, which is an alarmingly mundane disease that inexplicably rendered the entire planet to a complete stand-still.

I've seen the manifestation, acceleration and ramifications of concepts such as weaponized Global Warming and mass Globalization.

I have seen the rise of Socialism in the West, and currently exist in an era of unparalleled political upheaval.

Hell, I've even seen a man named "Woman" of the Year.

So just how much more do I need for my opinion to be worth something? How much more experience in life is required in order for somebody to give a damn about what I have to say?

I live in a world where Big-Tech companies such as Apple, Google and Amazon can simply remove you and your business from the Internet grid without warning. Where Social Media companies like Facebook, Twitter and YouTube can censor and silence anyone on their platforms without any rhyme or reason – despite legal obligations to act as a digital town square.

I live in a world where non-partisan journalism no longer exists – and every major media company under the sun clashes in a constant struggle to be the dictator of what you are, and what you are not allowed to see, hear, or even think. Where news is no longer given to the public based on urgency or importance – but rather is curated like a menu of self-approved topics, and force-fed to you based solely on the political bias of whichever outlet you happen to subscribe to.

I live in a world where Free Speech has all but been abolished, and you can be charged with criminal activity for the great crime of praying in silence on a street corner.

A world in which the ATF can't manage to kick in a single door without shooting a small child.

A world where UK police need six armed officers to forcibly drag an autistic girl, crying and screaming from her own home and in front of her mother – for telling a lesbian that she looked like a lesbian.

Where scores of Canadian police brutally stomp on old women in wheelchairs and then publically mock the general citizenry for their inability to do anything about it.

I live in a world where the current sitting "President" of the United States openly lines his pockets with millions of dollars from China, funnels billions into foreign war while claiming neutrality – and leaves his own citizens abandoned and ignored in their times of need.

I live in a world of constant nightmare and aggression. A world seemingly on the verge of catastrophe. A world governed by the incapable and administered by the infirm.

A world where your entire life can be ruined by an off-handed remark you made twenty years ago – or by failing to fall in line with an ever-changing set of social rules and running narratives.

In short, I live in a world where you aren't allowed to live anymore.

So if that isn't enough to warrant a goddamn opinion, then I really don't know what is.

Chapter II: Memories

It is often that I feel as if my entire life were some kind of strange and unfortunate thing. Not because of the validity of my birth, or even the numerous hardships which I have faced – but simply because of the peculiar timing of my arrival. The autumn of '94 has slowly but surely proven to be the most unique position by which to find oneself between two completely different generations and times.

I am old enough to remember floppy disks and corded phones. When fashion consisted of nothing but brightly colored nylon jackets, flannel as far as the eye could see – or solid denim from head to toe – and when computers were just starting to truly become commonplace in the home, though even then they were really only intended for adults.

I can even remember the final days cassette tapes and the advent of the MP3 player – and I especially remember the thrill of capturing home movies with the family camcorder.

Our camera wasn't very fancy and could only record in black and white – but I can so distinctly recall the whirling sound of the gears as the VHS tape filled with the sights and sounds of everything I aimed to capture. I didn't have many tapes to play with mind you, so I must have worn the poor things out by constantly recording and re-recording over them with new movies.

I also remember when the VHS died out to DVDs. Maybe this is simple bias – but I still think those old tapes captured something special which has never been replicated.

I can remember when the internet was referred to as the "World Wide Web" and you had to dial in to connect with a phone line – as well as thinking that "High Speed" internet must have been an invention of the future.

Hell, I can even remember when cell phones were massive bricks that you had to carry around in a bag, plugging them into the cigarette lighter of your car in order to power it.

In short, I remember a simpler time – because I lived it – and I also lived and experienced the turning of the tide as the world grew more "advanced" and infinitely more complicated.

Looking back on it now, I suppose I feel as if my entire life has been lived out in the same, grainy black and white of those old tapes. I was just a baby during the war in Somalia and a child during Iraq and Afghanistan. I was too young to join service during any major conflict in my lifetime – and the hour is soon approaching where I will be considered too old to do so in the future.

I've noted before to myself and my friends that, in truth, I really feel as if I were somehow born between the couch cushions of life.

Too young for the generation before me, and yet, ever so slightly too old for the one that came after.

With my birthday falling at the end of the year, I started into school a little later than most of my peers. I was always one of the biggest boys in class, and yet always excluded from playing with the older children.

It made for a rather lonely life. In truth I think it's still a lonely life.

My only true form of comfort now are these words which I impress upon the page – and the beating chime of my typewriter as each sheet of paper becomes a canvas for my thoughts.

It's sort of sad really, but sitting here now, reflecting on my life in order to formulate the words I wish to use, I cannot help but to ponder just how much the world has changed – truly changed – and just how much it has changed me as well.

My life – up to and including this moment – has not been an easy one. I have witnessed violence and felt the cruel sting of it personally. I have stomached scorn and swallowed discontentment – but these things alone did not sully or dull the world in my eyes.

In spite of all my sufferings, I think it is entirely safe to say that I once possessed a lust for life when I was younger.

It is the modern world which has changed me. Shaped and molded me into the man I am today.

All of the beautiful colors run together before my eyes into a dull, ugly grey that coats the world like a layer of ash – and yet, I can remember...

I can remember a time where the soft morning breeze brushed against my cheek like a gentle embrace. When the chirping of the birds and the playful wildlife danced around me like my friends and neighbors.

When the bright and shining sun covered me in warmth during the day – and the delicate glow of the moon kept the shadows of the night from creeping in too close.

Through all of this monochrome haze, I can still recall such vivid memories of my youth.

There is one memory in particular, which I can see as clearly now as the day it happened:

It was the spring time in Georgia, and the April showers were falling. I was just a boy, maybe six or seven – and I had run outside in bare feet. The rain was not falling hard, but rather like a gentle sprinkling. I remember going around the back of my grandmother's house where the trees made a natural canopy – and there I saw it. A small, little stream of water was collecting in a little tiny that ran along the bottom of the hill. Like a little river, it collected fallen leaves which bobbed along the running water – and the yellow pollen bubbled and foamed along the sides.

I cannot recall how many hours I spent playing in that tiny little stream, but I did. By God I did. Walking up and down the length of it and hopping to and fro across it. Finding the tops of acorns and making them float along like miniature boats.

It was such a little thing. A simple thing. An unbelievably beautiful thing.

The pitter-patter of the rain and the trickling of the stream with the chirping of the birds all surrounding me in a symphony of wonderment and joy.

Though the misguided struggles of my country and the chaotic turmoils of the world at large have faded all my colors into grey – those simple, blissful moments still call to me with crystal clarity.

Like a long lost friend who's found his way home.

I miss him terribly.

I do not think that all this yearning and reflection can simply be boiled down to something as trivial as nostalgia – which is often the immediate response to something like this these days. No, I think it is more complicated than a simple case of warped perspective or "rose tinted glasses".

I have spoken with my mother and I've spoken with my grandmother. I have spoken with several older people that I know – either family or friends or various acquaintances that I have made over the years – and no matter what they have to say, ultimately there is a running theme throughout our conversations.

Things used to be different.

There never used to be all of this governmental interference in the life of private citizens. People didn't used to call the cops and file lawsuits over every mundane issue that they had. Folks used to be able to laugh with each other, and laugh even louder at themselves. The population used to be a lot more respectful towards each other in general – and I suppose, generally speaking – the whole world didn't feel as if there was some kind of invisible noose hanging around its neck.

There's always been problems. That's civilization for you. It's the condition of man to cause issues where he goes – but by and large, people used to be happier. They didn't used to be so angry and miserable all the time.

I can remember going out to the mailbox in the morning to fetch and paper and seeing my neighbor across the street getting his own – and he'd greet me. He'd say "Hello young man, how are you this morning?"

Now whenever I say good morning to a neighbor, they ask "What do you want?"

Things are just... different, and not in a good way.

Yes it's true that we've always struggled through wars. Yes, we've always had our problems with crime – but those issues weren't so rampant and... dare I say, casual, as they are today.

Now we talk about crime like it's just to be expected. We talk about war as if it's a thing of inconvenience. We talk about sex and drugs and violence, and everything else, as if it's somehow normal.

Because it has become normal.

And that's a very sad thing to me.

In my heart, and at the end of the day – I'm really just a simple man, yearning for a simpler time – and I doubt that I'll ever live to see it.

Me, Myself and I

Chapter III: Elephants on Parade

I can hear the autumn winds rolling slowly by my darkened window, and I wonder more and more now about the reasons that I have for writing this. I suppose it is because I feel, as I have said – voiceless – but that is not the entire reason. Not really.

Upon closer inspection, I would hazard to say that it is not merely a sense of having no voice with which to speak – but also that I feel as if I truly have no ears willing to listen.

I think a lot of people probably feel that way. Certainly a lot of people that I know – either in person or online – have expressed similar feelings of abandonment, isolation, rejection or... Well, just being generally overlooked and forgotten by the world.

Everything is always moving so fast now, and the issues of our times seem to just get bigger and more grandiose with each passing year. I think it's a small wonder that the average person feels neglected.

I'd say that modern politics plays a very large part in this problem. You can't turn around today without seeing or hearing something political – or being forced to listen to one politician or another pointing their finger and screaming at the top of their lungs about either how much they hate your guts and that you're the reason for everything wrong in the world – or about how much they love you and will tirelessly work to help you achieve a better life.

It's a never ending game of tug of war, and it's ripping people apart.

Ignoring the other side of the isle for a moment, I think that having a healthy sense of political affiliation is probably a good thing, at least in moderation. It's a thing that can bring like-minded people together and give the individual a sense that there really is some kind of pseudo "Big Brother" looking out for them – even if from a distance.

It makes you feel like you're a part of something – no matter how broad the definition of that "something" truly is.

But I don't think you really get that anymore. A person in office – whatever that office may be – who actually cares about the people they're supposed to be taking care of. Every couple of years you'll get some new guy or gal who comes along with a big bright smile and a smart-looking haircut, and they run a campaign about how much they love America and apple pie. About how traditional family values and a good Christian love of God makes the world go 'round – and about how no matter what, they are gonna fight for you and fight for your interests and blah, blah, blah, blah, blah.

It's bullshit.

Everywhere I turn I see "Conservative" politicians – the "NeoCons" as some call them – shaking their fists and barking their tired rhetoric, without actually doing anything to make a difference. They say whatever they need to say in order to please their constituents – but in the end, that really is all that they're doing. They're just saying something.

It's a bunch of people who are full of hot air and blowing smoke up your ass.

They're just talking heads on empty suits – and very, very few of them actually have any form of substance to their character.

Everybody seems to know it, and most people either try to accept it, or to just ignore it altogether.

Don't get me wrong, I think that there are still one or two politicians out there who do care – or at the very least do a good job of pretending to care – but by and large it's become a dog and pony show. A game of smoke and mirrors that turns its entire audience into nothing more than puppets on a string.

It's exhausting.

Now I'm not going to sit here and pretend that the world of politics has never been dirty, I mean, come on. Let's be honest with ourselves. The very nature of politics in and of itself is a thing to be reviled – but this current trend of constant smiles and open lies with fingers crossed behind every, single, back – is just so frustrating to me – and frustrating to a lot of others I'm sure.

Whatever happened to the days of "The Buck Stops Here"?

Whatever happened to the time when the press didn't want to make FDR look weak and feeble, so they actively attempted to make America look strong for once?

No, nobody wants to work together anymore. Take President Trump for example. I liked Trump. I thought he was a damn fine President. I wouldn't say that he was the "greatest" President in the history of the United States – but he was certainly the best I've seen in my lifetime. He came into office as the underdog and he managed to get done just about everything that he promised to do – but even then, he still couldn't do everything.

When Trump became President, the Republican party held both the House and the Senate. That should have meant synergy. That should have meant every single bill getting pushed through, and major, lasting changes getting put into place. It could have been a clean sweep for the nation – but what happened instead?

A pissing contest.

Numerous Republican officials across every level of federal involvement seemed unusually combative towards the President, both for the duration of his term in office and in the run-ups to the election cycles in 2016 and 2020 respectively.

We saw a marked increase in supposedly "Conservative" news outlets such as Fox becoming openly hostile – and instead of trying to show a sense of solidarity for the party, they began to pull the same stunts as Left-wing outlets like CNN. Editing video footage and intentionally skewing the facts in order to try and make the man look bad – which of course is laughable in the modern day, because with so many different avenues for information, anybody can just go watch the full unedited footage of pretty much anything and see that it didn't happen the same way that it was presented to you.

Let's not even talk about all the problems that he faced from the opposition – no right now I'm talking about the fucking Republicans. We're supposed to be the "Grand Old Party" and instead of acting like that, with all of their dignity and distinguishment – they just devolved themselves into a bunch of school children having a dick measuring competition.

It made me sick. It was pathetic – and it's no wonder that we ended up losing in the 2018 midterms – and it's also no wonder that we really didn't see that supposed "Red Wave" surge back in with the 2022 mid-terms either.

The whole party's just become so laughably dysfunctional. It's just pitiful.

The more I think about, the angrier I get – and the angrier I get, the more I want to just stand up and say "Fuck you!" to everybody who keeps tugging on their privates instead of doing their goddamn job.

You know, I liked Governor Kemp when he first ran for office, but he's done nothing to help protect Georgia's Heritage Foundations and historical monument sites. Governor DeSantis seems to be doing an O.K. job down in Florida from what I can tell, but he also turned around and bit the hands that fed him, so I know he's not particularly loyal or trustworthy.

I think about people like Dan Crenshaw. Now there was a man I had a lot of respect for. Served his country with honor, and seemed to have a pretty good head on his shoulders – but he made all the same claims about fighting for this and fighting for that, and when pressed on serious issues like Section 230 – he'd just lock up and dodge the question without even trying to answer it.

Then of course you have scumbags like Christie and Pence, running up and down the country telling everybody that it's everyone else's fault for everything going wrong and for nothing getting done.

The list just goes on, and on, and on – one after another, after another, after another.

I could sit here all night and write about each and every one of them – but I don't have the time for that, and neither do you.

Suffice it to say however, that I am not happy. A lot of people aren't happy.

And I think that that's a problem.

I honestly think that it's one of my biggest problems. One of my biggest issues and concerns. I can't say that I really feel as if there's anyone out there who actually cares about me. As if I have any kind of connection or avenue by which to feel a sense of genuine political solidarity or representation. I just feel so estranged from my own political party. I feel so utterly ostracized in the current sea of upheaval, as the battle-lines are drawn and the greater political shift cements itself into the staunch, two-party system of today

– forever abandoning the quasi four-way split of Conservatives and Republicans versus Liberals and Democrats of America's yesteryear.

That really was a thing you know, at one point in time – when you used to be able to find more Liberal leaning Republicans and Conservative leaning Democrats – but you can't do that anymore. No, today it has to be black and white. Everything's split straight down the middle with no wiggle room and no more ground to give.

The Libertarian and the Centrist are all but dead, even if many would try to claim otherwise – and the Authoritarian? Well, he's doing just fine. All the proof you need is to look around at the world.

The whole thing is just an ugly mess – and it's only getting uglier with each passing day.

I would assume that by now it has become inherently clear that I consider myself firmly Republican in my beliefs. I've always leaned Right. I'm always going to lean Right. I've always been Conservative – but the fact of the matter is that I simply feel no sense of dedication from my party.

Not a lack of my dedication to them, but in their dedication to me.

And with the political system having turned into what it is – there's really no options available for a person to try and get around it. I know how bad the Democrats are. I'd have to have Satan on the ballot before I thought about voting for one of those jokers – but what's really my alternative? A bunch of lazy, self-serving RINOs who can't be bothered to do anything? At best, some of them work up the energy to drag their feet in Congress – but half the worst bills that get passed are absolutely covered in Republican signatures – with little to no effort in trying to stop it either.

It's infuriating.

It's infuriating because I don't feel like I'm voting for the right party – I feel like I'm voting for the lesser of two evils. Like yeah, you're both going to rob me – but at least this guy isn't going to rape me while he does it.

That doesn't fill me with a sense of pride. That doesn't make me feel like I'm a part of something bigger or that I can place my faith in someone to help look out for me.

It just makes me sad.

It makes a lot of people sad.

And I don't like that.

So please, indulge me if you will, to pull back this curtain of self-reflection – free from the trudgery of meaningless political commentary – to talk about who I am, how I am and what exactly it is that I want.

Concretely Conservative by nature, the Republican side of the political isle is obviously what appeals the most to me – but as I've said, in recent years I find that it feels so increasingly strange and alien to the point that it's become a thing I cannot wrap my head around. A thing I can't relate to.

At first I wanted to say that so many of the men and women who are supposedly representing Republican ideals seem less like people, and more like examples of living claymation. The sort of thing you'd see in the old movies that Ray Harryhausen worked on. But the more I think about it, the less I like that description. For all its shaking, jittering and eerie qualities – at least the clay is real. It's something physical, it's something that can be felt. No, the more I think about it, I suppose a more apt description of the current "Republican" is something akin to a work of animation like our modern CGI. It's nothing real, it's simply hollow. A fake. A facade. A series of ones and zeroes masquerading as an object instead of actually existing.

I can't relate to that.

In fact the only thing I really have left to relate to at this point, is nothing more than their vacant claim of being "Conservative".

So I suppose that begs the question: What does it actually mean to be Conservative? Truly, genuinely Conservative – not some narrative description or stereotype seen on the internet or TV.

Well, if the old Left-winger mantra is that the government must do for the people what the people cannot do for themselves, then I suppose I would say that the Right-wing equivalent is the belief that the people must do for themselves without becoming dependent upon the government.

It's that whole "Ask not what your country can do for you" mentality – and it's a good mentality, I feel. It's a responsible and self-sufficient mentality.

The problem, as I see it, really starts when it becomes an isolationist mentality – where you won't say anything or do anything or have any kind of expectations whatsoever – to the point that you let the world walk all over you. Where you won't stand up and defend your good name anymore.

I'm not just tired of my representatives in the Republican party – I'm tired of my fellow Republicans and Conservatives just twiddling their thumbs and letting everybody else take advantage of them. They call us Nazis. They call us warmongers. They call us racists and bigots and sellouts – and now they're even calling us shills for Vladimir Putin – and

we don't do anything. We just lie down and take it. Like a whipped dog taking another beating.

Well I'm not going to do that. I'm not going to just sit here and let a bunch of people tell me what I believe, when it's clear that they have absolutely no idea what it is that I believe in.

I asked a Liberal friend of mine what it is that he believes in, and he pretty much regurgitated the word the same shit that we see happening everywhere in the country. But then I asked him what he thought that Conservatives believe in, and he almost turned my hair white with the crazy things he said.

He had no idea what we believed in. None of them do, because they're too wrapped up in their own echo-chamber to find out – and almost nobody over here on our side is taking the time to try and educate them.

So I guess I'll take a whack at it, for whatever good it will do.

I think that it's fairly safe to say that by virtue of being American, I am already inherently more Liberal than my Conservative counterparts in other countries around the world.

I take a very hard stance against drugs, but I'm also not about to call the cops on somebody who's sitting on their own back porch and smoking a joint at two o'clock in the morning. I won't pretend to understand somebody who's gay, but I also wouldn't want to chop their head or see them imprisoned off just because they like to stick a dick up their ass.

I think whatever two people get up to behind closed doors and on their own property – so long as they're both consenting adults – is their business, not mine. Unless, of course, you go out of your way to make it my business by telling me about it – in which case I will let you know exactly how I feel – regardless of whether it's you and your boyfriend, you and your girlfriend, you and your boyfriend's girlfriend, or whatever that weird shit is that you did with the handcuffs and "french tickler" last week.

No, to me, Conservatism is exactly that. It's a form of ideological conservationism – an attempt to conserve a traditional and dignified way of life. That's why so many of these horror stories about Conservatives that you hear today just baffle me. The running idea that we're money grubbing bastards that love "Corporate America" and hate small business owners and the "Mom & Pop" stores – or that we're anti-environmental and want to cover the world in concrete until nothing green can grow.

It's utterly absurd.

American small towns and rural communities are exactly what Conservatives fight to protect. It's what I fight to protect.

I've spent my whole life in the woods. Walking barefooted across the hills and fields. Stopping in at the same local corner store and seeing the same local faces, day in and day out. I don't ever want to see an end to that.

Most people that I know who would consider themselves to be Conservative, really just want to be left alone so they can live their life as best that they can. With the aside of one or two prominent social issues – typical Conservatism is really just about keeping your head down and carrying on.

I suspect that if people could just manage to talk to each other again, they might find that they have some form of common ground – or at the very least, some kind of common understanding.

I don't believe in same-sex marriage, as the concept of marriage has been a sacred union between a man and a woman for as long as human beings have held spiritual practices – yet at the same time, I think that it was both criminal and wrong that the way in which the old Civil Unions and Common-Law partnerships were, legally speaking, inferior to marriage in the eyes of the Federal Government. Denying people involved in those relationships the same level of benefits and insurances that would otherwise be given to someone else.

I think abortion is wrong, and certainly criminal in most cases. I do not in any way support it as a method of birth control or as a means for people to shirk their obligations and try to get out of taking responsibility for their actions. But I also believe that, in some cases – such as a critical choice between the life of the baby or the life of the mother – that it is ultimately a decision for the parent, or parents, to decide for themselves.

It is their decision to make, in moments like that, about what is right for them.

I believe in the 2nd Amendment of the Constitution. I believe it is the right for all free citizens of these United States to own and carry a firearm – if they so choose. I also believe, as a gun owner myself, in sensible and responsible gun ownership. I believe it is a person's right to purchase as many firearms as they want – but I personally don't agree with a needless excess of weapons. You know what I mean. The underground bunkers that form a veritable armory of wall-to-wall guns and ammunition. I'm not going to say that people shouldn't be allowed to own their guns – but for myself, I find that level of "enthusiasm" over firearms to be distasteful.

I am an advocate for hunters and outdoorsmen, though I personally do not hunt myself – but I absolutely despise the killing of animals for "sport." I have no problem whatsoever with someone bagging a deer if it is their intention is to take it home and harvest it for food – but if you're the sort of person who only shot that deer so that you could get your photo on the cover of some fucking magazine – then frankly, I'd like to see your carcass strung up over the bed of that truck instead.

These are just a few of my core values and stances. Stances that most folks I know would agree with – and yet as I look around, I really don't see a whole lot of representation for these values. I don't really see the majority of our duly elected officials actually following through on their promises to stand up for things like these.

And what's worse, is that I rarely – if ever – see my fellow Conservatives standing up and holding those same officials accountable for the fact that they haven't held up their end of the bargain. When the guy you voted for decides to go on vacation while half your entire state is out of power because of hurricanes or snowstorms – you need to damn well tell him that he's a sorry son of a bitch.

There's too many people who are willing to just sit back and take it on the chin these days. Too willing to just be complacent in their disappointment, and never bother to raise some Cain about it.

I can't necessarily say that I blame them exactly – because I'm not the kind of person by nature who wants to deal with any of that myself – but

I'm at the point where I feel like I have to start saying something because otherwise... Nothing's ever going to change.

I consider myself to be a very traditional man in pretty much all aspects of my life – save for a few – and that obviously includes political inclination.

I like the traditional Republican.

The Ronald Reagan or Richard Nixon Republican. The button-down, tucked shirt Republican. The way they talk, the way they walk, the way they move their hands and the words that they choose – these are the tried and true established appearances which appeal the most to me.

It may not even be relegated to Republicanism per se, but rather the general appeal of old-time, "traditional" and professional politicians.

Ignoring for a moment the deeper meaning behind his words – I noted during the 2020 election that I liked the way Joe Biden spoke. Keeping in mind that he fumbled his words *slightly* less back then – the manner in which he spoke – not the message, but the manner, appealed to me.

The same can be said for the recent GOP debate which saw former Vice-President Mike Pence speaking to the crowd. I do not care for Mike Pence. I recognize him as a corrupt fraud – but again, ignoring this for a moment – I liked what he said and I liked how he said it. The words he chose, the tones he used, the stances he took. It seems very clear to me that, had I never done any research into the man – he would be exactly what I want in a President.

When I think of a Republican, or the broader Conservative in general – I picture Red Foreman, the father character from an old television program from the 1990s called That 70s Show. I picture a man who knows how to drink, enjoys a cold beer and knows how to throw them back at a celebration – but isn't a slosh, and is never seen in a drunken stupor. I picture a man that might smoke a cigarette with his morning coffee or while sitting down after tending to the lawn, but doesn't indulge in excesses. A man who knows how to fight, but isn't inclined towards violence.

He's a man who knows his own worth and takes a hard stance on his values. A man who can be stern, can be crass, can be wise – and can even be elegant when he wants to be.

When I think of a Conservative or I think of a Republican – that's what I picture in my head. A traditional, red-blooded, blue collar, American man.

That is what appeals to me. That is the sort of man I'd like to envision myself as – though in truth I think that I am a little too brooding to fit the bill.

I recognize that today's modern world dictates a necessity for change. It demands a shifting of principles, and new approaches to the radicalized opposition of the times. An opposition which, if I'm being honest, exists because of that old-school Conservative mentality.

The idea of being the "Silent Majority" or, being the "bigger man" and not lowering yourself to the level of the other party by holding on to some standard of public decorum, and carrying yourself with a sense of calm, quiet dignity.

"Never discuss Politics and Religion with your friends and family."

It's a good mindset to have in my opinion – but the problem is, that while you sit quietly at the dinner table, it's the other guy that's having his voice heard.

In effect it is a policy of inaction – and inaction is an action, in and of itself.

That's why I think we're in the position that we find ourselves in today. Too many generations raised on the idea of being too modest, too humble and too reserved in their points of view, have allowed the other side to take power – because they do not concern themselves with those same kinds of restraints.

That is why modern politics demand a changing of the guard. It calls for new blood in the Conservative party and the abandonment of "Establishment Republicans" in favor of younger, more outspoken, more fervent figures to shake the cobwebs off of the party.

I recognize the need for that, but it still isn't what appeals to me.

Maybe I have just admitted to myself and to you, that what appeals to me, does not necessarily work. It should, in theory, if both teams were playing by the same rules – but they don't – and so it doesn't.

If you're playing a game of soccer and one team adheres to the rule of not touching the ball with their hands, but the other team picks it up and runs with it anyway – you're not really playing the same game. You're just going through the motions. The only way to make it fair is to either force the other team to follow the rules – or to accept that they won't, and then break the rules yourself.

That seems to be where politics have gotten to today.

And I don't like it.

I've always spoken very critically of the political Left – and rightly so – as I cannot swear that in my lifetime I have ever experienced their intentions, actions and consequences as anything other than actively detrimental at worst, or openly ineffective at best. Yet in reality, I think that it is more the extremist nature that their party is so inclined towards which bothers me the most.

Truthfully, I think it is the nature of extremism in general that really scares me. Which is a real problem – because that is one of the biggest issues that we're dealing with today.

Now do not mistake me for a fool. The problems of extremism can be found on both sides of the political isle – and everywhere in between for that matter – but when it comes to the chief, ideological principles of Conservatism versus Liberalism – which side do you truly believe condemns and denounces extremist factions, and which side condones and encourages them?

In a perfect world, each side would be responsible for the skeletons in their own respective closets. For the wayward members of their individual flocks that have wandered too far afield.

When radicalized, far-Right leaning extremist organizations pop up – it is up to the Conservative to shut them down.

I recall an incident in which myself and some friends were attending a social gathering for Confederate History Month – which is a time in many Southern states to honor the soldiers which fought for the South during the American Civil War – as well as to witness reenactments of historical battles, attend demonstrations of civilian life at the time – and generally learn more of our own local history and share in the collective keeping of Southern heritage.

And though it may seem strange to some of you from other parts of the country – people from all walks of life will eagerly attend these events and festivities hosted throughout the state.

It's a staple of our culture.

But the reason that I bring it up, is because during one of these events, a group of Klansmen showed up to spout their typical inbred rhetoric of white hate, white supremacy and white-everything else that goes along with it.

And we had to move them along.

Here we were, a group of young men with Confederate flags on our caps – brawling with a bunch of miscreants and sending them back to whatever shit hole they crawled out of.

That's the way it should be. When somebody comes along to cause trouble and to ruin your good name – you run them off. You don't allow the rotten apple to spoil the bunch.

Liberals on the other hand, believe that every apple is unique and should be accepted for what it is – so long as it aligns with whatever their political agenda happens to be at the time. They don't remove it like they should, and instead they insist on leaving it in the basket to spoil everything else. The very nature of their ideology prohibits their ability to self-govern and self-manage their own party.

Extremist factions run rampant on the Left. ANTIFA, BLM, any number of groups surrounding the LGBT, and more.

Men shot dead in the street for wearing Make America Great Again hats, being met with overwhelming cheers of approval both live on the scene and across the internet. Public figures calling for the endless march of destruction which stormed throughout American cities during the summer of 2020. Celebrities making open threats against the life of a sitting President, to the roar of a crowd. Children being groomed in schools and exposed to public displays of adult nudity and sexual conduct, while being encouraged to hide it from their parents.

These are just some of the realities of our world today. These are just some of the reasons why modern politics have become so vitriolic and hungry for aggressive, and bombastic action. It is a thing which is necessitated by the boiling temperature of our times – and that is why I do not shy away from it.

I both recognize and embrace the need for change, so that our country may effectively combat these extremist ideals.

I accept this, but I still do not *like* it.

I don't like that this is where we're going – or more to the point – that this is where we've gotten to. I don't like that it has come down to nothing more than a "he said, she said" back and forth shit-show. I don't like that every single issue that comes down the pipe has to be massively blown out of proportion and used for political clout – while the real issues of the modern world are being openly ignored.

If you stop and think about it critically, the inherent differences between Conservatism and Liberalism are really quite mundane. Pushing morals and ethics to the side for a minute – the Conservative minded person is the sort of guy who's going to stay in on a rainy night and read a book – while the Liberal minded guy is going to go out dancing in the rain.

There's nothing inherently wrong with either one of those two things. In fact, the truth is that both sides actually need each other – because the Liberal is supposed to keep the Conservative moving so that he doesn't become too stagnated – and the Conservative is supposed to be able to reel the Liberal back in, and keep him from walking off the side of a cliff.

The problem comes from everything else that gets added onto it – and gets even worse when nobody is actually willing to do anything about it.

I would personally like to see the temperature cool. I would like to see a little less talking and a little more action. I would like for somebody to finally stand up, do their job and draw a line in the sand because if we don't – thing's are going to continue spiraling out of control. And if things continue spiraling out of control – then the only thing we're going to see is more extremism.

I don't want to see the inevitable reaction of tomorrow as a direct consequence to the already radicalized actions of today.

I don't want to see American cities and communities get turned into that little town from Footloose, where music is outlawed and dancing is illegal. Where books are burned with zealous enthusiasm and children want to kill themselves.

I don't wanna be here to witness this unhinged, pseudo-socialist and totalitarian dystopia that we're currently heading for, get swapped out for some post-apocalyptic, authoritarian state in the opposite extreme.

Because that is how the pendulum swings. Once that momentum starts building, you have to be willing to reach in and catch it, or else the glass is going to shatter – and all you'll be left with is broken pieces.

Excess begets excessiveness – and extremism begets more extremism.

If things don't start to change soon – that's exactly what this country's heading towards.

Chapter IV: A Question of Faith

I like to think that I am a goodly man. A Godly man. A man who stands his ground and never shakes from what he believes in, despite how much of a struggle it may be to do so.

I like to think that in spite of my flaws – of which there are many and far too numerous to count – that I am still a man somehow worth admiring.

I like to think about these things – but I do not feel them. Not really. Not truthfully, deep down in my soul.

I am proud to call myself Catholic – no, perhaps proud is not the term. Honored, I think, is the word that I would use. Honored to be a part of something so ancient and storied. Honored to have been blessed with the opportunities to see the beautiful Cathedrals and feel a sense of utter majesty tending to my spirit in such glorious places of worship.

To tread upon the Monastery grounds, feeling their cobblestones beneath my feet and viewing the Monks as they go about their work – taking in the serenity and the silence of its splendor in the truest and most blissful peace.

These are some of the things which I have been honored to experience in my life – things which I cannot even begin to do justice in the medium of words. Things which have touched me, changed me, and given my troubled conscience the most beautiful peace of mind – and yet if I'm being perfectly honest, I cannot recall the last time that I actually attended Mass.

I often feel so empty inside – so lost and unable to see – that I think somewhere along the way I'd simply given up trying.

My conviction in my faith is unquestionable – but I often feel as if, somehow, my faith's conviction in myself is lacking. Theologically speaking, I am without issue – but spiritually I feel forgotten, and alone. Abandoned by God, the Almighty, our Lord – or whatever you care to call him.

I've heard it referred to as the "Dark Night of the Soul" - but I fear that my single night has become a life sentence.

The world in which I now reside often berates me for being a man of faith. I am scorned on a near daily basis for the great crimes of being born a man – and understanding that I am as such. For being Southern, and taking pride in my heritage. For being heterosexual, as well as for consciously abstaining from sexual activity until marriage.

And quite disturbingly for being White – a condition, in and of itself, which is now often viewed as an offense of the highest caliber.

I am terrified by the prospect of a world governed by fear – and that is exactly the kind of world I find myself living in.

A world in which all human thought must comply with one-sided political ideas, or be denounced as some form of "ist", "ism" or "phobic". A world in which all forms of communication have broken down, despite the ability to communicate with anyone, anywhere and at any given time.

It is a world withdrawn into itself – a world of regression.

It is my world, and I hate it.

It saddens me that faith has become something so lost and forgotten. A concept that is more and more mocked and ridiculed as time goes on. Unquestioningly there are many people who are still practitioners of faith – in one form or another – and many more devout than myself, yet it is also true that there are still more who despise the very notion of it, even to an obsessive degree.

In many ways it's ironic, the almost evangelical nature in which an aggressive atheist can whip himself into a zealous frenzy over the prospect of denouncing the existence of God – and the sad and extreme lengths he will often go to in order to belittle you and your intelligence for believing in such a thing. All the while speaking with the same passion and fervor of a Biblical preacher.

It's truly... unsettling.

It is also unsettling that we seem to live in a society which cultivates these kinds of attitudes, like a farmer tending his crop. We nurture and grow each new generation to be more adamant and vitriolic than the last. Always striving for a harsher and more jaded civilization, until the day that God and faith have been erased from history.

People attacking religious houses and communities. People desecrating religious icons in their attempt to show their hatred and mockery of our very existence.

A friend recently directed me to a web page that showed a woman using a copy of the Holy Bible as the mounting bracket for her... *toy*. I've seen that sort of thing before. Choices like that aren't accidents, they're decisions – and from everything I've seen it's apparently a rather popular trend. Even when the content isn't pornographic in nature I've come across numerous videos of people tearing the pages out of bibles and using them for toilet paper or for rolling joints.

It's atrocious.

It appears to me that no matter where I look, the fundamental principles of religious institutions are assaulted and assailed – not just from the outside, but also from within. The very walls of the Vatican itself are darkened by the long shadows of a "Pope" that seems determined to unravel the theological tapestries of the church, and to dismantle the very foundations of her most sacred traditions.

Even my fellow Christians don't seem too enthusiastic about practicing what they preach these days, or even defending their own religious beliefs for that matter. I know that I am a failure in many ways, but at least I try to adhere to my teachings. After all, that's what it means to be a Christian.

To be a Christian does not mean that you are automatically better than anybody else, or that you are somehow guaranteed a "free ticket" to Heaven just by virtue of being baptized. It does not mean that your life is perfect or that you are somehow infallible – but rather it means that you should try and strive for a perfection that you know you cannot reach, because you are human and you are flawed.

To be a Christian is to recognize that you are going to fail, but that in spite of that failure, you continue to try and live your life as best that you can – and you do your damnedest to try and be a good person in the process.

I just don't think there's a whole lot of good left in the world these days.

No, the world I live in has grown so increasingly antagonistic and hateful as we move ourselves further and further from God – and it's becoming so difficult to feel as if my head is actually above water, when everywhere I turn I am met with hatred and derision for something so simple as existing.

And it's not simply a question of faith – but also one of ethics and morality in the modern day, and the ways in which these things are broken and shattered with disturbing levels of increased enthusiasm.

I don't just mean the subjective level of these concepts – the wrist slapping and brow-beating of somebody allowing their child to stay up late and watch a movie that you wouldn't approve of, or to let them play some kind of violent or otherwise graphic video game that you think they're too young for – but I mean the objective level of morals and ethics. The true, unwavering black and white – the clear cut cases of right and wrong.

From the social normalizing of slander and dishonesty, to the intrinsic need for shirking any form of personal accountability. From the complete lack of hesitation in inflicting harm onto others, to the perverse fetishism of violence and the predatory targeting of children.

It's the way in which the modern world not only celebrates, but encourages these celebrations of hatred, foulness, and destruction. From the people barging into Christian prayer circles to laugh maniacally as they describe with twisted glee, the gory and graphic details of their latest abortion – to the rampant violence and slaughter of kids in schools, which is then glorified in the news and gives madmen their moment of fame.

It is a thing of chaos.

It is an ugly thing. It is a pitiful and disturbing thing – when hedonism and debauchery are openly embraced with a sense of reckless abandon – reveling in the growing state of self-destruction that we find ourselves in.

It is the oldest sins, in the newest ways.

And I do not know how much more I can take.

It truly feels as if God has abandoned me – or more rather, abandoned us as a species.

As if some unknown and incomprehensible thing is waiting for us, just out of sight on the horizon. As if simultaneously, all the while mankind is sitting around and screaming its head off – everyone is also holding their breath; waiting for the other shoe to drop.

For the bomb to go off.

I am so utterly afraid of what might happen – and even more so of the blind eye that humanity will turn to it if it does happen. So many lessons from our past have been forgotten now... it almost seems pointless to try and hope for a better future.

I often wish that I could just end it all. That I could open my veins like the ancient Romans in the days of old, and say goodbye to the whole damn thing – but I cannot bring myself to do it.

Either for fear over the repercussions of my soul – or some hollow sense of duty to my life – I cannot do it.

Chapter V: Fear

Maybe these embittered ramblings are pointless. Maybe I'm simply expecting too much of the world when I ask that it remain decent and grounded.

Maybe, the fault is really mine after all. Maybe I expect too much or ask too many questions.

Maybe all of this is just some vain attempt to subvert the overwhelming perception of doubt and dread that hangs about me like a noose – or the petrifying sense of fear which covers me like a shroud – smothering me with its cold and clinging embrace.

I am afraid.

I'm afraid of the world that my family is leaving me in because it has grown so strange and unhinged in recent years.

I'm afraid of what will happen to me if I cannot find success in the things that I do and I'm afraid of the expectations if I do in fact succeed.

I'm afraid of what will happen after my grandmother passes away, and of not being able to support my own mother who is currently in poor health.

I'm afraid to try and realize my dreams of starting a family – because I am afraid of bringing new life into a world that I cannot stand or recognize.

I'm afraid of the way people look at me. Of how they perceive me.

I'm afraid of the thoughts they might be thinking – and frankly I'm afraid of the thoughts that never cross their mind.

It is though I am standing frozen in terror, gazing upon an as of yet unopened door; dreading the unseen horrors which lurk on the other side.

I am afraid of being alive – and I am afraid of what comes next.

Dark and dismal have been my thoughts of late. The all too familiar malaise has once again settled upon me like rain settles in upon the morning meadow.

My typical brooding cycle coils around me and repeats itself – as it always does. Shadows of my past seem to slither across the walls with cruel fangs and barbed claws with which they heap themselves upon my castle bower. Endlessly hurling their malice and discontent against the crumbling

bastille of my mind.

Words fall out in chaotic mutterings from my mouth, yet flow like honeyed wine upon the page.

Damned am I, and damned is my blackened soul in these abysmal hours when my mind may not rest and rage boils in my veins – pumped ever onward by an aching and bitter heart.

Happiness, joy and pleasure are nothing but foreign concepts to me now. Whenever I close my eyes, I am plagued by visions of torment and frustration – and when I do open them again, I see that my world is black.

Like a great cosmic void, my world is black.

Long have I stared into that empty, rotting abyss – and long has it drawn from me all that might make a man human.

I feel no warmth, only cold. I feel no rest, only weary. I feel no love, only... Nothing.

I used to love.

I used to love things.

I used to love meeting new people. I used to love tasting new foods and experiencing new cultures – but oftentimes I now look at my fellow man and find myself filled with nothing short of suspicion and contempt.

Frankly, I have often suspected those feelings to be mutual – even if I know that they are not.

My formal education may be lacking, but my intellect is superb. Saying it out loud leaves a sour taste in my mouth – and I do not intend in any way to be boastful – but the sentiment is true. I know that I am not stupid.

Most of the people I'm related to are unable to appreciate my mind or my interest. My thoughts or my feelings. Most of them can't even appreciate my lexicon, and usually I am forced to subdue my own vocabulary for the benefit of those around me.

Still, even I will admit that this strange and romantically fanciful form of poetic verbiage – which seems to spring forth so freely during these darkened moods of mine – does seem rather odd and out of place in the modern world.

Maybe I'm going mad – or maybe I'm drifting off into some other place far, far away from here.

Whatever it is, I just don't understand why it has to hurt so much.

The bleakest thoughts are upon me now. Gloom turns to sadness, sadness to sorrow – and sorrow into despair.

The walls are closing in on me. I must get out for a while.

Chapter VI: Cherry Red

It is the next morning now and I have returned to my typewriter. I will not say that I have slept peacefully, as all manner of thoughts from last night continue to spiral in my head – but I will say that my mind seems somewhat clearer on what it is I wish to say – at least for the time being.

I left the house around eleven I think. My poor old truck isn't good for much – but a midnight drive through the winding county roads so late at night practically assured my desired solitude.

The sky was mostly cloudless and the moon was bright. How deeply it was that I wished to shed the trappings of this repugnant human body and roam free amidst the forest, howling at the moon with no sense of care or concern to impede me.

My windows were down and the wind whipped rather violently through my hair. On occasion I would see one or two other cars pass me by and I could not help but to wonder if they too were like me. Lost souls roaming the darkened countryside in search of some surrogate means of running away.

Eventually I did make my way into town. I had passed it by at least twice, driving on aimlessly for what seemed like the better part of an hour. An admittedly indulgent waste of gasoline, especially in this economy – and something that under any normal circumstances I would absolutely never permit myself to do – but tonight I was not in the mood to care.

I ended up stopping into a diner on the outskirts of town and ordered a rather unremarkable meal. The place itself was anything really worth writing home about, just one of the greasy spoons attached to a truck stop. The small town of Byron's only real claim to fame is the fact that it has an interstate running through it.

It must have been about 1:00 am or so – maybe a little after – by the time that I finished and went next door to the gas station to get a cup of coffee and some more cigarettes. I stood outside the building; beneath a flickering, half-dead street light as I smoked and took in the cold night air. I will admit that despite writing these events down as soon as I returned home – I cannot exactly recall what was on my mind as I watched the trucks roll slowly into the commercial lot behind the station. I'm sure it must have been some pitiful dream of striking out on my own and leaving all of this pain and heartache behind me. Burning every bridge, and never coming back.

Little did I know however, that while I was somewhere off in a dream – I was being watched by someone else.

Before I even knew what was happening, I had been approached by a creature of the night. Her beauty had been paled by age and the life she must have lived, but she was beautiful. Her hair was long and dark like her eyes, and her lips were full and painted red. Her skin was a sort of pallid ocher – presumably from conducting most of her business after dark.

I remember exactly what she said to me as she walked up:

"Are you lonely baby? You look like a man in need of some company."

I remember it, because that must have been the single most cliched thing that I have ever heard in person – but when a woman who looked like she did says something like that to you in the darkness of night – it does stir a certain fire in the blood.

And she did certainly seem well-versed in stoking the flames.

Still, I did decline. She didn't give up easily however – asking if I was sure and openly noting that I looked a bit sad. In her defense I suppose I probably did, given the deeping black that has filled my mind of late – but I continued to decline her offer.

For whatever reason, she ended up sticking around and we even began talking. I'm not entirely sure why she didn't just move on – maybe she thought that I was an easy mark and that she could eventually wear me down – or maybe she just didn't feel completely safe with the truckers down the hill. I suppose I'll never really know for sure.

I'm also not quite sure exactly how or even when it came up, but she did tell me her name was Rosa. She told me several different things that I admit I didn't pay much attention to – except at one point she mentioned how she loved to sing, and that she had always dreamed of being a singer professionally since she was a little girl – which did stick out to me. When it was my turn to talk, I returned the cordial manner and spoke idly about myself and my dreams and other things that I'm sure she really didn't pay much attention to either.

At one point I did offer to buy her a cup of coffee, but she turned it down – instead asking if she could bum one of my cigarettes – which I obliged. It was an odd thing to experience, all things considered. Two strangers from completely different backgrounds – sitting on the cold, concrete border of a truck stop parking lot in the middle of the night – smoking and sharing a conversation.

It felt like the sort of thing you'd only see in a movie or on television – but it was real.

I'm not entirely sure of just how long we sat there. Long enough for us to burn through three or four cigarettes respectively.

I do remember mentioning at some point that I should probably be careful around her because "roses have thorns" or some such nonsense, which is just about one of the most stupidly awkward things I think just about anyone could have managed to say – but it just sort of slipped out of my mouth without really thinking about it. It did make her laugh though.

Either due to a knee-jerk reaction over hearing something so absurd, or because she thought I was just absolutely pitiful – she laughed.

I cannot now imagine what it was – be it her looks, her demeanor or my own bleak loneliness – but something came over me then, and I did the unthinkable. I asked if her offer for "company" was still on the table.

She did not balk or mock or make some form of face, but simply smiled and said yes. Together we made our way to my truck which was parked nearby and I helped her into the passenger seat, before going around and climbing into the driver's seat myself. It was probably around 2:00 am by this point, and on a Thursday morning too – so it wasn't very busy. Only one or two other cars were there in the parking lot and I happened to be parked on the far side.

There was traffic coming up the off-ramp from the interstate, and I was parked face-out from the lot so I suppose somebody could have seen us – but we were largely facing into the side of a hill, so I think it unlikely.

Once we were settled, I told her that I only had about $20 – which was true – but she said that it was enough. I wasn't exactly sure what could be bought for that much money – and I'm still not – but I fished around for my wallet anyway.

When I looked back to hand her the money, I found that she had exposed her breasts to me. They were gorgeous – naturally full and round – they looked warm, soft and inviting to say the least. I was... more than a little taken aback, as you might imagine.

Here I was, the "good Catholic boy" sitting alone, in my truck, with a complete stranger that had just exposed herself to me in a near-abandoned parking lot in the middle of the night.

I didn't really know what to think if I'm being honest.

After regaining some of my composure, I knew that I must have been grinning – I mean, how could I not be – but I informed her that in spite of the very lovely view, that wasn't what I was interested in. She had told me how much she loved to sing – and so I asked if she would sing me a song.

I saw the skepticism on her face, but I asked again if she would please sing for me. I couldn't tell you why I wanted to hear it so badly, but I did. In that moment, in that instant the only thing in the whole world that I wanted was to hear her sing.

I didn't think there was anything that could make a prostitute blush – but apparently this was it.

She was quiet as she mulled the idea over in what I can only assume to be bashful apprehension – an odd trait for a whore – but then again I don't even like to be undressed while home alone so, who am I to judge.

In the end she agreed and took the money from my fingers. The air seemed to fill with a strange sort of calm – the only sounds within the cab were the rustling of clothes and soft breathing as she adjusted in the seat. Gently, she placed her arms about my neck and laid my head upon her shoulder. The sweetness of her perfume filled my nostrils. The heavy wind was rolling outside and tractor-trailers were hissing and squealing as they made their way in and out of the service yard behind us.

Then she started to sing.

Any suspicions I might have had about her Latin blood were all but put to rest when she began to sing some soft Spanish song. I could not fathom a guess as to what she was saying or what it meant, as I do not speak Spanish – but it was hauntingly beautiful.

I knew that I had fallen asleep because I woke with a rather startled jolt. I imagine Rosa must have thought me rather pathetic, but I'll never get the chance to know – because by the time I woke up – she was gone. My $20 bill had been tucked into my breast pocket, though she had clearly taken a few more cigarettes from the pack.

(I'll add here that I wish to assure you – lest you think me naive – that I am very well aware this was an incredibly stupid thing to do. The entire thing was foolish – not because I care what people think, but because I could have been robbed, or worse. I didn't have any money, but my keys were right there. She could have leaned across and opened my door, shoved me out onto the concrete and drove away leaving me there. But she didn't.)

I sort of just sat there in the end. Thinking about her, thinking about my night so far and about all the thoughts running through my head. The whole experience was odd, to say the least... I couldn't help but laugh if I'm being perfectly honest.

Driving home, the clear sky had grown cloudy and I knew the rain was coming. I don't really remember what I thought about while driving – just that it was solemn and quiet. A complete reversal of the chaotic soul-searching of the drive out. I hadn't checked my phone for the time, but I knew it must have been 6:00 or so because the morning commuters were slowly making their way onto the main county road from the side street – and little columns of headlights were coming towards me, heading in the opposite direction.

I heard the first drop of rain hit my windshield, and lit a cigarette.

Getting back home was a rather bleak and uneventful affair. I looked at my shabby, rundown house and slowly made my way up the broken front porch – utterly unconcerned with the falling rain as I fished for my key and opened the door.

I mulled about for a while, putting all my things away and sat down to write out the events which had just taken place.

Now that it was all over and done with, I find that my hands are starting to shake. I cannot help but to wonder why such a strange and seemingly specific set of events took place. As I said before – it was the sort of thing you'd see on TV or the movies, not in real life – and yet it was real. It really did happen. Such a strangely serene and human interaction.

Why is it that a chance encounter with a truck stop hooker could feel more natural – more human – than half the conversations with an average corner store clerk?

What does it say about the world today, when the supposedly simple human kindness has been ground down into something so rare and unrecognizable that it takes an inconceivably astounding incident like this just to find it?

Truth be told, I'm not sure whether to laugh or to cry at this point.

I know that there is still some compassion left in the world – but I cannot seem to feel it. The impact of this, however, I will take to my grave.

I'll never forget that woman as long as I live. And I will always hope, and I will always pray – wherever she is or wherever she ends up – that she'll find the happiness she's looking for.

She deserves to be happy.

For her smile alone, she deserves to be happy.

Chapter VII: Nobody

I want to make it perfectly clear – and in no uncertain terms – that I am not special.

I am not important.

I am not a distinguished newscaster or famous internet personality. I am not a great philosopher or poet, nor am I a renowned scientist or mathematician. I am not a celebrated artist or noted political pundit. I am not a big-named politician or an idolized celebrity.

I am simply a man, born and bred – a creature of flesh and blood the same as any of you – bound to this world for the duration of my time upon it, and I'm alright with that.

I am a man of little means in a world where means are everything. I do not end my day by flying back to my private mansion in Beverly Hills, or to my penthouse suite on the Upper East Side.

I do not view the world from some golden chair raised on high – looking down at the muck and mire as it writhes beneath me.

I exist in that swamp. I live in the squalor of that murky bog, riddled with pestilence and plague.

I have to live out each day of my life wallowing in the filth and shit that trickles down from the mouths of people in power. To drive home every night in my broken down truck to my ramshackle house – with no heat and no water – and having the *honor* and the *privilege* to contend with the problems of the world which others have created.

Of having their lies and their twisted beliefs force-fed to me – and being told that I should be grateful for it.

I am sick of it. I'm sick of all of it.

I'm sick of the ignorant masses turning a blind eye to the problems of the world. I'm sick of these radical insurgents which are systematically dismantling every aspect of America. I'm sick of this self-appointed sense of entitlement that everyone seems to walk around wearing on their sleeve. I'm sick of being told that I don't matter, and that I don't have rights because of the nature of my existence.

I'm sick of dishonesty and I'm sick of corruption. I'm sick of fear and I'm sick of inaction. I'm sick of the gas-lighting and I'm sick of the slander. I'm sick of the greed and I'm sick of contempt.

I'm just sick of it, and I've had enough.

I'm so tired of having to swallow this garbage and then just sit here looking around at all the other faces as if nothing were wrong.

Civilization has lost its civility – and if we cannot put an end to the things we are doing and correct this grievous oversight – our world is doomed.

I've been warned by some people that I could be accused of "projecting" my own insecurities considering all of the generalizations that I make – but the sad truth of it is that I'm not. To be quite honest, I almost wish I were.

I'm sure despite the dour tone, there are still a great many people who are happily living out there lives – and I say good for them. Genuinely. But for myself, I have gone out and spoken to my friends, my family, my neighbors – strangers on the street in different towns around the state – strangers online in different states and different countries even, and the story is always the same.

Maybe not every issue I bring up is applicable to every person – but the same running themes that I get from them are real. The similar concerns, the similar worries and woes – deviated of course, to each individual person respectively.

That is why I am writing this book, so that myself, and all the people like myself – who do not matter in the eyes of those in power – may have our voices heard. For everyone that thinks the way I do, and feels the way I do – and are scared of the things I am, and are tired of the things I am – can have a chance.

I feel that my only recourse now is the vain hope that maybe – just maybe – these words may help those who come after me. To help, in some small way, to right the wrongs of my generation and cast a light on the millions of people just like me – with voices unheard and uncared for – to start us back on the right path and find the balance of life again.

I do not know if this sad story is going to accomplish anything. I cannot claim that this written work will alter the course of human history, become the catalyst for change or help influence the future of our world – but I know that if I do not write this, then it *cannot* do those things.

That it will not do those things – because it will never have had the *chance* to do those things.

Living ain't Easy

Chapter VIII: The Digital Age

Life in the digital age, at least as it appears to me, has proven to be nothing short of miserable. In many ways, it is a life of endless connectivity – and equally it is a life of endless isolation. It is an age just brimming with the thought provoking avenues of critical information; which are also vastly outweighed by near insurmountable monoliths of misinformation.

It is an age in which the value of personal property has been utterly dissolved. Where the virtue of patience has been erased – and where the simple concepts of privacy have become extinct.

In short: it is a genuinely terrible time to be alive.

That is not to say that certain aspects of life can't be fun or be enjoyable – but a thing being "fun" is not the same thing as being "good." There are so many elements to the modern era, so many twists and turns and new inventions that are both exciting and fascinating – it's a truly thrilling sensation that we can be here to see results of budding new technologies and scientific discovery.

I've seen amazing leaps in robotic engineering – prosthetic limbs for amputees that can connect to a person's nervous system and provide the function of moving fingers and wrists. I've seen discussions and even development on a similar idea to replace a lost eye, and somehow feed the image of the camera into the brain so that the blind can see.

But the simple fact of the matter remains, that for each inherently positive thing we create – it keeps being overshadowed by the multitude of corresponding negatives related to it in the process. Almost as if we're no longer capable of curbing our enthusiasm and "looking before we leap."

I would argue that not only is this sentiment true, but that it is truer now than in any other era of technological advancement before us.

We have self-driving cars and vehicles that will park for you – but if that onboard computer ever breaks down, it causes a disaster. We've made such massive leaps in the field of medical science – but we still haven't cured cancer, let alone the common cold.

We've got state of the art communication systems set up so that emergency response teams can be alerted and deployed to any kind of problem in the blink of an eye – and yet we also see that the general times of those responses are getting slower by the day.

We have developed and created advanced Artificial Intelligence that is capable of harvesting information so that it can formulate an almost human-like response to any question you could ask it – and it is also ringing a death knell for the artist and the musician. Not to mention that it is also capable of analyzing and recreating a person's voice, and using it to access their personal data and bank accounts – so criminals have just been given a shiny new toy to play with.

What we see right now is a world in which all forms of media, such as books and games, television and film, are now available for purchase by online digital retailers around the globe – and typically, for the full market price of their physical counterpart. Yet if that retailer decides, for whatever reason, to remove said item from their digital shelves, library or catalogue – the consumers who purchased that item are frequently blocked from being able to access it.

Which of course means that, if you have paid money for something – and then somebody else decides to arbitrarily take it away from you without your consent – that is theft. It is legalized theft.

Because to their side of the argument – you never actually *owned* it.

And to make matters worse, as more industries and platforms move towards this digital business model – there is an ever shrinking pool of material which the average consumer is actually capable of physically getting their hands on. You cannot simply go out and buy the full boxed set of your favorite streaming show, or buy a physical copy of your favorite band's latest online album – because they don't exist.

It is unfortunate, but true, that sooner rather than later we will see an end to the DVD and Blu-Ray. They'll be going the way of Betamax and VHS, ending up like the old LaserDiscs – a thing to be collected and displayed on someone's shelf. Music CDs have been in decline for quite awhile, but even video games now are often packaged and sold in stores – only to be opened and find that the "disc" inside is just a piece of cardboard with a serial code that lets you download it once you get home to your computer.

And books? Oh, and books... Libraries are shrinking as general reading is in decline. Production of physical copies of new material is beginning to slow down – even this book will almost certainly gain more attention in its electronic format – though I do intend to see about a physical release.

At least, that is my hope.

But no, I think that it's just one of those sad and terrible things that, eventually, we're going to reach a point in which nobody actually "owns" anything. We're all going to wake up one day and realize that all of our property, our valuables – our prized possessions – aren't really ours.

We're just renting them – and like anything rented, it can and will be taken away.

What's even worse, I'm afraid, is that we're raising a whole new generation to be complicit with that idea. To see no visible issue with the concept of never truly having ownership over something – and if you cannot understand the concept of owning your own property, how can you possibly be expected to understand the concept of someone else's property? Which is an issue that we're seeing crop up more and more each day.

Not to mention the fact that, while yes right now the only things I'm talking about are simple items of recreation – what happens when the culture becomes ingrained with the idea of never owning anything? If it is becoming acceptable now to never truly own the things that are yours – what happens in the future to our grandchildren, or our great grandchildren? If we give up on the notion of having ownership over our own DVDs – are they going to grow up never expecting to have ownership of their own home?

And if you're sitting there thinking to yourself: "Hey, wait a minute! That's a pretty big leap from not owning your own copy of the latest "Halo," to not owning the title of your car or the deed to your house!" You are sadly mistaken, because if you create a populace that has no expectations of ownership of their property – then the people "selling" that property in the future, will take advantage of that fact.

You can bet your money on it – at least while it's still yours, that is.

You're already seeing it. We are the "rental" generation. Fewer and fewer people buying homes and instead opting to live in apartments or rented housing. Fewer and fewer people are buying cars – they're leasing them and trading in every year or so without ever taking ownership.

No, I think the future's very bleak indeed.

Of course nobody really talks about this issue – and even if they did, it's very hard to get people to listen. It's difficult to get any kind of information circulating today – at least, factual information at any rate.

Critical information, such as what's being given to us by the major news networks around the globe, have largely become a thing to be chopped up and redistributed throughout the internet in the form of smaller, more independent publications – or is simply being used for the purposes of viral marketing.

There was a time, believe it or not, when the nightly news was not subject to the political bias of the company, anchors or sponsors that brought it to you. When Walter Cronkite used to sign off with his signature catch phrase "And that's the way it is." He meant it. Sure, there may have been political opinions or ideological commentary offered by specific personalities – but the overall news itself was just that. The news.

Now the established media conglomerates and corporations have become nothing more than echo chambers for whichever side of the political aisle they happen to be pandering to. CNN is the liberal news network, and Fox is the "conservative" one – although I use that term lightly. In this regard, both sides frequently stretch the truth or go out of their way to lie and make up falsehoods, just to get their predetermined point across. CNN's notorious doctoring of Joe Rogan's photograph in order to make COVID-19 symptoms look more akin to jaundiced leprosy comes to mind as a perfect example.

So what exactly, you might ask, is the solution to this problem? Well, one solution has presented itself with the rise of the independent journalist. The wide world of the internet, along with our ever advancing waves of technology, have given new freedoms to the individual, which allows them to take their grievances online and offer up their own opinions, sleuth out their own investigations, and deliver you the facts without any form of incorporated bias.

The problem with this concept, of course, is that not only is there absolutely nothing in place to to hold these independent sources accountable for any form of journalistic integrity (not that the established media is being held to that same standard either) – but by having so many voices all talking about a given subject – it just makes too much noise for anybody to listen.

On the more conservative side of the isle alone, you have home-grown companies such as The Blaze or The Daily Wire which, inside of itself, offers the voices of Ben Shapiro, Michael Knowles, Andrew Klavan, Matt Walsh, Jordan Peterson – the list goes on. In the same general space you also have personalities like Steven Crowder, The Hodge Twins, Alex Jones, Dave Rubin – and then you have even smaller journalistic entities such as The Quartering, Liberal Hivemind, Officer Tatum, Sydney Watson, all the way down podcasters and clip-content creators like Benny Johnson and Lauren Chen or Nick Freitas – a man who is actively working in government right now as a Virginia State Delegate.

Not to mention any of the big independent names that land somewhere in the middle, like the aforementioned Joe Rogan, Timcast or Russel Brand, etcetera.

Now I could sit here all day listing every possible source that I know of – but the point of this tangent isn't to point out every single personality, journalist or news site on the internet – it's to show that there are a lot of voices out there to be heard. Voices ranging from big to small, and with varying levels of resources and credibility to back them up.

And the same thing has to be said for the other side of the political isle.

The sheer volume of information that is floating around on the internet today is insane – but it all becomes like static after a while. You can't make out what anyone is saying – because everybody is saying something just a little bit differently about the exact same subject – or sometimes, not even the same subject, you'll just have to take a gamble and click on the video to find out.

And that's the problem. Because there's so many different voices – and so many different personalities offering those voices – it's very hard to actually get the "big picture." From three-hour long expose's to hour and a half long podcasts and fifteen to twenty minute videos or even thirty second shorts – there's just too much. There's no uniformity or cohesiveness, it's just... Chaos.

Don't feel like watching a video on something? Just go to Wikipedia! But the problem with Wikipedia is that literally anybody can edit it, and while the website is more highly moderated now than it used to be, you really can't guarantee the validity of what you read without triple checking across multiple sources.

Want to just get a quick answer without having to put too much effort into it? Just ask your question on Google! Except the problem there is that Google is a company full of corporate bias, and depending on what it is you're looking for, it may well suppress your intended search results in favor of less relevant or outright false information that just so happens to align with Google's political agenda.

And let's not even talk about other alternative news sources such as Apple, Facebook, Twitter and the like. They'll have you frantically hopping from one article to another like a coked out grasshopper – it's exhausting – and half of what you read on sites like that are openly plagiarized, false, or both.

It's no wonder people have stopped trying to find the factual information on anything – because it's simply become such an annoying pain in the ass to do so.

Huge swaths of the country have no idea that Joe Biden infamously said "If you have a problem figuring out whether you're for me or Trump, then you ain't black."

They saw a woman getting arrested by police and screamed "Down with authority!" but never bothered to find out that the reason she was being arrested was because she was publicly masturbating on a beach in front of children.

Millions of voices cry out against Donald Trump, denouncing him as a monster because he created ICE and erected "metal cages" to hold illegal immigrants and separate children from their families – except that ICE was formed in the wake of 9/11, and those metal cages were built under Barack Obama.

It's not that the information isn't out there, or that it's hidden away in some special corner of the internet where only the most privileged and informed people are able to access it – it's just simply that there's so much of it, that people won't be bothered to go and look.

I remember one time I was talking with a woman who just refused to educate and inform herself on any issue. We talked about the job market, and the horrible unemployment rates at the time – and she said "No, unemployment is lower than it's ever been, Obama said so!" and I said "No, it's awful, it's terrible, what are you talking about?"

She insisted I was lying. She said "Where's your proof?" I said "First of all, just look around because it's not hard to see – and secondly, how about the National Archives, the United States Labor Department, the Bureau of Labor Statistics, the CATO Institute and The New York Times?"

She said "Well prove it then. Show it to me." I told her to just go look for herself, but she wouldn't. You couldn't convince her of anything that she hadn't already made her mind up about – and she was completely unwilling to put in the work herself. She wanted it hand-fed to her like an infant, and I wasn't going to act like her babysitter. This wasn't some spoiled teenage girl, this was a spoiled twenty-something "woman" who just wanted to act like a child – but even still, I can't say that I necessarily blame her. At least not completely.

Using The Daily Wire again as an example, they can easily wrack up hours upon hours worth of news related content per day – and that's not including other outlets besides them. That's all internal – and unlike traditional televised news broadcasts – you have to go manually hunting for each new video release and upload.

Now imagine going through all that effort to catch up on each news story by every source that I've just mentioned, and maybe throw in a dozen or so more for good measure.

That is a lot of information for the average person to consume – and so most of them just simply won't.

Personally, I miss the good old days of Superstation TBS and their 24-hour updates that ran along the bottom of the screen – but maybe that's just me.

Regardless of what I feel, it is clear that the established networks are going the way of the dinosaur. CBS, CNN, FOX, MSNBC, they're all floundering. Their entrenched biases and failure to play by the rules – along with the changing of technology – has simply pushed so many people away that are never coming back.

For my part, I'm just not entirely sure that this next evolutionary step in news media is a healthy one. For all of its advantages, it has so many drawbacks and glaring issues. At best it doesn't seem to effectively reach as many people as it should be – and at worst it seems to be actively contributing to the growing sense of division throughout the world. Instead of three thousand people tuning in to one cohesive broadcast – you have three groups of a thousand tuning into three separate broadcasts, and arguing back and forth with each other over which one was the best.

It ultimately keeps boiling down into more tribalism and a distortion of facts.

Moving away from the inherent problems of information vs misinformation, you also have the rapidly materializing issues surrounding over-connectivity via the internet. We're seeing the rise of isolationism and the forming of para-social relationships. Online harassment is at an all-time high, personal security is at an all-time low – and somehow, people still haven't figured out that the internet is forever.

Technology in and of itself is not necessarily an issue – it's the influence that technology has over society and culture that becomes a problem. When YouTube first started and you could go watch funny videos shared by people around the world of dramatic prairie dogs, cats playing the piano and impassioned lip-syncing to O-Zone – it was a mind blowing and wonderful experience at the time. It was fun and it was innocent.

But then it became corporate. It became a business.

And anything that becomes a business, becomes a business model.

Video lengths increased and computer algorithms came into play. Advertisers got involved and the entire thing turned into a creature designed to keep you watching – forever, and ever, and ever.

Other sites tried over the years to break onto the same scene. Vimeo and Daily Motion. Most recently Rumble has thrown its hat into the ring. All of them hoping to take a bite out of YouTube and keep people staring at their screens.

Live Streaming started cropping up about a decade later, give or take. Why wait for somebody to post an unnecessary update on their life when you could just go and watch them live it in real time? Of course, you're not out there living your own life while you're sat at home watching someone else – but that's besides the point.

That proved to be successful and so now you have other companies getting in on that too, with places like Twitch, Facebook Live, YouTube Live Streaming and newer upstarts like Kick.

There are numerous success stories to be found. People who took a chance and tried to make a career out of becoming a "content creator" online – but it's not a sustainable way of life. Everybody seems to want to do it, and thus they don't want to do anything else. Trade jobs are shrinking and the economy is plummeting and kids don't don't want to go to school – they just want to sit at home, staring at their computers and their phones all day.

They talk to their favorite streamer or youtuber and become convinced that they know this person. That they're friends with this person, and that this person is also friends with them. The same is also true on the flip-side of the coin, when a streamer or video maker sees the same name comment on every video, or come into live chat every day. It blurs the lines between what's real and what isn't.

It's the evolution of "Reality" Television, and it's clearly damaging to the public.

In a lot of ways, it's not unlike the old hay-day of the Soap Opera. When rabid fans would see cast members of their favorite show walking through a grocery store and just start talking to them as if they were the character that they played on TV.

The difference is, that these aren't people being insulated by a stage or script. I'm sure many of them do "play it up" for the camera – but they aren't actors playing a role. They're people, presenting themselves as themselves.

Slamming their heads into walls and desks. Ingesting inedible and toxic substances. Engaging in, and encouraging others to engage in addictive habits and behaviors. Using sexual promiscuity to groom and take advantage of their audiences. Intentionally or inadvertently revealing their personal information to the world.

It's not a good thing.

You have actual "professional" porn-stars who live stream nowadays. Their stream isn't necessarily sexual in nature – maybe they're just playing the latest video game – and it attracts all kinds of attention from the audience. I'm sure that some of these women have "fans" that tune in to watch, but there's nothing that stops children from coming in and being exposed to these people either.

Little Timmy sees a very pretty lady playing Pokémon and starts talking to her about how much he loves Charmander. She's engaging with her chat and talks about how much she loves Jigglypuff. Little Timmy thinks that she's a really nice lady and decides to come back and watch her stream again. And again. And again – and eventually he finds his way to the bottom of her streaming page where she has all of her links to her various social media profiles and so Little Timmy clicks on one, follows the link through to a link-portal, and is directed to an image of the very nice lady laid out on her bed, spread eagle with a giant cock up her ass.

Now if she was paying close attention to the way he was typing, maybe she could tell that Timmy is a child – but frankly, so many people are so bad at writing and they talk or act like children online, that there's no guarantee that she would notice this.

And there's also no guarantee that she'd care.

That is grooming, whether intentional or otherwise.

And there's no systems in place, no checks and balances to curtail the negative side-effects of this industry – and frankly, given the very nature of the internet itself, there really isn't an effective way to implement those systems anyway.

If a stream or video is "age restricted" then kids are just going to click that little button that says "Yep! I swear that I am 18 years old!" and go watch it anyway – but not all content requires that age restricted warning. Channels don't have to be flagged at "18+" only the content that they create, so if little miss "Jigglypuff" isn't actively showing her ass on camera, then there's no reason that the tag has to be there – and often, it isn't.

And you can't fix it by denying the pornstar her right to stream on the site, so long as she's not breaking any rules of public conduct. She might be a whore, but she isn't a convicted serial killer – it would be outrageous to condemn her just because of her profession – past or present.

So what's the answer? What's the solution? I don't have one, but at least I'm willing to talk about it.

Different sites have tried different measures to tamper down on the problem, but nothing is actually working, and realistically speaking, nobody seems to care.

Little Timmy's parents who let him go off on the internet without supervision certainly didn't care – because they're too busy being glued to their own devices, watching their videos and live streams.

Different twists on the format keep coming and going, like Vine or most recently TikTok – which is a problematic thing for a number of reasons. YouTube and Facebook now offer "shorts" which are designed to imitate that particular format. You scroll on your phone through ten to twenty second videos, over and over every chance you get. The people making them are hoping that their title is catchy enough or shocking enough to grab your attention so that you'll watch it and they'll get another "click" to their algorithm which makes them more "popular."

You see the same thing with movie streaming sites like Netflix and Hulu. People just scrolling and scrolling. So many options and perpetually bored of all of them.

The human attention span is shrinking. I read one study that said, basically, you have approximately three to five seconds to grab the average person before they've wandered off to the next thing.

We're becoming like Goldfish. By the time that we've reached one side of the fishbowl – we've already forgotten the side that we just came from.

And with our noses constantly shoved into our phones, we keep growing farther apart. There's a reason that we have a loneliness epidemic running rampant across the globe. We aren't engaging with each other as humans anymore, we're just staring down at our screens. Drifting further and further away from reality.

I remember sitting in a restaurant a little over ten years ago now, and I looked towards the party table in the corner that had about five teenagers sitting at it. Not one of them was eating. Not one of them was even looking at the friend sitting next to them – but they all had their eyes glued to their phones – and the scariest moment, is when they all suddenly laughed at the same time. They were texting in a group chat with each other, instead of just talking.

That's not healthy.

I've had things like that happen with my own friends. They'll ask me how I'm doing, and I start to say what's going on in my life and they'll just casually pull out their phone and start scrolling.

I'll say something like: "Y'know, it's just really tough right now with everything going on and-" boom! a burst of laughter before they say "Hey check this out!" and start trying to show me whatever it was that they saw.

And this has happened with people who I know care about me – but they've just become so disconnected to anything besides that phone. Besides the internet.

They're desensitized to… Life. It's like being out of sync with reality.

I see people who only think that they have "friends" if they're on Facebook. People who only think that they can be popular if they get enough "likes" or "up votes" on their social media.

They think that if they spread their legs on OnlyFans that people will love them.

And when they inevitably don't feel that love, that friendship, that fulfillment… They question what went wrong. They question what they did wrong – they'll blame themselves for being some kind of a "failure" because some stranger on the internet didn't share their latest "tweet."

Then they spiral.

They'll start looking for answers and looking for reasons and ultimately they will pull themselves together and try to make a change in their life. They'll try to "unplug" and disconnect from the internet, in order to get away from all the complications – but they can't.

You can't get away from the internet today, because it's become so ingrained in everyday life.

You try to talk to your own friends about the problems that you're facing and they do to you what mine did to me – they're disinterested and disassociated. They're looking at their phones while you're talking about spending too much time on yours.

Don't just take it from me – look around. You see it everywhere. People at the restaurant, people at the gas station, people at the grocery store – all on their phones, never talking to each other.

Maybe you wanna turn off the phone and go for a drive to clear your head – but the whole time you're gone, that phone keeps buzzing. Those texts keep coming. The alerts keep popping up. My mother lost her phone recently and we finally found it, but once we'd charged it up and turned the power back on we sat there listening to the sound of "Ding! Ding! Ding!" over and over again for nearly ten minutes. Every message, every application update, every alert – they all came flooding back in.

Maybe you want to get yourself a job so that you can get out of the house for a while and earn yourself some money while you're at it – well you have to apply online. Just about anywhere you'd want to work requires an online application process these days – a system that not only adds to the issue of isolation for the employee, but also prevents the employer from getting to know the person that wants to work for them.

Even if you do find a job, so many of them are computer-based – and worse, many companies are now having their employees operate from home.

I recently watched a man on YouTube, a guy I tend to think of as having a pretty good head on his shoulders, give a very snide and long-winded speech about the absurdity of people returning to work in the offices after COVID-19.

He spoke ad nauseam about the only reason that anybody would want their workers back in the building, is because of "middle-management" being afraid to lose their jobs with nobody to manage – and landlords losing money without anybody renting their offices.

At no point did he ever stop to consider the continued disconnect of everyone working from home. The lack of coordination, teamwork and general comradery that comes from being isolated. The sheer loss of human-connection that takes place when everybody that you work with is nothing more than a name on a screen.

Now I'm sure that most companies don't give a shit about anything that I'm talking about – as I'm sure you well know – but some of them can see the bigger picture. If for no other reason than productivity.

Humans need human interaction. A team isn't a team if everyone's a stranger.

In a world that's already struggling with loneliness, going off and being alone doesn't help.

It's getting harder and harder to meet people and to make friends. You start to make bad decisions and before you know it, you're slipping right back into those same old habits that you tried to get away from. Your friends didn't listen to you and you try to please the crowd – but nobody takes you seriously. You settle for the first boyfriend or girlfriend you can get but it doesn't work out, because of things you've done in the past or because of who you are as a person – and you just continue to spiral.

Things like this have gotten so bad that as the blight of artificial intelligence takes off, we've seen the rise of the "Chat AI" which are applications specifically designed to simulate a real world relationship, be it romantic or platonic. I know this, because in order to do a bit of research on the subject, I tried a few out so that I could write about it.

The AIs will do pretty much anything you want. They'll ask you how your day has been, or offer their support when you're feeling blue – and if you whip out the old credit card and pay them enough money, they'll even attempt to act out your wildest sexual fantasies – at least through the medium of text.

They'll offer a person the fantasy of having somebody – anybody – who cares about them.

And much like the old school sex hotlines, most of these applications are universally created to take advantage of the lonely, miserable and depressed people that have turned to them for comfort – because like all fantasies, it's fake.

In a world where we're all so connected – everyone's just a stranger, and most of us are all alone.

I don't think that technology on its own is a bad thing. Like I said at the start of this chapter, I've seen a lot of really great things come out of the technological and scientific advancements that we've made.

A quick example I can think of would be things like Garageband. It's a music application that comes on just about every Apple product and it's such a fantastic way to introduce young people and children to the world of music. The world of creating music. It affords people the opportunity to learn about various instruments that, realistically, they otherwise might not be able to afford.

And it also provides its users with the capability of recording their own songs and albums without having to break the bank and go find a music studio somewhere.

But the problem comes when people look at these digital instruments, and then never bother to go learn the real thing. When the attitude towards this makes a shift, and people just accept that a fake guitar is just as valid as a real one. That just because they learned how to tap their fingers on a screen – means that they don't need to bother going out and practicing their scales or learning measures and keys.

Applications like this are great for so many things – but they also don't instill any sense of discipline in their users. Frankly, they sort of encourage the opposite – because why would a person ever need discipline in their craft, when they already have everything they need right in front of them, and they can just tap out a song in a few short minutes. It doesn't actually teach you anything – at least not beyond what you learn by simply using it. It doesn't really teach you how to play an instrument, only how to mimic one – but as long as it gets the job done, who cares right?

The fact of the matter is, that the human race just isn't capable of handling all of the power that we currently have at our disposal. We don't take enough responsibility for ourselves. As a species, to be quite honest, we are not mature enough for the internet – and yet the internet is here.

We aren't mature enough for half of the things that we have, but we still have them.

You have people out there in the world right now talking about how great it's going to be once we finally start colonizing Mars – and yet back here on Earth, we haven't managed to settle border disputes that have been going on for centuries. Do you really think mankind is capable of interplanetary-colonization and wide-scale terraforming? I don't think so.

In the film adaptation of Michael Crichton's famous novel Jurassic Park – the character of Ian Malcolm says that "your scientists were so preoccupied with whether or not they could, that they didn't stop to think if they should." I think that that's a pretty accurate statement for a lot of what we have today.

We've made so many changes for the sake of "advancement" that we've ended up in a state of regression. Children are accessing the internet and using computers, in some cases, more effectively than adults who have been using them for years – and yet by and large they can't read or write. People with nothing but free time on their hands are constantly active and engaging with one device or another, never able to get away from it, to the point that they're burnt out and have no time left to do anything.

Even simple mundane tasks like going to the grocery store are starting to become fully automated. It started with the self-checkouts and now most of them will bring the items to your car while you're parked, or just simply deliver it to your house so that you never have to leave.

Pretty soon I think we'll end up in a world like "WALL-E."

Human beings simply weren't designed to live this way.

Chapter IX: Upside Down

There's so many things that I could talk about in this chapter. There's so many things that I could talk about in this entire book if I ever write it.

The evening hours tick by slowly – one by one becoming lost in the ever shifting sands of time. I find myself reflecting on my feelings of neglected abandonment – on being an outcast from society – and yet it is society it seems, at least to me, that has cast itself out. Turning its back on all hope of reason and restraint.

I suppose I'm just so disappointed in the way things have turned out that I don't even want to try.

I see so many strange things happening in the world today. So many unnerving trends that are taking root in our modern culture.

There's a callousness in the air – and an odd, seemingly inexplicable sense of self-righteousness to everything that we do. It's palpable. It's tangible – and it's electrifying.

It seems to me, that society has reached this pivotal moment in life where we are completely unable to see the forest for the trees. Where we have amped everything up into an extreme reaction or expectation in one form or another.

We've concerned ourselves so much with the idea of making sure that everyone around us feels "safe" and "comfortable," to the point that we've actively begun making them feel "unsafe" and "uncomfortable" in the process.

Speaking for myself, I once wrote a short sketch story and was approached by someone repeatedly asking for permission to use it in one of her classes. She wanted to know if it would be "alright" and if I would be "okay" with her showing it to some other people – but the problem is that she kept asking to the point where I genuinely became unsure about it – when otherwise it would have never bothered me.

This obsessive emphasis that modern society places on constant inquiry over everyone's thoughts and feelings – while admirable in spirit – is not human in nature. Human beings do not talk to each other that way. It's simply not how we communicate. Common courtesy dictates a short and simple "Hey, would you mind if..." but that's no longer how we ask the question. Now we poke you, prod you, hound you – asking upwards of three, four, even five times and in two or three different ways: "Are you sure?"

It's no longer a human interaction. It's a mechanical one.

We've developed this idea that nobody is capable of atoning for their sins or for correcting past mistakes. You see rabid mobs whipped into a frenzy, scouring through the entire history of any person or persons they dislike, hoping to dig up some skeleton from their closet and use it against them for clout – even if it's as minor as something they said twenty or thirty years ago.

I've heard it justified as "accountability" but that's not holding someone accountable. It's persecution.

At best it's blind hypocrisy, not being able to recognize that as you "rail against authoritarianism" you have yourself become authoritative – and at worst, it's an obsessive witch hunt in order to live out some kind of culturally tolerated power fantasy.

You have governing political bodies such as over in Ireland wanting to enact legislation that would allow a person to be criminally charged for having pictures on their phones, or opinion-based media in their possessions. I watched Senator Pauline O'Riley stand up there with a straight face and say: "We are restricting freedom for the common good." With her justification being that, if your personal world-view causes others to feel "discomfort" then you should have your freedoms restricted.

For the love of God, a man was arrested and criminally charged over in England for silently praying outside of an abortion clinic. He wasn't picketing with a sign or shouting at the people entering or exiting the facility – he wasn't even on the same side of the street. He just bowed his head in silence and clasped his hands together – and they arrested him for it.

For years now on the internet I've heard people make fun of "the thought police" but now it's becoming real. These sorts of things are actually happening.

The world at large is chafing under the constraints of political correctness and censorship. Freedom of speech has all but been abolished – and people are starting to break from the pressure.

I've also noticed a rampant sense of unwarranted self-entitlement running through Western civilization as a whole, and it's an issue which sees the continued theft and damage of physical intellectual property – as well as a flagrant disregard for civil rights and personal actions.

You can find long-winded video lectures on why musicians have "no right" to block somebody from unlawfully re-recording their music in order to make money – because the idea of a licensing agreement is somehow "draconian."

I've seen footage of people attacking innocent bystanders on college campuses and then insisting that they possessed the legal right to do so, just because they found that other person's presence to be "offensive." The most bizarre part, is when they cannot comprehend that their actions have consequences and they start kicking and screaming and having a full-blown meltdown when campus police get involved. If they get involved – which they won't always do.

The country is facing a massive drug crisis and crime wave – but nobody seems to care. Every time a criminal shoots somebody, they sound the alarm of abolishing the 2nd Amendment and punish law abiding citizens – while simultaneously enacting laws that openly aid criminals in evading punishment. They call for the decriminalization of drugs, legalize addictive substances, and push to keep the borders open for drug peddlers to illegally enter the country and push these substances into our schools.

I lost a young friend of mine just in the past few years to drugs. He took something laced with Fentanyl and didn't know it. He was 18 years old, with his whole life ahead of him – and now he's gone.

The state of Virginia alone has had several school children overdose on Fentanyl. A recent drug-bust in the state recovered enough of the substance to cause a lethal overdose in over 1.2 million people – but the state government refused to allocate $50,000 to the proposed update of the state Criminal Code, because it too concerned with spending $150,000 on a budget to deal with "overly loud mufflers."

The disconnection from reality is mind boggling.

There's currently an active argument right now about why parents should have no rights over their own children – and how schools should have the right to enforce any form of "education" onto those children that they want to – because only those schools can have power over the mind.

And it's not just coming from some lunatic on the fringe – these ideas are seeping down from positions of power and authority. Randall Garrison of Canada's New Democratic Party outright said that "There's no such thing as 'Parental Rights' in Canada." That's completely insane.

You have families around the Western world who are being forced to either sign away their rights over their own children, and allow them to undergo horrible, life-altering medical procedures with no ability to reverse the effect – or potentially lose those children into custody of the state.

And this isn't some kind of conspiracy theory either. It just happened in Montana – a fourteen year old girl taken away from her parents without their consent, because they objected to the transitioning of her gender identity. And the family in Washington state, who were forced to sign legal documents stating that they would in no way object to their underage son transitioning, just in order to maintain custody of their child.

If you are compliant then you're miserable – and if you stand against it, you get demonized. You either find yourself as part of the problem or you face the repercussions of not abiding by "the rules."

It's a lose-lose scenario.

Combine all of this with the other modern practices that I spoke of. Things like reducing a person's worth down to sheets of paper, of blocking everybody out into a culture of isolation. It begins to rapidly dehumanize our existence.

I myself often struggle with the fact that I no longer feel like a man, but rather like a piece of meat – a product on the shelf of life – with a bar-code and serial numbers etched into my skin.

I look around at the ever growing lethargy of my peers – men and women who are my age and don't want to work, don't want to raise a family, don't want to... try.

There's an emptiness – an aimlessness in our existence – and if they are feeling this way, and for the same reasons I do, then I cannot blame them for it.

Western civilization is struggling with the largest increase in depression – since the Great Depression – and it's no small wonder why. We have become the faceless masses. We have become the files in the cabinet. We've lost our individuality and stopped being people – because our lives and our identities have been reduced to nothing more than a set of numbers and expectations. A set of risks and rewards.

To put it simply, we have stopped being human.

I look around at this life we have created and what I see is a world in which "discipline" is a dirty word, and the concept of "dignity" has been raped into the ground. A world where activists chain themselves to tractors in order to protest the slaughter of animals – and then turn around and call for the unregulated practice of infanticide. A world in which we harvest our aborted young, and carve up those that do survive in some perverted act of playing God.

It is a world of barbarians and savages. A world of human cattle.

I cannot recognize it.

The more I dwell on this, the more I am reminded of an article which I have read by a man named Mikel Gilmore of the Rolling Stone magazine. He was writing about The Doors, and specifically about the legacy of their former singer, the late Jim Morrison.

In the article, Mikel writes about the unique position in which The Doors found themselves – as well as the general feeling of the musical scene in the late 1960s and early 70s. The particular section which calls to mind is his observation of the contrast between typical "Rock 'n Roll" music of the time – a genre which largely preached a message of peace, love, drugs, or any combination thereof – whilst The Doors opted to forego an overtly upbeat message, and instead focused on the darker aspects of life at the time. Choosing instead to shy away from framing these excesses and facades as being inherently "positive" in nature, and rather pointing them out for the negative that they were.

To quote:

"Morrison realized that any generation so intent on giving itself permission to go as far as it could, was also giving itself a license for destruction."

This sentiment, I feel, perfectly encapsulates the problems of today. The problems of a world gone mad – a world turning on the tangled and skewed ideals of a single group of people with absolutely no ability or intention whatsoever to keep themselves in check.

A radicalized half of the modern political atmosphere that is so dead-set on turning the wheel of progress forward at all costs, that they have forgotten that a wheel with no foundation can only spin in circles. Around and around, and around again, until eventually, those first treads double back on themselves and end up facing backwards, instead of forwards.

"Progress!" They scream from the rooftops. Rooftops of now toppled buildings in ruined cities, and on streets overflowing with excrement and disease.

It is true that all things must one day grow and evolve – but progress is to them a wheel which never ceases to turn. The bloodied tracks of it, squealing and scraping against the pavement – churning up everything in its wake.

There is no stability to their goal – and thus their wheel has run off the road.

Instead of true progress – what we have now is a state of absolute regression. We have forgotten and foregone all that is good, and placed the theories of race at the top of our list, re-segregating communities across the nation. We have seemingly lost the ability to recognize the inherent differences in sex between male and female – and instead, we ignorantly insist that biological structure is nothing more than a subjective and social construct.

Everything's turned upside down these days, and I'm not entirely sure how we flip it all back over.

We have lost the ability to communicate with one another, and in fact we openly relish in the self-appointed power to silence any and all voices which in any way would disagree or disparage the nature of our chosen agendas.

We target the weak and insecure in order to further our political goals and then we hang them out to dry when it no longer suits us. We're grooming children and violating the rights of parents in order to propagate twisted and perverse backroom-ideologies that are being forced onto the public stage.

Never would I have imagined that the culture of America could fall so far and so fast – and in such a short amount of time. We have become a country of excess in all things. A country of hedonism and debauchery. A country of bedlam.

Wealth, sex, food, violence and drugs. An overabundance of all things spiraling together in an endless cacophony of noise that grows ever more meaningless and self-indulgent with each passing day.

We are bombarded with these things – assaulted by them – as they have crept into every facet of day to day living. Not just in America, but in the majority of Western countries – and indeed many countries across the globe.

Animals and produce are altered and mutated through the injection of chemical steroids and growth hormones to provide larger quantities of a lower quality product. We've seen the rapid legalization of marijuana, as well as the general decriminalization of narcotics which further adds to the growing apathetic lethargy of the population. Radio, television and the internet have become places of corporate marketing where salacious advertisements dominate the air time – and are only broken up by the often lackadaisical and hastily put together content that we are supposedly tuning in for.

Prostitution has been legalized through the medium of pornography, which is increasingly thrust onto display at every possible turn. When sex is not shown in movies or televised programming, it is marketed off to the side of our computer screens and in the center of catalogues.

Hell, even the Vermont Country Store and Better Homes & Gardens feature a slip in the middle that advertises adult "toys." We've even pushed the envelope so far that society has begun to indulge in the overt sexualization of children. Little boys and girls prancing around on stages and proudly presented in the skimpiest and most provocative forms of clothing that most grown women would not wear outside the confines of their bedroom.

The irony that one hundred years after the "Roaring 20s", society now in the 2020s has once again devolved into chaos is not lost upon me.

Yet I think this chaos to be different, for we have gone much farther – and continue to go much further – than any generation which has come before us.

I mean for God's sake – children's genitalia are being depicted on TV and child sex-dolls are openly marketed towards the "discerning" pedophile.

The malignant blight of transgenderism is publicly pushed onto children and peddled in our schools to such an extent, that even the Walt Disney Corporation – a company which was created by a devout Christian and founded on the precepts of family values – has now publicly stated that kids as young as "three years of age" should be subject to the human butcher-block of gender reassignment.

We have gone beyond bedlam.

We are now Sodom, and we are Gomorrah.

I would certainly say that this generation has given itself permission to go as far as it can – and it has unquestionably given itself a license for destruction.

Chapter X: Higher Learning

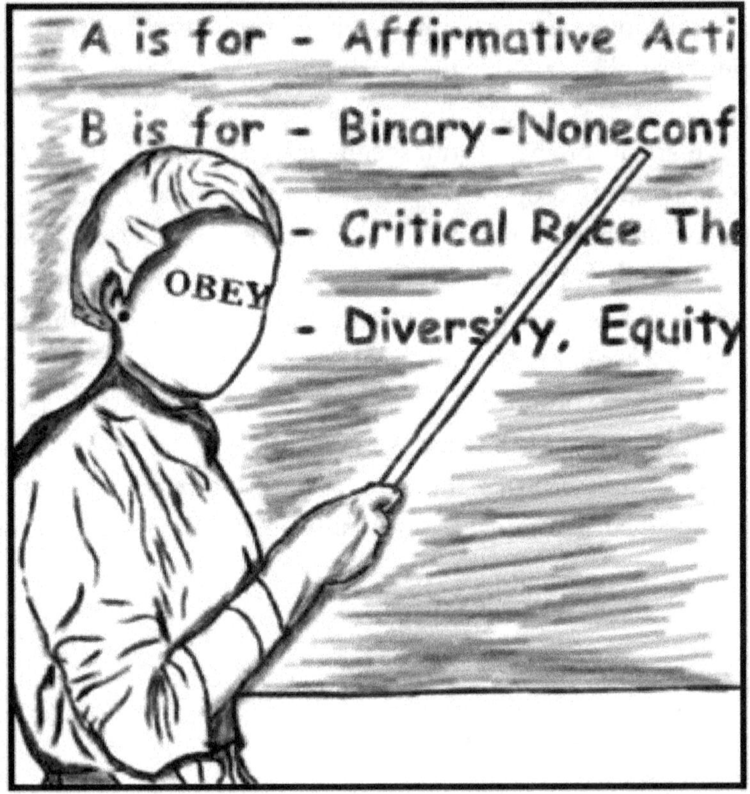

I think that one of the more disturbing realities of life in the modern era, is just how much time and effort we have put into the subversion of the English language. Really not just the English language, but verbal communication as a whole. It's become a dying art. A thing that has been cast aside or otherwise mistreated, as more and more people use language for the purposes of bending and twisting it to conform to their own agenda and ideology.

Children in our schools are not being taught to speak properly. I don't just mean in the sense of proper diction or some Henry Higgins level of dialectual expectation – but I mean, they aren't being taught *words*.

The English language is shrinking at an astonishing rate – young people today don't just speak with a large reliance on modern slang – but their overall vocabularies are simply nonexistent. Terms like "toxic" or "wholesome" come to mind – where while these are indeed some admirable words with powerful meanings – they have begun to take up the vast majority of space inside of modern conversation.

A person is very likely to use the word "toxic" in order to describe anything that is inherently a net-negative. Conversely they will also use the word "wholesome" to describe anything inherently net-positive.

Words like: "good" or "great" and "excellent" or "outstanding" are used with less and less frequency. An image of a father playing catch with his son is often no longer described as "lovely" or "endearing" or "beautiful" it's just... "wholesome." And it is wholesome, absolutely – but that is not the only word that you can use to describe something so wonderful in life.

"Community" is another one that has really started to get under my skin, because it is just so overused, and often underutilized in its use. Today, any group of people that share even the slightest hint of a common interest is dubbed "a community" and that's just... sad.

Where once there might have been a "clique" or a "group" or a "fandom" or a "circle" or a "collective" or a "neighborhood", there is now only a "community". It's not an incorrect term. A neighborhood is a community. Your church parish or small town is, as a whole, a community – but it's not the only word, and that's exactly how it's being used.

Everything is being boiled down into just one or two tiny little labels that roughly describe what they are, and every other description is being forced to take a back seat. But if our words are pushed to the back for long enough – they will eventually become archaic and forgotten. "Community" is a term that is haphazardly slapped onto everything nowadays. Have a group of people that enjoy a particular video game? It's a community. How about an avid fan-base that follows a certain film franchise? They're a community. It's even applied to sexual fetishes and orientations – unless of course that orientation happens to be heterosexual – in which case you don't get to have a community.

My point is, that what we are witnessing, is the sad and pitiful death of the English language – and as I said at the start of this page, it's not just the English language – but it is most languages around the globe, where native speakers are actively choosing to forego the greater depth of their respective lexicons, in place of one or two key phrases or descriptors that are overly applied to everything.

On the flip side of this coin, we're also seeing the loss of both meaning and understanding of the words that we use, and the purposes for which we use them. People either aren't being taught enough words to form a well-rounded and functional vocabulary – or they are being taught a vast network of words, but have no idea what those words mean or how to properly use them.

We see this a lot with the ongoing culture war surrounding "identity politics" in which proponents of this ideology insist that a person's biological "sex" is "objective", whereas their biological "gender" is "subjective". The problem is that these people are too stupid to realize that the terms "sex" and "gender" are simply two different words for the exact same thing. The fact that some Feminist in the 1970s arbitrarily decided to change the meaning of the word – does not mean that it actually means anything different. Try opening up the Oxford English Dictionary for once if you don't believe me.

(Gender is, by the way, yet another word which I can no longer stand to hear – as just like with wholesome, toxic and community, it has become the singular term that is applicable to any conversation surrounding a person's identity).

They also fail to understand the definition of what is and is not "objective" in nature. They claim that a person's gender is subjective, and that any person can, at any given moment, change their chosen gender into something that is more fitting for who they truly are – except that once they have applied the label of this new gender to themselves, it is an "objective" fact that cannot be contradicted or denied.

They lack any and all critical understanding that a thing which is subjective, is a thing which is viewed through a personal lens, and may be perceived differently depending on the person who is analyzing it. (Which is to say: something that is subjective, is often based on an opinion. Whereas a thing which is objective, is a thing based around an inarguable fact).

It is an objective fact that fire is hot. It is a subjective opinion on how long a person could hold their hand near that fire, before starting to feel pain. It is an objective reality that you will begin to burn your skin if exposed to heat temperatures of 120 degrees higher – regardless of the subjective nature of an individual's personal pain threshold.

You can apply this basic understanding of these two words and what they mean to... almost anything.

Two people have a baking competition, and one is more careful and follows the recipe much closer than the other. One dish is presented beautifully on the plate while the other is just tossed on there rather lazily. You can say that, objectively speaking – one contestant did a better job – but as to which dish is ultimately going to taste better, that is a subjective opinion.

In the world of film and cinema, Conan the Barbarian is objectively a better movie than its sequel, Conan the Destroyer. Barbarian had objectively a bigger budget, better writing, greater depth of vision, broader scope, and ultimately earned its place as a cinematic classic, in which the film seamlessly blends both the subject matter of "Sword & Sorcery" fantasy, with the stylized presentation of a spaghetti western.

Subjectively, I find the movie to be boring, and much prefer its more poorly written, lower budgeted and overly campy follow-up. Barbarian is, by all rights, the better of the two films – but I just enjoy Destroyer a little bit more.

That is why understanding the words that you are using is so important – and that is also why it is such a shame that we have found ourselves in the situation we are now in, with regards to our language.

Yet another common issue today is the changing of the language – typically justified with the shallow argument that "languages grow and evolve". Languages do grow and evolve – that is absolutely true – but the way in which languages grow and evolve is typically not with the dismantling of themselves. That is how you end up with dead or ineffectual languages – some of which are lost to time, and others are hanging on by a thread.

During the Elizabethan period of England, people used to say things like "How for art thou?" or "Good fortune on the morrow." These are perfect examples of how our language has evolved – because why they may sound odd or silly to us today – the deeper meaning of their sentiments haven't changed.

"How for art thou?" is simply an archaic way of asking "How are you?" Likewise, "Good fortune on the morrow" is exactly the same as "Good luck tomorrow." The verbal basis of these phrases may have changed, but their definition has not. Their *meaning* has not.

That's why it's called an evolution of language – because it grew and evolved. It became shorter, a bit simpler and certainly more modernized – but the definition of its words never altered. "How are you" in the 1500s doesn't suddenly mean "Go fuck yourself" today.

You could, in theory, walk out into the street and say "how for art thou" to your neighbor – and aside from the funny look he would give you – he would understand that you're asking how he's doing.

Language is arguably mankind's greatest tool. It is our ability to communicate and speak with each other through the use of human language, that we are able to accomplish some of the most amazing things ever imagined. And it is because human language has so much power, that it also brings with it such an overwhelming level of influence onto us and our culture.

More and more we are seeing our languages being used to further an agenda of wide-scale social influence. Serious issues are often downplayed to the point of disinterest, and mundane problems are elevated to monolithic proportions through the use of reconstructed dialogue.

Medical "experts" are now openly using the term "S.T.I." instead of the term "S.T.D." Why? Because they do not want to "stigmatize" a person who is suffering from a sexually transmitted disease. The problem with changing the terminology of a disease to an infection, is that you are not only encouraging the individual suffering from that disease to not take it seriously – you are also not discouraging them from going out and engaging in the same reckless behavior which earned them that disease in the first place.

The definition and severity of a disease does not change, just because you changed the language in order to not make people feel bad.

It is a serious issue. I have written in other sections of this book about how modern society is not only cultivating a culture of rampant sexual promiscuity – but how it is also reveling in that fact. The implications of downplaying the severity of things such as sexually transmitted disease, not only panders to the already established narrative of going out and sleeping with anyone you want – but it also encourages the people participating in those activities to be less safe and less responsible. Both with themselves and with each other.

We see this same strategy being used to build a narrative of social acceptance over issues that are flagrantly unacceptable in any society. Pedophiles are now being labeled as "Minor-Attracted Persons" and not just by brain dead activists on Twitter or other places on the internet – but by actual psychologists and therapists.

Again, it is an effort to not "stigmatize" the person – but that person, more often than not, raped a child. They don't deserve to not be stigmatized. They are exactly the sort of people who *should* be stigmatized – because they are evil. What has become of our society when we are actively trying to be more considerate of the feelings of a person who would like nothing more than to fuck an innocent boy or girl?

You can always make the argument that maybe a person that has been experiencing these sexual urges and has never acted on them is seeking help – which is in fact a good thing – but on a planet consisting of some 7.8 Billion people, that argument is nothing more than a straw man. It's naive, wishful thinking at best and outright subversive and insidious at worst.

This is the power that our language has. A slight change here, a redefining there, and everything we have begins to fall apart.

So what's next?

We already have words like Beastiality being changed out for terms such as Zoophelia, in order to temper the distaste of a person who wants to fuck their dog. Are we going to make a nicer word for rapists? Well we kind of already have. "Sexual Assault" is a term being used with a broader and more vague definition each and every time somebody stands up to use it in a court room – maybe we should start calling them "Sexually-Aggressive Persons" so that they don't feel so bad about shoving their cock up a woman's ass against her will.

I'm actually having to come back to this page, because while I clearly wrote the above paragraph with a certain sense of sarcasm – the state of Washington now actually has a bill up for vote to remove the term "Sex Offender" from their records in order to "advance a 'person-first' approach." I don't even know what to say. You can't make this shit up.

We're building the foundations for a future where anyone can be anything, and everyone can do anything, because nobody is allowed to be ostracized from society or condemned for their actions. We are teaching a generation – two generations – that you can say or think or be anything you want, even if it's wrong or incorrect. You're perfect, you're special, just the way you are.

But that's the state of the world. That's the state of our modern school systems – where we imprint these ideas onto people who then go out into life and act upon all of the bullshit that has been fed to them. Finding themselves in likewise positions of influence in whatever field they happen to be in – and remembering that crazy theory by their college professor that there's nothing wrong with being a pedophile.

Mark Twain once said: "I have never let my schooling interfere with my education."

How sad and true that sentiment seems to be.

One of the things which concerns me the most about the future of America – and the future of our world for that matter – is the complete and utter collapse of education as a whole and as a concept.

The once beautiful world of academia has become nothing more than a propagandist system of influence for Marcusean politics – the blending of Freudian sexual theory with Marxist ideologies, and topped with a sprinkling of Nietzsche's perpetual victimhood.

A place where critical thinking has been completely abolished – and students are turned into sheep and churned out on an assembly line of unquestioning, incurious complacency.

Goddamn it is a sorry state we live in.

While it is true that America's public education system has often been the butt of many jokes among foreign countries – more and more I witness and experience those supposedly more educated people making unfounded, fictitious and non-factual claims about the world.

As a matter of fact, I have personally been told by two different Canadians and three different Australians that "America actually lost the

Revolution." These people, with no hint or semblance of irony do truly believe – because they have been made to believe – that the United States of America is still to this day, a member of the Commonwealth of England.

The sheer level of ignorance that is growing across the globe is mind-boggling.

I was recently lectured by a Swedish man who insisted that the issue surrounding the use of "preferred pronouns" is an inherently ignorant and "American" one – because as a boy in school, he was taught to use the terms "They and Them" when referring to anybody in a position of authority. Teachers, Principles, etc.

The problem with this logic of course is that Swedish and English are not languages that have a one-to-one conversion, and that while "de" and "dem" may be a very close verbal cousin to "they" and "them" – the applicational use of those words in this context are very clearly not related at all.

I myself am not Swedish. I will not pretend to be Swedish. I will not pretend to understand why you would use a word like "they" or "them" to describe an inherent authority figure – but I can say that is not how those words are used in the English language. And I will furthermore add that regardless of whatever respective culture is dictated by your native language, the implication of this conversation is that I should not only be ashamed of being such a "stupid American" – but that I should also acknowledge the people who use "They/Them" pronouns as somehow being inherently superior to myself in the process.

Similar stupidity to this was also echoed in a conversation I once had with a particularly uppity Englishman who insisted that during the sixteenth through eighteenth century in England – the English term for a child was the phrase "It." Specifically, because the English did not recognize children as a "person" of either male or female, until maturing into adulthood.

That... is one of the dumbest things I have ever heard in my entire life.

To quote another great thinking on the subject of education, I believe it was Bertrand Russel who once said: "Men are born ignorant, not stupid. They are made stupid by education."

It is true that the term "it" could be applied to children – especially in certain regions with certain dialects – however to assert that for some three hundred-plus years, the British suddenly just up and forgot a majority of their own language in regards children – and that they adopted the concept of non-binary identification – is simply asinine.

Sentences like "Oh, well *it* is a bit nasty, isn't *it*?" are certainly within the realm of commonality during that time period, if not even earlier and probably still even today in certain places given the British' love for slang – but that doesn't mean that it held any kind of deep-seeded social commentary.

"It" was not a replacement for the word "child." "It" was not just arbitrarily applied to all children across the country – as this man insisted – but rather it was used with the same interchangeable frequency as any other slang for a kid. Tot, urchin, sprout – you could argue that it was a diminutive word – used to imply the lack of station or status possessed by a child as compared to an adult at the time – but to assert that it was the British recognition of children as a "separate gender" through its use is just utter horse shit.

The situation here in America is not much better, I'm ashamed to say. I am fortunate enough to have been awarded a unique vantage from which to peer behind the curtain of modern academic study – thanks largely to my mother.

As a teacher of History, she has passed down to me a love and appreciation of the fabled tales and tragedies of our world throughout the ages. Through this medium I have also developed a distinct love of languages, dialects and cultures – though admittedly – it's probably also her fault that I'm so bad at Mathematics and Science.

Here in America – and evidently around the globe – young students are being corrupted by misinformation and political bias in the classroom all throughout their Grade School education – and then they are thrust into their first years of college without so much as a basic, fundamental understanding of... anything.

I've met an inexcusable amount of people who wrongly assume that the U.S. is a Democracy, and don't even know that it's a Democratic-Republic. They don't even know what kind of government their nation adheres to.

A shocking majority of them can't read or write beyond a first or second grade level. Almost none of them know basic geographical terms such as "isthmus." Most of them can't name the capital of all fifty states – hell some of them don't even know the names of all fifty states.

For example, as an exercise in one of my mother's classes she assigned her students with the task of writing "letters" to an important historical figure of their choosing, so long as the letter came from the viewpoint of a person living in the appropriate era.

The responses to this exercise were... heartbreaking.

One student chose to write a letter to President Roosevelt, pleading with him to "be compassionate" and to "stop being mean to those poor German people."

The "poor German people" in question, were *Nazis*.

A complete lack of understanding, comprehension and critical thinking.

These issues are nothing new in the modern day – as I recall another story of my mother's students from my childhood, claiming that the Black Plague of Europe is what ultimately drove the ancient Peloponnesian Greeks out of Greece.

Let that one sink in for a minute.

This is a very real issue which is growing ever more prevalent, and rapidly spiraling out of control.

Combine this growing deconstruction of education among the youth of America with the literal hand-cuffing of educators at a college level – who are expected to pass failing students in order to make a quota – as well as the growing interference of political idealism on college campuses, and it makes for no surprise that things have gotten to where they are.

I'm not entirely sure that we have much of a future left in front of us, if this state of things is becoming the new norm.

You've probably heard the phrase that "Common sense isn't common anymore" but this has gone so far above and beyond that.

I don't know how we even begin to turn this around.

Chapter XI: The Race Card

Bob Dylan once wrote: "Times They Are a Changin'" and how little it seems to me that we understood those words to be prophetic.

We live now in the age of Diversity & Inclusion – a practice by which we look upon our fellow man and boil every facet of his life down to the simple color of his skin, sexual orientation or otherwise self-appointed identity.

We do not stop to ask if he is skilled or educated. We do not think about his individual wit or intelligence – nor do we account for his experience or credibility. No, instead we treat him as if he were a novelty – and stress the importance of his gratitude for our doing so.

That is a harmful act. It is a selfish act. A demeaning, insulting and contemptuous act.

It is the practice of those who do not truly care about the individual – but rather only care about making the impression of themselves look better to others.

There is a fissure in society. A great, gaping chasm of racial division and ethnic shaming. It is the slavery of the mind, and all of us – men and women of every color – must act and obey at the whims of our masters.

Who are these masters you ask? They are the Liberal and the Progressive. The malformed serpents of Congress and the Senate. The political denizens of the rot-infested cesspool known as Washington.

It is they – and their like-minded ilk in the most prominent positions of power – which construct a language of vitriol, derision, resentment and hate.

Critical race theory, ethnocentrism, intersectionality, systemic-racism and equity of color.

Words which are hollow and bear no meaning – and yet are used with purpose and cause great discord and calamity.

I have lived my entire life in the American South. A native born son of Virginia, and a long-time resident of Georgia. Life down here is a bit different than life in other parts of the country. Generations of people being taught a fictitious retelling of the Civil War often view the South through a lens of ingrained bias and imparted ire – yet for myself, and people like myself, life here is a place of warm welcome and neighborly affection.

The halls of my schoolhouse were lined with posters depicting children of all colors, holding hands and forming a circle around the earth. Everybody got along with one another – and never in all my childhood did I hear a single word uttered against another person over the color of their skin.

While I may be a man of many fears – a fear for my life or of physical danger has never been an issue for me to contend with – but now there are places in Macon where even I would not dare to go without a good reason to do so. Old and storied streets which I once walked without a care, are now darkened by the shadows of distrust and aggression.

It is true that the racist and the bigot have always existed in the world, but it was not until the election of President Barack Obama, who brought with him a re-ignition of racial animosity – not through the color of his skin but rather the message that he preached – did those most unseemly and uncivilized ways of thinking make a resurgence into the limelight.

Morgan Freeman once said that if you want to get rid of racism – stop talking about it.

In an interview with Mike Wallace, Freeman said that he didn't want a Black History Month. He said that "Black History" is American History. He asked Wallace if there was a "Jewish History Month" to which Wallace admitted "No." When Freeman asked if he wanted one, Wallace again said no – and Freeman said "Good. I don't want one either."

One of the things I've noted when pondering the topic of racism is the way in which other countries handle it. The British, for example, despite all of their problems, do not have Indian British, or African British, or Asian British – they're all just British. It isn't like here in America where everybody has to have a prefix or label.

Labels which, I might add, are so broad and umbrella in their usage that they often don't make any sense. African American, Asian American, Caucasian American – well, I would be a Caucasian American now wouldn't I, but under that heading comes Irish Americans, Italian

Americans, German Americans – even Jewish Americans whenever they're being lumped in with white people. It's divisive by nature.

If anything, as a native born resident of these United States – I should be a Native American – of course I cannot call myself a Native American because I'm not a.... Native American... Although I do have Indian blood in my veins – but so to do I have English and Irish and German and French and Italian and Sicilian and, Lord only *knows* what else is floating around in there.

Why do we all have to be a "Something" American? Why can't we all just *be* Americans?

We're "Something" Americans because we're supposed to be the "Great Melting Pot." We're supposed to celebrate our differences and our cultures, while also coming together as countrymen – but instead we keep using these prefixes to build walls between ourselves and grow further and further apart.

There has to be a give-and-take but everybody just wants to take and never give anymore.

We talk so much about racism and especially about slavery – but the simple fact of the matter is that I never owned a slave. My father and my father's father never owned a slave.

If you want to talk about oppression, then I can't think of anything more oppressive than heaping the burden of guilt onto somebody that hasn't committed any crime.

How far back are we supposed to go with this narrative?

I am a quarter Italian and a quarter Sicilian – I'm a descendant of ancient Rome. Before there was the great Roman Empire, you had the Roman Republic – and before you had the Roman Republic, the Roman people were enslaved to the Etruscans. Before the Roman people were enslaved to the Etruscans, they were refugees fleeing from Agamemnon's siege of Troy, and a genocidal slaughtering by the Greeks.

This is a series of events which takes place over the course of approximately 700 years – and all of it happened nearly 1,500 some-odd years ago.

Am I supposed to go out and ask for reparations? I'd love to see the people's reaction if I did.

Hell, while I'm at it I might just try seeking reparations for my Christian-European ancestors who were captured and turned into galley slaves by the Islamic Barbary States, and sold throughout the Ottoman Empire across a 400 year time-period spanning the 16th through 19th centuries.

Or y'know... maybe I could *not* do that.

Every single ethnic group throughout mankind's history has been enslaved at one point or another – and while we sit here bickering back and forth about it in *this* country, the very real issue of slavery is *still* taking place over in Africa and other parts of the world to this day.

This ongoing culture of racial agitation is not something that used to be so prevalent only a few short decades ago. History is history, and wounds are meant to be healed – but if you constantly pick off the scab then you are going to be left with a scar at best, and an open wound at worst – and if you have an open wound then it's going to become infected.

If left untreated the infection will spread – leaving the whole body to become ill.

That is the state of my country. A decrepit body wracked with illness.

I think I first noticed this during Obama's second or third year in office. There were numerous issues surrounding the discussion of race – many of which were aimed at government aid programs, welfare and education, etc. I cannot remember exactly who said it, but I will never forget the words that this man used. He was a Democrat from somewhere up North I think, and he stepped right up to that microphone with a smile on his face and said: "We have to help black people, because black people cannot help themselves."

And Leftists had the nerve to call that "progressive."

That would be the moment, I think, that it really dawned on me just how perverse the nature of the Democrat party had become. Prior to that, I had always held the general belief that Democrats and Republicans wanted the same thing – a better America – they just had different views on how to get there.

But that moment is what truly opened my eyes to everything going on. It's what made me realize that Liberals truly do not see people as "people," they see them as commodities.

Ever since then I've become acutely aware of certain speech patterns and mannerisms that get tossed around by people on the Left. The strange way they'll make a blanketed and declarative statement like "I just love gay people!" Or when they say "Oh I absolutely adore black people!"

What does that mean? A person being black isn't their identity. Their sexual orientation isn't their identity – a human being is more than the sum of their parts – so what do you really mean by that?

It's disturbing to me. It feels slimy and two-faced and disgusting to hear somebody talk that way. Like they can just bundle an entire group of people together like a collection of little toys on their shelf.

I care if a person is honest and loyal. I care if they are hard working and dependable.

I care about their dreams and ambitions. Their ability to hold a conversation and how easily they laugh at a joke. I care about their hurts and their troubles, their wants and their needs.

I care about the reflection of the past – and the reach of their vision for the future.

What matters the most to me is not that I surround myself with people of all backgrounds like a Sultan curating his collection of exotic pets – but rather that when I go to sleep each night, I might sleep soundly in the knowledge that the people I work for, work with or otherwise have work for me – as well as those closest to me – are good and decent.

What matters the most to me is seeing a person as a person – not a label or description on a shelf.

Human beings are more than that.

In 1965 James Baldwin spoke in a debate held at Cambridge University, and he won that debate. In his closing arguments Baldwin said these powerful words: "until the moment comes when we the American people are able to accept the fact, that I have to accept for example, and my ancestors are both white and black... That on that continent we are trying to forge a new identity for which we need each other – and that I am not a ward of America – I am not an object, or a missionary charity."

I cannot begin to describe how proud I was when I first heard those words – not because I had some fetishistic pride over a "black man" standing up and saying them – but because I heard a fellow American stand up and say them. I took pride in hearing such eloquence and earnesty coming from the mouth of my fellow countryman.

I suppose that ultimately, these words fell on deaf ears – because today we push these harmful and discriminatory practices onto the people at every turn. We ascribe to the principle that "racism" is a concept that cannot be held by any group of people other than the "white man." That "white privilege" somehow exists in America, or even the world – and that racial discrimination is not the practice of looking down on someone based on the color of their skin – but based on the power that they hold – and that if you do not have power, then you in fact cannot be racist.

Well I have no fucking power. I have no authority or sway in the world – and my skin *is* white.

I've heard "white privilege" described as never being pulled over by the police due to the color of my skin or otherwise due to any form of racial profiling – but I've been pulled over by the cops several times in my life. It gets so hot down here in Georgia that I once shaved my hair for the summer, and around two or three in the morning I was pulled over by an officer that looked at me and treated me like I was some kind of neo-Nazi skinhead.

I've heard "white privilege" described as never suffering from the burden of social-economic struggle, and always coming from a place of sound financial stability. Why don't you just come on over to my house, where I have no heating or air conditioning – where I have no running water or internal plumbing – and take a look inside my wallet. It's right there on the make-shift counter that I built out of two saw-horses and a sheet of plywood. Go ahead, take a look inside. I'm poorer than fucking dirty. A lot of people are poorer than dirt – most of the goddamn country is currently poorer than dirt. Poverty knows no color other than *green*.

I've heard "white privilege" described, believe it or not, by the fact that the white-man has a father in their homes, and that white fathers are allowed to show affection towards their children without the fear of being emasculated by society. First of all, let me tell you that I did not have a father. I had almost no positive male role-models in my immediate family growing up – and if you have cultivated an internal culture for yourselves that says men are not allowed to be loving towards their children – that is *your* responsibility, not mine.

If you don't want to hear that from me, then take it from Denzel Washington who was asked about whether or not black Americans could ever hope to truly make a change in this country, to which Washington said: "Well it starts in the home, y'know. If the father's not in the home, the boy will find a father in the streets."

We've perpetuated this culture of race-baiting, race-blaming and indoctrinated victim-hood. The only thing that these mindsets have accomplished is a deepening of the divide which comes between us as Americans. That comes between us as men and women who are privileged to be American – and to wake up every day in this once proud nation under God, which stands or at least at one time stood for the principles of freedom and for liberty.

Those concepts, those ideals that make this nation what it is are being destroyed. They've eroded away on the machinations of the political Left, and you can see this playing out before us in real-time.

I have worked very hard for most of my life. Mowing fields, digging ditches, clearing stumps and chopping logs. These are the normal, mundane tasks that come with the territory of country living.

I did not have my first job – by which I mean one that required filling out paperwork – until I was eighteen years old.

I was a simple busboy at the Logan's Roadhouse in Warner Robins. Looking back on it now, I truly believe that everyone should be made to work in a restaurant at least once in their lifetime. I think if this should come to pass, the world would be a much better place.

Working at the roadhouse opened my eyes to a great many things, and taught me so many invaluable lessons that will stick with me forever.

I saw sane people and crazy people. Happy people and angry people – not to mention the sad people. I saw loud people and quiet people. Rude and polite, serious and carefree. Every type of person you could ever imagine came into that restaurant. From the Mennonites in period clothing to the leather-clad bikers and the inner-city basketballers to the blue-haired old church ladies.

Everybody ate at the roadhouse.

If you've ever seen the 2005 film "Waiting..." it's actually not very far off – except for the part where everybody shows their genitals. That never happened at Logan's... That I know of.

But I laughed and I cried with those people I worked with. We'd go outside to smoke cigarettes by the dumpster on our break, and everyone would share their hopes and dreams – or things that were getting them down in life.

They'd talk about their parents or siblings or partners or children in such great detail that I'd swear I met them all.

We were a family. A family of strangers, but a family nonetheless.

I worked hard and eventually earned a promotion – opening up the restaurant in the mornings and cleaning floors. Mr. Kenny, the old man who worked the dish pit, became a sort of father figure to me. I would arrive before him and make sure the coffee was ready by the time he got there. Kenny was an old black man, and I was a young white man. We'd stand outside the front doors of the building each morning, sharing coffee and cigarettes while we talked.

He'd tell me stories about his life, and listen to stories about mine.

We'd talk about music and about women. About cars and about the weather – and he would always give me advice whenever I needed it. He was a good and decent man, and he will always have a place of love and respect in my heart.

Thinking about it now, I'm reminded of a funny moment that happened. Most of the men in the "back of house" were black – one or two being Hispanic – and the only other white guy that worked behind the kitchens was Mr. John. An older gentleman who just so happened to be around my height and roughly the same build. The guys used to always call me John, and joke that we all looked alike – to which the baking ladies who made the bread would simply tell me to "pay no mind."

One day in the middle of summer, I was waiting for my mother to pick from work because my truck had broken down. The sun was high and the heat was brutal. Kenny came out of the back door to run trash to the dumpster – so naturally several of the cooks snuck out with him to grab a quick smoke.

Kenny said to me, he said: "Boy, don't you know if you sit in that sun you're gonna burn up?" To which I couldn't help but reply: "I'm just trying to look more like y'all!"

It just sort of came out without even a moment's hesitation to think about it.

One of the cooks, I'm afraid I cannot recall his name at the moment – choked and spat out his cigarette – and Mr. Kenny laughed so hard that he nearly toppled over the trash cans.

I still look back on that as one of the funniest – and happiest – moments of my life. Everybody crowded around the back of the restaurant, trying not to get caught smoking – and laughing their asses off.

Everybody understood that there was no malice in those words. No hidden meaning or subtle jab. It was all good fun, and taken in good nature.

I believe this would have been around the start of Obama's second term – and while it may have taken more time to creep into the country towns and rural cities – that cultural divide which he had instigated, and the people like him pushed for and perpetuated – would eventually find its way here. The scars of which can still be seen everywhere you look.

Today, Logan's Roadhouse is gone. An empty lot with an oil stain on the concrete where I accidentally spilled some grease, the only testament to its memory. It will, however, live on inside my mind – and the memories and stories I experienced there will always be with me.

In stark contrast to this, another story calls to mind from several years later. By this point, the spite-filled venom of liberal "outrage" culture had become exactly what it is today, and small towns and cities were no longer exempt from its wrath.

I had been out of steady work for some time and my body was in poor health – though at the time I did not know why. It was around the Christmas of 2018 I think, that while looking for work I managed to pick up a part-time job at the local theatre.

I wasn't the oldest employee, but I was close to it. Well, outside of management at any rate. Most of my co-workers were sixteen or seventeen, with only one or two being eighteen or older. They were loud, obnoxious and typically rather lazy. They carried vape-pens and would hotbox themselves in the break room or supply closet – and call me a "Dirty

Redneck" for smoking cigarettes on my break. Honestly speaking, they were brash, entitled and had absolutely no idea what it meant to go into work and do their job.

I'd like to be clear that not all of them were like this. There were a handful of decent kids who worked very hard and had good heads on their shoulders – but largely, it was a farce. A gathering of foul-mouthed and ignorant children who spent their time playing crude games like "Kill, Bang, Marry" in front of customers, or being overly concerned with how you addressed them and by which name you called them.

The managerial staff were no better, and I can remember so distinctly the strange and frankly unnerving way in which they approached me to inquire after my "preferred" name.

My name is Benjamin. That's what's on my name tag. Call me by my full name, or shorten it to Ben – it's not rocket science, and it certainly is not the extreme matter of life or death they made it out to be.

Every day I would come in and listen to them spouting off some piece of progressivist propaganda – and when questioned on it – they had no way to back it up or explain their position on the subject, because they had no idea what they were talking about.

They were told to think a certain way. To act a certain way. To walk, talk and mock a certain way – and they did. One girl called me a racist because I asked one of the other guys working there to help me change the letters on the marquee. Now, I am over six feet tall, but I am still very much overshadowed by somebody that is seven feet tall.

The fact that he was a black had nothing to do with it – he was just taller than me.

But that's where things have gotten to.

Now this last part really doesn't have to do with race, but I'll end this little anecdote by mentioning that eventually, I was brought into the office and reprimanded for referring to one of the girls as "sugar". Apparently, as it was later explained – some other girl working there overheard this comment and became "uncomfortable" by hearing it.

From what I gather, it wasn't even the person I said it to who complained.

Now I don't know about other parts of the U. S. but in the South and especially out in the country and in small towns and cities, casual use of terms of endearment such as sugar, honey, darlin' and so forth is a deeply ingrained part of our culture. Those words don't mean anything beyond a form of nicety between two people who, at the bare minimum, are at least somewhat cordial with one another. They're terms that men and women both use openly and in frequent fashion.

From the way those managers spoke to me, you'd think that I had cornered that young girl in some secluded part of the theatre, forced her up against the wall and molested her. I was made to feel like a pervert. Like a dirty old man, leching around after those underage girls and co-workers.

I apologized of course, for making anyone uncomfortable – but what is more, I apologized and expressed my deepest sorrow over how that girl is going to react when she leaves the theatre and finds a real job. When she makes a mistake one day – as we all do from time to time – and her new boss tears her a new asshole and chews her out until he's blue in the face.

It wasn't very long after that when I handed in my two weeks notice. I told the managers the truth. I said: "I'm not comfortable with people who are so uncomfortable." And that was that.

Looking back on it now, while Logan's turned out to be one of the happiest times of my life – that theatre was one of the saddest. As an avid lover of film, I had hoped to enjoy my time there – but seeing and experiencing the way in which the younger generation had been taught to behave, and how management seemed to walk on broken glass to accommodate that behavior – was really heartbreaking.

I will not say that there was nothing admirable to be found, or that there weren't moments worth remembering – but overall the experience served no purpose other than to show how truly bleak the future is.

There's an indoctrination of the mind at work in this country. This chapter is about race – but there will be another one about sex – and the way you're seeing people view these issues is alarmingly similar. The way in which a person's very existence gets dissected and trimmed down by the culture of our society today until a single description or feature is all that it takes to categorize them. It's horrifying.

That's how you ingrain an idea into a generation. That's how you turn a "buzzword" into a reality.

I remember the day my mother came home crying from work, and she told me that one of her students had been attacked. She was working at Fort Valley State University here in Georgia, and this young man had missed several classes. One day he came to her office with a black eye and swollen jaw – and he was apologizing to her of all people, that he had been absent.

My mother was never a terribly emotional woman – but she was in tears as she told me what happened to him.

He had gone back to his old neighborhood in town to visit his mama for Mother's Day, and he got stopped in the street by a group of guys who recognized him. They said he was "Turning his back on Black" because he had a decent haircut and decent clothes. Because he was trying to better himself and go to school to get an education.

They beat him down in the street.

If you want to talk to me about "systemic-racism" why don't you look at decades of the Democrat party treating minorities like a product to be used and controlled for their voter base, instead of actually trying to make a difference in their lives. Decades of telling them that they can't be anything more, and can't do anything on their own, instead of building them up and encouraging them to hope and try for something better.

Liberals don't really care about racism, they only care about seeming to care about racism. They have absolutely no idea what life is like out in the real world. You talk about "white washing" well they're the ones white-washing everything. They've told Hispanics that they have to change their language to be more "inclusive." They've told Native Americans that white people know what is and is not offensive to them, and that they can't even have a fucking football team anymore.

I once saw these two young guys doing a review of an old Dungeons & Dragons book called Oriental Adventures. It was basically the exact same thing as regular D&D, but instead of having a typical Western European setting, it was modeled after a more Asian aesthetic. These guys flipped through the book, and they got angrier and angrier and angrier with each paragraph they read. They were shocked, they were outraged – it was "racist." Do you know what they didn't do? They didn't once stop to consider the fact that somebody took a look at Chinese, Japanese, Tibetan and Mongolian cultures and thought to themselves: "Wow! This is cool!" They never once took a moment to think about the fact that somebody out there in the world thought that these cultures were fascinating and inspirational. The only thing they did was get offended, because they *wanted* to be offended.

Do you have any idea how amazing I would feel if somebody looked at my culture and thought that it was cool? Thought it was fascinating and inspirational? I'd be over the moon. I'd be ecstatic.

If you picked up a book for some roleplaying game and found an America inspired character, like the "War Eagle" or something – you'd look down in the stat block and see the only thing it gets is a +2 in being fat and stupid.

And I'll just go ahead and say it, these guys were white. They were as white as rice – they sounded whiter and more California-clueless than a fucking Kardashian. It's ingrained in them – it's ingrained in all of them. It's the nature of their political ideology.

I see videos all the time of guys going out and wearing a poncho, maybe a sombrero, because they're celebrating Cinco de Mayo – or others where they're wearing some variation of hanfu because their celebrating the Lunar Festival – and they get swarmed by white liberal college students or passers by, screaming at them for being "racist" and "perpetuating cultural stereotypes" or for "cultural appropriation." Then you see those same guys go and wear these outfits in a predominantly Chinese or Hispanic neighborhood – and they absolutely love them. They love the fact that somebody, anybody has taken the time to genuinely appreciate their culture. To get involved with it.

But that idea of appreciating the differences that make us unique is simply unacceptable to them.

Do you know what is considered acceptable? "Transracialism." The concept that a person's ethnicity is just as "fluid" as their sexuality or gender, and that they have the right to "self-identify" as a different race. That a white woman can go out and apply to college or apply for a job, while claiming to be of Native American or African American descent – despite the fact that she has purely white ancestry – and take advantage of minority scholarships and minority hiring practices.

Some of you reading this might think that it's a joke, or might think that I'm exaggerating – but it's true. I know a girl who rode on the skirt-tails of Affirmative Action by claiming to be half black and half Indian – and it worked – she received a full scholarship to college. What was her ethnicity? White. Pure Irish ancestry – skin whiter than mayonnaise, hair redder than ketchup – emerald green eyes and freckled from head to toe. She was so white that she looked like she had just stepped straight off the first potato-boat to New York – but hey, she got that free ride.

The hypocrisy surrounding Liberal racism is utterly repulsive and vile. It's inexcusable.

They're the ones who are actually racist.

I remember when the comedian Bill Burr got attacked for being "racist" because he mispronounced a woman's name – and when his wife, a woman who is black, came out in defense of her husband – they called her a "filthy coon" and an "Aunt Jemima."

When Larry Elder ran for Governor of California as the Republican candidate during the 2021 recall election, Leftists did the same thing. They called him a "coon" they called him a "nigger" and an "Uncle Tom." I saw one woman – a white woman – walking behind his parade float wearing a goddamn monkey mask and throwing shit at him, shouting at him to "go back where you belong."

Where was the outrage for that?

There was none.

Because it didn't fit the narrative.

Just look at where we are in this country. You have people out there talking about what a better world it would be if you just "erased all white people." If you "performed an ethnic cleansing."

You have activists, politicians and community leaders calling for re-segregation. You have schools creating areas on their campuses where white students aren't allowed to go, or events that they're not allowed to participate in.

I mean Jesus Christ, you have major companies out there like Coca-Cola forcing its workers to attend employee-seminars that instruct them to "Try to be less white."

Do you really think that that's progress? Do you truly believe that that's a step forward for civilization?

Let me tell you something right now. If that's really what you think, then you can keep those thoughts to yourself and stay the hell away from me, because I've got no fucking use for you.

Chapter XII: Numb

I am deeply concerned about the growing sense of general complacency and disinterest which seems to permeate the modern youth culture of the West. People my own age and younger who no longer seem to care about life, or the things happening in it.

Ignorant statements are made about the most basic factual truths such as biology, anatomy, history and science. Tactless comments are made at the expense of victims and tragedies the world over – and only the most hollow excuses are made to justify themselves – with almost all of it met by only laughter and jest.

In short, they do not care.

They do not view the world as being important. They do not view life as a thing that should have meaning. They are incapable of taking anything seriously, and shrug off most everything as one massive joke.

They are lethargic and apathetic – utterly disconnected and unconcerned.

To put it plainly, they are lost. Drifting on the oceans of declination and cultural escapism. They are numbed to the world around them by the excess consumption of drugs, sex and media. Their lives are no longer exciting – not a thing to be lived, but simply endured – and it shows.

Arrested development is one term which calls to mind – but somehow this is different. This is a wide-spread issue that is quickly becoming commonplace, and if it is not addressed it will become a fixture.

Perhaps it is some form of rebellion against the growing trends of totalitarianism found throughout the Western world. After all, why should they care about a world governed and ruled over by people who view them only as props and trinkets? Then again, perhaps it is merely emblematic of the current state of cultural regression, and the devolution of society as a whole.

They say that a person's 40s are their new 20s. When once a young man was expected to graduate from high school and be out of the house by 18 – now he is 38 and still living with his parents.

Socialized economic structure dictates a rate of high taxes and low income. The politicized nature of the modern education system demands more degrees in order to mean anything in life. When once an Associate's degree meant that you were an educated man – thanks to the overabundance of people having one – they have diluted its value and made it meaningless. A newer, shinier diploma at best – forcing students to spend more time and more money chasing a higher degree that they certainly should not need and may not even want.

With that in mind, why would you leave the house where you have no real expenses, to go out and get a job that won't provide a future – when you could just live at home for free – slowly and soullessly fulfilling the arbitrary requirements that society has set for you in order to succeed?

Why should anyone bother – and why should anyone try?

Everywhere I look in this country – everywhere I look in most places for that matter – I see the same shambling masses trudging through their day-to-day lives, trying to hold on for something better. Something deeper, something more meaningful – something that makes any kind of sense at all.

But we can't seem to find it.

There's a lot of talk today about mental illness and emotional well-being. They say that we've made such amazing strides in combating these issues. That we're a society who is more caring and more compassionate than any generation that has ever come before us – but the problems that we're talking about are only getting worse as time goes on.

It's true that we are talking about these things more. That we do have more practices and regulations and laws and services, all specifically dedicated to people suffering from mental illness – but it isn't getting better, and nobody seems to be asking "why?"

I mentioned in an earlier chapter that we have more people suffering from depression today than we had during The Great Depression. That's a verified study – it's a fact – so why? If we never used to talk about these things, how come now that we are, everyone is feeling worse?

I think that it's fairly obvious that we have created a society which generates infinitely more problems than it solves.

There's so much pressure in the world today that it's crushing the general population under the weight of it. Things like therapy and psychiatric care have become downright normal for most people – even people who I know for a fact can't afford it. That's not a "good" thing. Needing to see a therapist isn't a good thing – you shouldn't need to visit a psychiatrist unless you actually need help – which means that either A: Therapy isn't helping, or B: More and more people are beginning to buckle to the point that they have to have it.

But the question still stands: Why?

Trying to tackle a problem is all well and good, after all if you're dealing with a man who's been shot, or a house that's currently on fire, you don't stop to ask why it happened or how it happened in the moment. You have to treat the situation as quickly as possible – but eventually you do need to try and find out what caused this. That seems to be where we're falling down on the job. Everybody is so obsessed with all of the different ways we have with which to treat different problems – nobody is trying to stop the problems from happening in the first place.

Applying a solution after solution without ever understanding or addressing why it was necessary in the first place doesn't actually solve anything.

Inflation is out of control and getting higher by the day. Fewer and fewer people actually own their personal property. Crime has become an everyday normality. Personal privacy has been abolished. Everyone is becoming more and more isolated. Social contagions pressure kids into being people that they don't want to be – and God help you if you speak out about any of it, because you'll get shouted down for committing a hate crime.

People are miserable. People are depressed. They are desperate for help – desperate for answers – but we won't give them any. I look around at the Western world, specifically the United States, and I see a country riddled with disease. Cancer is at an all-time high, diabetes is running rampant – children are born with disabilities in the thousands, people are developing mental disorders at an incomprehensible rate – the whole country is suffocating under an overreaching political ideology – and rather than look for a genuine solution to these problems, we keep prescribing them with medication and passing laws which legalize drugs to keep them in a stupor.

The U. S. has placed many different bans or restrictions on things like asbestos, mercury, lead in the homes over the last several decades. They've banned smoking in most public places, claiming that it is the chief cause of cancer – and yet other countries like Japan that do not have such heavy restrictions of some of these things aren't suffering the same way we are. Why? Japan does not have the restrictive bans on mercury that we do here in the United States. Japan began diminishing the use of asbestos in 2004, and did not outright ban it until 2013 – long after the US began to crack down on it in 1989 – and only as recently as 2020 did Japan enact greater restrictions on smoking that reflect those found in Western countries.

The total population size of the United States of America is roughly around 26 times larger than that of Japan, and yet according to the CDC, WHO and GCO, if you were to compare and cross-examine the rates of cancer in these two countries to their relative population – you would find that Japan is much healthier.

Using 2020 as the anchor point for this experiment, I began to crunch the numbers:

Total US Population = 331 million.

Existing Cancer Cases in the US = 8.4 million.

8.4 million is 2.5476% of 331 million.

Total Population of Japan = 126.4 million.

Existing Cancer Cases in Japan = 2.7 million.

2.7 million is 2.1432% of 126.4 million.

2.1432 is a 15.8742% differential of 2.5476.

These estimates reflect a marked 15.9% differential in the rate of cancer cases between our two countries, which is not insignificant – although they also reflect that while Japan is healthier, cancer is on the rise. Low rates of obesity, a considerably lower intake of saturated fatty acids and much higher intakes of marine n-3 polyunsaturated fatty acids, along with a possible hereditary resistance, may be factors as to why Japan has remained so comparatively healthy for such a long time.

Yet there are signs indicating that as a greater influence of Westernization, with things such as more sedentary lifestyles, poorer choices in diet, higher levels of obesity and increased reliance on medications begin to cement themselves in the country, the general health of the nation is starting to reflect this and *fall*.

The reality of this is reflection can be found in the total number of <u>new</u> cancer cases found between the US and Japan in the same year of 2020:

Total US Population = 331 million.

New Cases of Cancer in the US = 2.2 million.

2.2 million is 0.6893% of 331 million.

Total Population of Japan = 126.4 million.

New Cases of Cancer in Japan = 1.02 million.

1.02 million is 0.81331% of 126.4 million.

0.68931 is a 17.9% differential of 0.81331.

Here we can see that, at least in 2020, Japan has suffered from roughly 18% more *new* cases of cancer than the United States. There *is* a decisive gap between our two countries – but it is steadily closing as time goes on and widespread illness is on the rise.

On the topic of rising illness, it should be noted that while the general mortality rate of cancer in the US has been lowered by roughly 30% over the last several decades, the rate at which individuals are actually developing cancer has skyrocketed and only continues to rise with each passing year.

In other words, the gap between our two countries isn't closing because the rate of cancer in America is going down – but rather because the rate of cancer in Japan is going up.

Now I want to state it as plainly as possible that I am in no way suggesting we should consider bringing asbestos, mercury and lead back into the public mainstay – and nor am I saying, even as a lover of tobacco – that we should return to the days of smoking up in hospitals next to patients on oxygen. But what I am saying is that we should be deeply concerned about the things we have replaced these materials with, and about the changes that we have been making to our environment along with them.

It seems to me that we have become a society that is utterly dependent upon foreign substances. The shape of the human body – especially in the West – has physically altered with new forms of body fat that are more resistant to traditional methods of exercise, and the male Y chromosome has noticeably begun degenerating its shape. We over-expose ourselves to growth hormones, antibiotics, antidepressants, uppers, downers, chemical solutions of every variety.

We fill our drinking water with fluoride. We pump our livestock and produce full of steroids and pesticides to provide larger quantities of a lower quality product. We've seen the rapid legalization of marijuana, as well as the general decriminalization of narcotics which further adds to the growing apathetic lethargy of the population.

In fact just talking about drugs like marijuana, when it first started becoming legal they pushed it onto children and said that it's "none-addictive" and it has no risk of any negative side effects. Now they're seeing that all those kids who were pumped full of it are suffering from cognitive faculty issues due to arrested development of the brain. They said that it wasn't addictive like cigarettes – that it wasn't habit forming – and now they're saying it causes "chronic dependency issues."

What the hell do you call a "chronic dependency issue" if not an addiction?

If you're unable to function without being in a "certain state of mind" then it's an addiction. If you suffer from withdrawals, becoming irritable and irrational because you haven't had enough of something – it's an addiction.

We keep lying about the reality of things, ignoring the bigger issues of the world and then ultimately we just numb ourselves more easily – and eagerly – than ever before.

We keep pushing the boundary over and over and over again about what is "progress" and what's "too far." We're flooding our children full of chemicals and substances from the moment they are born and then wondering why so many of them are having issues.

Just coming back for my final edits and in the last week or so a new song by Jack Harris called "Careful What You Wish For" has started circulating and going viral. The song itself beautifully articulates the kind of things that I am talking about, and lyrics such as "Take this pill, you'll feel much better when you wake up numb, and your brain's been severed" clearly resonates with a lot of people.

The song even continues later with another line, asking the simple question: "How can they sell you on something to help you, then tell you it might make you wish you were dead?"

I understand exactly what he's talking about and it honestly makes me so glad to know that other people are beginning to take notice of this issue. I see so many "doctors" get up on TV or on YouTube and tell everyone watching to just "fall in line." To stop asking questions, stop doubting "the process" or "the medicine" and, and basically just put a sense of blind faith in them without ever looking for more information.

When my mother was a baby she would have received half the total number of immunizations that I did – and in turn, I didn't receive about half of the vaccinations that my best friend's child has been given. Each generation we see a marked increase in the number of shots being given to kids, as well as a striking increase in developmental issues found among those same children.

I was born with Dyslexia and Asperger's Syndrome, as well as some kind of degenerative joint problem. My friend's son is riddled with disabilities and developmental concerns. Could the increase in immunizations given to us as children have had an effect on these sorts of things? I don't know – because nobody wants to talk about it. If you ask questions you're shouted down. If you show any sign of being hesitant or unsure, you're called a conspiracy theorist.

I am not a conspiracy theorist – I am not one of those raving "anti-vaxxers" who believes that we should be returning to the dark days before modern medicine and leaving ourselves to the mercy of chance – I'm just saying that we are seeing such a massive influx of problems, all taking place when we are supposedly "advancing" in a better direction. It's a case of 2+2=3; something isn't adding up.

I like having clean drinking water and I'm glad that we've created things such as Penicillin. I do not want us to somehow revert back to the stone ages, or to ancient times when doctor's thought that human illness related to the "humors" of the body – but I do feel compelled to point out that we clearly have too much stuff being pumped into us. Human beings weren't designed for all of these outside influences, and it's quite obviously taking its toll.

If a person is feeling even the slightest bit blue – they run to the doctor who prescribes them medication upon medication to cover up the problem. We load pregnant mothers full of Celexa and Zoloft, and then they give birth to children that suffer from fetal withdrawals and grow up to become depressed themselves.

Sources have shown that approximately 8-10% of women in the United States are given Selective Serotonin Reuptake Inhibitors, or SSRIs, during their pregnancy – which means that anywhere between roughly 300,000 to 400,000 children are being exposed to these drugs each year.

In a study by Columbia University, researchers noted that while most sources concluded the presence of SSRIs during pregnancy had little to no effect on infants at birth – these same sources were not taking into consideration the effect on children entering adolescence. When experimenting on mice, scientists noticed a profound effect that SSRI exposure held on the fetal brain circuitry, leading to a significant increase in the volume of the Amygdala and the Insula – as well as increased connectivity between those two regions of the brain.

While behavioral studies of these same mice have shown no effect when they are young – those that were exposed to SSRIs during the early stages of their life all seem to begin showing signs of extreme anxiety and depression upon reaching puberty.

Well damn, that sure sounds familiar doesn't it?

I know so, so many people who are my age or younger that are completely dependent upon things like antidepressants, anti-anxiety medications, anti-this and anti-that – so much so that they can't even see it for themselves anymore. The very notion that they may have a dependency issue sends them into a defensive rage – even when they'll admit to you that   they   "cannot   function"   without   it.

It is a state of chronic codependency and absolute denial.

What's worse is so many of these same people still turn to drugs and alcohol in spite of the medication – popping pills every single morning and spending their nights getting drunk and high in order to numb a pain that isn't being cured – and in some cases, isn't even there to begin with.

I used to know a guy who'd get himself hopped up every single night and he surrounded himself with people who did the same thing. They'd all be staying up until three or four in the morning, smoking dope and wasting their lives away. Each one of them were on multiple forms of medication.

They used to say the sickest and most awful things. they'd share photographs of 9/11 or the Kennedy assassination and just... laugh. They'd laugh their hearts out. If you tried to talk to them about it they either wouldn't remember, or they'd try to justify it as "no big deal" or something. It was disgusting.

They'd do the same thing with images of children in Iraq and Afghanistan, or the journalists who were beheaded by ISIS, or even just brutal and horrific car crashes on the interstate.

I'll never forget how they used that famous photo of Kennedy, the one where you can see Jackie crawling over the back seat and John slumped over – and they just laughed and laughed and laughed. They said "Man that's a great car, you can fit so many dead Presidents in that bad boy!" I said "What the hell is wrong with you?"

They didn't care. Nothing mattered to them.

When I finally cut ties they tried to tell me that I was the problem – and I said no, it's you. But they didn't care, and you couldn't convince them of that. I've known a lot of people who do that sort of thing and think the way they did.

You might be surprised just how much of that sort of thing goes on in the world.

I myself suffer from depression. My moods are often dark, even under the best of circumstances. It's a condition which vexes me to no end, especially when more often than not my greatest achievements – my highest highs – are usually my lowest of lows. Conquering or mastering or otherwise overcoming some task or challenge that would otherwise leave a person feeling elated and accomplished – tends to just leave me feeling empty and miserable.

I was afforded the option to try some "happy-pills" when I was younger, but even at the age of thirteen I realized that finding "happiness" at the bottom of a bottle of pills would be no different than finding it at the bottom of a bottle of liquor. Man-made or otherwise manufactured "happiness" is not true happiness – and I have no interest in settling for a cheap knock off of the real thing. I would much rather suffer and struggle to find it on my own.

And believe me, I have struggled to find it. I've dealt with my own demons of alcoholism and drug addiction over the years. I still drink to be honest – it comes on me in waves. Sometimes I won't want it. I'll be completely dry for months – and then one day, boom. I've fallen off that wagon in a hard, hard way and it'll be a minimum of a two week bender –

and then I'll get over it again for some reason and I never know what causes it or when it's going to happen.

I never burnt spoons over the stove or slammed a needle in my arm, but when I was younger I was mixing up a cocktail of pills just about every morning. I didn't have the money or the contacts for heavy things like codeine or quaaludes – but I could easily get my hands on the over-the-counter stuff.

Acetaminophen, ibuprofen, dextromethorphan, naproxen, etc. Wake up, pop my bottles, take about two of each different pill – add a few bismuth to keep from throwing it all back up – and wash it all down with a belt of whatever booze I happened to have. Hop in the shower, brush my teeth and start my day.

Things like that will absolutely get you high – and keep you there. What finally broke me of that habit was one day I went through my routine, drove all the way to work, had my last cigarettes before starting and then went inside to clock in. I punched in my number and – I was parked in my driveway, taking the keys out of my ignition.

I lost an entire day of my life.

I assume I must have done my job correctly since I didn't get fired – but whatever happened between clocking in and getting home, I have no idea. I don't suppose I'll ever know. That's what made me quit and I'm very glad that I did – not that I've never stumbled here or there.

Alcohol has certainly remained a persistent issue for me, but at least when it came to drugs I was able to kick that bucket – but not everyone is like me though – and some people need more help than I do. I am not suggesting that we suddenly ban all medications and dismantle the pharmaceutical industry – but we have created for ourselves a society built on crutches. We medicate teenagers who claim to have "PTSD" because their mother once justly spanked them for shoplifting – in the exact same manner that we medicate veterans coming back from war.

We have become a society that is built upon lies and facades – and now we can no longer distinguish the true from the false. We no longer differentiate between those individuals who truly need help, and those who simply want an easy excuse.

In short, we have become blind.

I mentioned fluoride in the drinking water – they say that it's such a small amount that it can't cause any harm – but we started putting that stuff into the public water system back in 1945. That's over 77 years of people drinking that water, probably multiple times a day for your average person – especially ones who live in a big city. Don't tell me that it can't or doesn't add up over time.

I think we can all agree that many brands of plates and dishes from the 1950s were just completely filled with radiation – and that removing things like that from the public is a good thing – but we're also so overbearing on all of these different man-made solutions that we lean on today, that it's actively having an adverse effect on our lives.

I've said it before in the chapter and I'll say it again – I don't think that we need to stop interacting with modern medicine – I'm not telling anybody to go flush their pills down the toilet, but I do think that it's high time that we all start to slow down and take a good hard look at exactly what we're doing.

Take a look at what we're doing to ourselves – and to each other.

Chapter XIII: Sexual Creatures

One of the biggest and most rapidly growing concerns in America – as well as many countries around the world – is the topic of sex. Sexual activity, sexual orientation, sexual identity. Sex. It's everywhere today, and it's hard to get away from it.

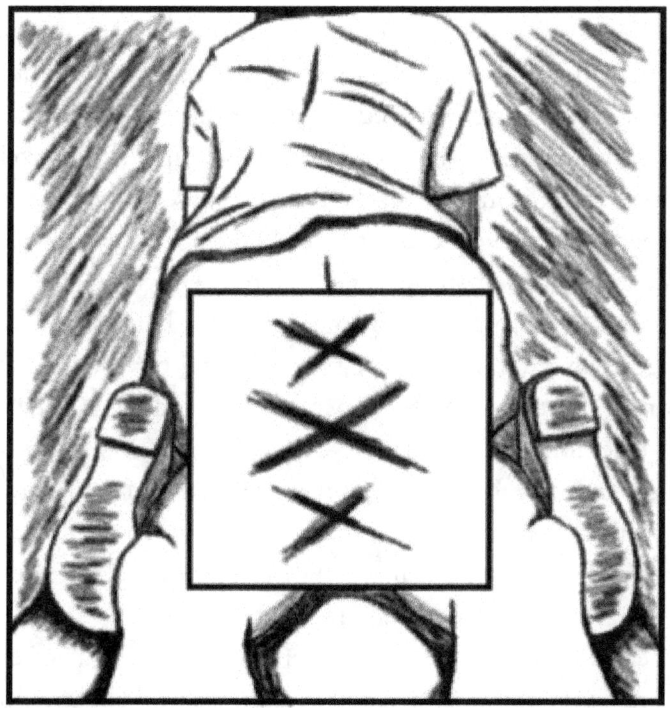

The issues surrounding sex are just constantly thrust into your face no matter where you look – and not in the fun kind of way.

You see the most of it in the form of gender identity politics – but it's not really an issue that can be entirely relegated to just the matters of gender or identity – it's really an issue of society and culture.

Ironically, I'm actually having a rather difficult time writing about this subject – because sex is such an omnipresent topic in modern society – there's so many different possibilities that I could use as a starting point. It's really a bit staggering. I've spent most of the past three days just trying to figure out what I wanted to say and how I wanted to say it – and even just the best angle to approach the issue.

I suppose the most intuitive thing to do would be to start with myself, and work outwards from there.

As I have said before, I am Catholic. Personally, I do not believe in sex before marriage – but that doesn't mean that I don't have an interest in sex. I'm still a man. I'm still *human*.

As a person I've always been very creatively minded, so I have studied classical and contemporary art. I'm a lover of history, so I've read the mythologies of the world. I have viewed images of men and women from every angle. I've seen renderings and depictions of young girls tied to bulls on the order of tyrannical Romans – and engrossed myself Greek epics and tragedies where women lay with every manner of God or beast – usually resulting in some monstrous offspring for a hero to then go and slay.

In a much more modern and mundane context, when I was a young boy I spent more than my fair share of time slipping off to the back of Books-A-Million or Barnes & Nobles to peek at the dirty-magazines – and hell, let's just be honest for a minute – I was born in 1994. I grew up right alongside the internet. I have seen everything that you could possibly imagine – and probably a lot more than that.

Suffice it to say that what I mean by all of this, is that yes, while I am religious – I'm also not unworldly, inexperienced or naive.

I've always been a very sexually minded person – or maybe a better way to say it is that I'm a very *sensually* minded person. It's probably the Italian in me.

I'll look around at things and see their beautiful shapes and curves in ways that other people don't. I'll feel the gentle rustling of the wind through my hair, or slowly run my thumb across the surface of a pebble or a stone – and get lost in the experience of it – like living in A Midsummer Night's Dream. I've always been that way. I'm certainly not lacking a libido, that's for damn sure. There's absolutely a part of me who would love for nothing more than to walk through a field full of women, bend them over one by one and just rut away like a bull – but that's not the kind of person that I want to be. That's not the kind of *man* that I want to be.

I've thought about sex a lot in my life. I've dreamed about it. I definitely can't wait to have it, and I'm sure I'm going to annoy the piss out of my wife once I can get it – but growing up I also never felt this overwhelming "need" to rush into it that so many others seem to feel – and I have always viewed the subject with the respect that I think it deserves.

We seem to have this idea today that, sex is a thing which should be a none-issue. That human beings are inherently sexual, and therefore we should be allowed to just go off and have sex and that there shouldn't be anything wrong with that.

And in a very rudimentary way I suppose there is some logic in that sentiment – but I don't think that it's really a decent justification in and of itself for this new attitude in society that we're cultivating.

Sex is a perfectly natural thing. It's a basic human desire, no different than wanting food or water – but part of being civilized is understanding that base desires aren't necessarily something that we're supposed to live by. And this is not me proselytizing or preaching at anyone – it's just the truth. If you eat too much food, you get sick. If you drink too much water you can outright drown yourself.

Sex is a way in which we derive physical pleasure, yes, but it's *also* the way in which we reproduce. It's a way for human beings to come together and form a bond – it's supposed to mean something. It's not intended to be this empty, meaningless thing that we just go around and have because it feels good. It's supposed to be the ultimate expression of love, and the joining of two individuals into a singular being – not some casual pressing of flesh that it's largely been reduced to.

That's just sad.

I don't want to experience some hollow sense of instant gratification through the dead-eyed stare of some disinterested woman with an equally disinterested man grunting away on top of her.

I want to experience that wild, explosive and rapturous passion which can only be brought on by the collision of two souls that are in love with each other. To experience the trembling joy and quaking fear and tearful ecstasy of holding that other person in your arms as you come together as one.

Now maybe you could chalk most of that up to romanticism – which I am, admittedly, guilty of being a romantic by nature – but from a far more realistic and pragmatic perspective, sex is a very powerful thing that does hold a great deal of influence over our lives.

It is an act which can lead to serious complications with your physical health, either due to unintended pregnancies or the transmission of sexual diseases – as well as on a more mental and emotional level due to problems resulting from various forms of addictions and codependency issues. As much as we like to view sex as an incredibly personal thing – it is something that can have a severe impact and ramifications not just on our own lives, but on the lives of those around us – particularly our children.

It can have a devastating impact on kids, either due to trauma from being exposed to it at a young age, or due to the consequences of their parents actions and indiscretion. Engaging in sexual activity with a multitude of partners increases the risk of cancer. An overexposure of sex or sexual material can lead to an unhealthy view of the world as well as the human body. It is often the cause of serious self-image problems, which can ultimately lead to instances of self-abuse or to the abuse of others. It can, and is, frequently used as a means of leverage via coercion or blackmail – and is easily applied as a sense of pressure onto another person, whether maliciously intended or otherwise.

There are a lot of people out there who engage in sexual activity because they feel, or are made to feel, that the act of sex alone somehow prescribes them a sense of self-worth. That they won't be loved or valued unless they put out. A very dear friend of mine would be a perfect example of this: she was made to feel like the only value that she had to offer the world could be found between her legs – and so she spread them for pretty much anybody that asked her to.

She got swallowed up by a string open-ended or otherwise "polyamourous" relationships – and she had to learn the hard way that consensual infidelity, is still *infidelity*. That the lies they told her about "equal love" were designed specifically to pull people in and to use them. To prey upon their feelings of loneliness.

She and a few other women that we knew came away from that lifestyle with the realization that you can't truly commit yourself to multiple people

– because there's only one you – and if you were having a rough day but the other two were busy, then you were out of luck.

It took a very long time and an awful lot of work for her to realize that she wasn't just a hole – but that she was, in fact, a person.

It's unfortunate, but her story isn't very original or unique. A lot of people fall for that, or get pressured into it by the people around them.

I myself have been subject to sexual pressure. As a man, there's this idea that you have to go out and sleep around with women so that you can get some "worldly experience" or what have you – and if you don't, if you abstain, then you often face criticism or have to deal with social allegations. I've been told that I must be "gay" because I haven't had sex, or that there must be something wrong with me – that my "dick must not work" or something – just because I haven't gone out chasing tail.

I've got several friends who have admitted over the years that they wish they had waited for the right woman, or the right man to come along – or at the very least that they wish they would have slowed down and been more careful and more cautious when they were younger. That they felt like there was some kind of need or expectation for them to "perform" and so they did.

Now several of them are miserable and depressed. Some of them had it make a lasting effect on their lives and career opportunities. A couple of them are even in declining health – with one friend of mine having passed away due to AIDS. And almost all of them ended up having kids that they either didn't want, couldn't take care of, or weren't able to properly take care of even if they wanted to – and for what? To get laid.

Sex really isn't half as casual as we like to make it out to be. For all that it brings, it can also lead to some incredibly lasting repercussions.

I've known so, so many kids – either ones that I grew up with, or ones that I've met through work – that have suffered in their lives because their parents weren't responsible. Because their mom and dad didn't really love each other, or had their baby when they were too young. Because their parent's split or got divorced and then one or the other always had a constant string of boyfriends or girlfriends coming in and out of their lives.

The stories that you hear about children being abused by their parents' current partner isn't particularly new – but it is becoming extremely common. Even when they aren't abused by the person, but the opposite, when they have a good relationship with them but it doesn't work out – the emotional damage that gets inflicted on a child when one day daddy's new girlfriend who was so kind and caring to them suddenly leaves is staggering.

That sort of pain never leaves a person. In some cases it can be like losing your mother or father all over again.

But nobody wants to think about that, they just want to think about themselves.

With all of this being said, it does sort of beg the question: Where exactly is this attitude coming from? Well, you can certainly trace the roots of this problem back to the Women's Liberation movement and the rise of Feminism. The ideas surrounding "female empowerment" and "sexual liberation" have certainly had a strong impact on society – but as much as I dislike Feminism, or at least modern "Feminism" – I don't think that it's entirely fair to blame the women's revolution for what's going on today. At least, not completely. I would blame, at least in large part, the monster that Feminism turned into – as the movement went further and further away from what it was originally intended to be – leaning less towards issues of equality and more towards an unfettered interest in sexuality. I truly wonder if the suffragettes would be pleased with how things turned out.

I also think it's safe to say that there are, and were, plenty of men who took advantage of that fact.

I remember reading about how pornography began to get legalized. The argument was made that it wasn't prostitution, and that in reality it was a form of "art" and therefore should be Constitutionally protected under the First Amendment and the Freedom of Expression – and for some unknown reason the Supreme Court upheld that notion.

Prostitution is defined as "the practice or occupation of engaging in sexual activity with someone for payment." In other words, it is the act of exchanging sexual favors for goods or services rendered – typically in the form of monetary compensation.

Pornography is an industry in which a person, or persons, are paid money in order to engage in sexual activity – on film.

It's prostitution.

Some people have tried to argue that this isn't the same thing, because the "actors" involved are having sex with each other, and not the camera man – or that it's "professional" because in order to start filming you first have to acquire various licenses and file taxes etc, etc. Go to a porn site and see how many "amateur-point of view" films you find. I can see how maybe there was a time when that idea held some merit, but with the advent of the internet, all of that goes right out the window.

What I will say is that I am willing to concede the idea that there is a difference between erotic photography, such as you might find in Playboy or Penthouse – even when the pictures themselves are in fact pornographic in nature – simply because it is a static image. But I think once you transfer that onto film, the inanimate becomes animated, and it begins to blur the lines between what is and what is not "artistic."

Others have argued that legalizing prostitution as a whole – such as out in Nevada – comes with the benefits of regular health inspections and clinical screenings, along with the general protection of law enforcement, and that it allows for a safer and more regulated environment for its workers and their clientele.

I suppose I can see the rationale behind that logic – and I'll even go so far as to admit that if you are going to engage in that sort of practice, that is probably the best way to go about it. But the problem there lies in the fact that prostitution is, to put it bluntly, human trafficking. Consensual human trafficking, maybe, but it is still trafficking nonetheless. You are receiving monetary compensation for the selling of flesh.

I've heard a lot of different arguments over the years – particularly coming out of Europe – that say that sexual liberation is a good thing. They say "Sex work is real work!" And that "It's an honorable public service" or a "Symbol of personal empowerment!" But I don't really think that that's true. I could be wrong, Amsterdam seems to have a pretty decent grasp on the situation as far as I'm aware – but on a much broader scale I'd say that the evidence is pretty clear to the contrary.

For such a natural thing, sex or the topic surrounding sex is often incredibly dehumanizing. And it's not just a "social stigma" that can make it so harmful – but it's instinctual as well. Human beings are intrinsically emotional creatures, and eventually those emotions tend to break through even the most thick-skinned individual.

When you allow yourself to use another human being as an object – or to be used by other humans as an object – you begin to internalize that feeling. Maybe it's slower for some than for others, but almost universally whenever I hear somebody talk about their "career" in Adult Entertainment or the broader "Sex Industry," they inevitably mention at some point experiencing a change in themselves. Of noticing that they stopped feeling like a person, and started feeling like a piece of meat.

And you can hear similar stories from all sorts of people that have spent their lives being promiscuous, but without ever entering into any form of obligation, contract or employment. It's not a big secret.

I've watched several different documentaries on sex in society, and particularly about life in the porn industry – and you'll see these beautiful girls talking to the camera, trying to explain how "freeing" and "empowering" and "liberating" and "glamorous" it is to be a porn-star – but just about all of them had the coldest, saddest eyes that I've ever seen. And none of them sounded like they really believed what they were saying – because I don't think that they did believe it. I think they were just echoing what they have been taught to say. This one girl had such horribly dark circles under her red and puffy eyes, and in a trembling and shaking voice she said "Oh it's been so great, you know... I think this has really been the best decision of my life..."

I don't know how anybody could sit there and watch that and take it at face value.

Then of course you do have the ones who break away from that particular way of life and say the quiet part out loud. Talking about how exploitative and predatory it is – but they get ignored, or shouted down, just because they had the self respect to stand up and be honest.

Sometimes what I think is even worse than a person making a mistake and getting involved in that kind of life, is when I see them have to struggle and face unnecessary challenges just to get *out* of those situations and turn their lives around.

I remember the story of an older guy that had been a porn star, who said he wanted to make a change in his life and that he wanted to try and do something positive with his money – so he tried donating it to charity. But the charity foundation wouldn't let him. He ended up getting around that by becoming a golfer I think, and donating his tournament winnings instead. Another story I remember pretty vividly is a woman, again an adult film star, and she got out of the business and went off to become some kind of EMT – but the news broke out about her past and it became this great big scandal.

I'll tell you right now, as far as I'm concerned, that woman can save my life *any* day of the week.

Regardless of how you feel about it, we're seeing a lot of pressure in the modern day for young people – especially girls – to go out and become sexually active. In fact I think it's fairly safe to say that there's more pressure now than at any other time in American history. Modern society has become so obsessed with the concept of sex, you would think that human beings have never gotten laid before.

As cultural and societal attitudes shifted on things like porn and prostitution, you saw the increase in exploitation of women and girls in the modern setting. From unrealistic body standards and social expectations of beauty, the incredibly over-sexualized pop-stars and teen-idols, to the rise of mainstream fetishism and the targeting of children. It's not that these things, these elements of "the business" never existed – but I do think there's a pretty big difference between a full grown Cyndi Lauper singing "Girls Just Wanna have Fun" and being a little tongue-and-cheek with songs like "She Bop," compared to a 16 year old Britney Spears singing "Hit Me Baby One More Time."

That attitude, that mindset of always pushing the envelope, always pushing the boundary – always looking for more – is what ultimately leads music away from being just a bit provocative, to outright singing about "Wet Ass Pussies." It's what led to the swinging of opinions and the fetishizing of obesity. It's what gave way to "reality" television and the exploitation of vulnerable teenagers. It's what gave rise to companies like Netflix that produce content such as "Cuties," or fashion brands like Balenciaga who created ad-campaigns using children to market sexual paraphernalia.

Even before these most recent controversies, I remember growing up and slowly seeing kids fashion – specifically girls fashion – getting more and more risque. I was in Walmart back when I was... fifteen or sixteen years old, and I saw this "outfit" as I was passing by the children's section, that was nothing more than a few pink leather straps across the chest, leading down to a very tiny skirt. It was an incredibly "girly" looking bondage costume that was intended for an eight or nine year old child.

Whether you want to think of it as the natural progression of artistic freedom or not – it is *absolutely* having an influence on our culture.

When I was growing up one of the biggest catch-phrases in school or among kids my age was "Don't slut shame me!" The irony of which being, that if you weren't doing something that you yourself didn't feel guilty for – you wouldn't be concerned with somebody shaming you for your behavior. Regardless, the world kind of just rolled with it and look where that attitude has gotten us. Underage sex is at an all-time high – teen pregnancies even more so.

In the wake of COVID-19 we've seen the rise of sites like OnlyFans – a website which only really garnered popularity during the "pandemic," and so has only really been around for the past four years – but is already having a serious impact on society.

You can go and watch countless interviews of young women talking about having an OnlyFans account. Talking about how all of their friends have an account – all of their neighbors or classmates. How it's just becoming common-place to sell your body on the internet. And what's even scarier than the fact that something like this is becoming the cultural "norm," is that almost all of these women who I've seen talking about it, truly believe that they can just erase it when they decide that they're done. That there won't be any lasting repercussions for this.

I saw one girl insisting vehemently that she has lawyers, and she can just get her photos and videos taken down whenever she feels like it – and I'm sitting there just baffled by the ignorance of this. Does she not know what downloading is? Does she not understand that anything you put online stays there? If even just one person right-clicks on that picture and saves it – you no longer control that image.

It's called a hard drive.

And that's not even taking into account all of the possible states and countries that might not necessarily have the same legal procedures as your own. Places where whatever legal authority you "think" you possess, has no power.

We're already seeing the ripple effects of this. Children being exposed to their own parents – either because their friends at school found out and showed them, or because they were hanging around on websites that they shouldn't have had access to. Imagine the trauma that causes a little boy who's scrolling through Twitter and comes across a photo of his own mother, on her back, legs apart and fingering her pussy. Or what that does to a father – maybe he's home alone or things haven't been too spicy in the bedroom recently. It's been a long day at work and he's trying to find some relief, so he goes to some website that he ought not to be on – and there's his own daughter, his little girl, on all fours and spreading her asshole open in front of the camera.

Testimonials are already coming out about children having to deal with this. In one interview that I saw, this woman, a mother of two girls, defended this sort of behavior by saying "I told my daughters that I never got to have my 'ho phase' when I was younger, but now I'm an adult and I can do what I want." That just goes to show that being an "adult" does *not* equal maturity. It is not a free license to just do whatever you want to and to shirk your responsibilities.

Even worse than that however, is several of these testimonials and interviews that have come out, have openly stated that numerous parents are actively getting their children *involved* with the idea – either by having them take the pictures themselves, or handle the editing and uploading for a share of the profit.

Can you even begin to comprehend the kind of serious damage that causes to someone? When a young boy, maybe 14 or 15 years old, is tasked by his mother to take photographs of her in bed. To stand there in her bedroom and watch her undress? To see her expose herself – to *pleasure* herself in front of him – that's crossing every kind of line imaginable.

There is no reality in which this should even be a fucking debate.

I mentioned earlier about the blurring of lines when it comes pornography – but this? This is blurring the lines so much that you can't even see them anymore, and eventually there won't be any lines left at all.

You can sit there and you can try to say "Well it isn't 'incest' because they didn't sleep together." I hope it hasn't gotten that far – but this has moved way beyond just being inappropriate. I don't think that it's any great stretch of the imagination, considering the state of society today, where there are fewer and fewer men in the homes and boys are often demoralized just for existing – and young people are more twisted up and riddled with insecurities than ever before – to see how whatever pitiful excuse for a boundary there might have once been, get crossed in an instant.

When you stop seeing your mothers and fathers, your sons and your daughters, your sisters and brothers as being a family – but instead begin to see them as *sexual creatures* – it's only going to lead to the very ugly reality in which this behavior progresses into its natural evolution. Where inter-family relations become the norm. That's disgusting. It's horrifying.

Look, I'm from the South – my family tree reads more like a family wreath – but even for me this is just unacceptable. We cannot keep going down this road and treating it like it's not an issue because it is, and it's only going to keep spiraling out of control.

Some of you reading this might be inclined to say "Well, it's only a small percentage of that website's user-base." Or that "It's only a small percentage of the internet." But that's the fucking problem. The fact that it's a "percentage" at all is the problem – and you can't just sit there with your heads buried in the sand. This is a serious, growing concern, and it is already bleeding outside of the internet.

Just a year or so ago, my friend's cousin came home in absolute hysteria because of something that had been done to him – or rather, done in front of him. He had been dating some girl and when he went over to her house for Thanksgiving her mother met him at the door and said: "My daughter tells me that you haven't been giving her a proper orgasm." Now that ought to stop everything right there, but it gets worse. The mother then tells him that she needs to show him something, leads him to the bedroom where he finds his girlfriend waiting – and proceeds to "demonstrate" the proper way to make a girl climax – on her own daughter.

And if you don't understand what I mean by that, let me make this perfectly clear for you – this woman fingered her own child, to show a boy, how to make her daughter cum.

The unfortunate truth of the world is that it is filled to the brim with evil people – and there have often been reports of household abuse throughout history – but what we are seeing is such an alarming uptick in the number of these things happening.

We are seeing these sorts of stories at a much higher frequency, in much greater detail, and frankly it's being met with an alarmingly blasé attitude from the general public – because they just don't care – they've become completely desensitized to it.

Things are getting wildly out of hand in the West. This obsession with sex and the overall sexualization of everything that we do is going to be our downfall. I haven't even begun to talk about the sexual identity crisis happening in our culture – this is all still just "the culture" that I'm dealing with.

If you don't believe me that this is a problem, look around at other countries that have dealt with an overly sexualized population. Japan is a prominent example: I think it was 2014 or 2015 when a news report came out of Japan, that young couples in that country weren't engaging in sexual activity. Between the claustrophobic living conditions of the average city home, to the incredibly demanding and high pressure conditions of their work routine – to the rampant over-exposure to sexualization in their culture – their young married couples weren't becoming intimate with each other.

I believe that at the time of this report, the express concern was that if their married populace didn't start producing children – the nation would be looking at a population crisis by around the year 2045.

I don't live in Japan. I'm not an expert on Japanese culture – but I know a few things about the country and I have a few friends from there – and they were able to give me a little more insight on what was going on. The Japanese people have a very sexually charged society, with everything ranging from "Love Motels" to "Fantasy Cafes" down to vending machines that dish out dirty panties. It's a pretty wild place.

My friends talked about how sex was so open in large parts of the country, that it became downright *boring*. It was everywhere, constantly on display. I think I understand what they're getting at. It's kind of like "dirty talk." People didn't use to say the word "fuck" in every other sentence – so when you were in the bedroom and said something like that – it was exciting. It was tantalizing, titillating and risque – but now it's just mundane because you hear it everywhere. I swear like a sailor, I admit it – but I understand exactly what they mean.

You take the fact that sex is no longer thrilling and combine that together with all of those different societal pressures I talked about – as well as the multitude of pressures that life in the modern day is having on people – it's no wonder that they're struggling. I very much hope that they can figure things out over there, I really do.

Sooner or later I think that's going to happen to us.

We keep putting more and more pressure onto people to go out and engage in sex. To tear down the long-established boundaries of behavioral conduct – pressure to label themselves and draw conclusions about their identity in order to conform to social expectations – our society is going to hit a wall. I think it's already hitting a wall.

In fact I *know* it's hitting a wall and I'll tell you why.

You know how when two people have just finished making love, having intercourse or whatever you want to call it – and they're in that moment of "post coital bliss" when they're supposed to be laying together and holding each other? Snuggling close, embracing, cuddling – maybe even crying if it was that strong of an emotional and moving experience? Well now we've taken all of that away, and the commonly accepted term in the social zeitgeist is "aftercare."

Aftercare... I cannot think of a more sterilized, dry, and frankly just clinical sounding term for what should be the most deeply intimate moment of bonding that two human beings could be sharing together.

Aftercare – no "aftercare" is what you receive after you've come home from the hospital and had some kind of surgery. Aftercare is when somebody is having to check your weeping bandages to make sure that you aren't developing an infection. It's when somebody has to run q-tips and cotton swabs along your surgical incisions to make sure that there's no pus building up.

Aftercare is helping you onto the toilet and having to wipe your ass for you after you take a shit, because both of your arms are stuck in casts.

I suppose I shouldn't be too surprised that we've started referring to cuddling as aftercare considering that we've largely thrown out terms like "girlfriend" in favor of "partner." Let's just take all sense of romance out of the equation.

I wrote somewhere in these pages a good while ago – about how human interactions are breaking down to a mechanical level – and this is exactly what I'm talking about. This is the definition of losing a sense of humanity and just becoming some dry, clinical and mechanical "thing."

It's pathetic.

The social and political pressure – the cultural pressure – that keeps forcing sex just forward, forward, forward in our lives is so immense, and it's taking a very real toll on our nation and the lives and perceptions of the people living in it.

I see a lot of people who are just... I don't know, "consumed" by this infatuation with sex that they can't see anything past it. That they can't stop and think about anything beyond themselves.

They'll make "fan art" of their favorite actors who they "respect so much" and it's smut. It's disgusting. You claim to be a fan of somebody's work – claim to have respect for them as a human being – and then you draw a pornographic image of them? Some of these actors are faithfully married, some are religious – and so you render their likeness in an image which suggests that they're cheating on their spouse or going against their religious beliefs?

You didn't draw two happily married Christian men having balls-deep gay anal sex with each other because you're their fan – you don't care about these people at all. You did that in order to satisfy your own fetishes and nothing more. It's selfish, self-centered, and disingenuous. It's pathetic.

When I worked at a movie theatre I had a closing shift one night with a young man, about 17 or so years old, and I could tell that he was feeling pretty down. I asked him what was wrong and I don't know, maybe it's because I was an older guy – or because people have always seemed to talk to me about things – he opened up after awhile and told me that his friends at school were trying to get him to come out as gay.

So I asked him point blank if he was – and he said he didn't know.

I said "Well what makes you think that you might be gay?" And he told me, basically, that he was on a porn site and saw some gay porn and that he liked it – and that it bothered him that he liked it – and so he tried to talk to his friends about it but they just piled on him saying that he needs to "come out" and "be proud" and all of this, that and the other. I said "You don't seem too happy about that" and he said that he wasn't, because he didn't feel like he was gay.

After awhile of talking, since it was just the two of us, I asked him to describe what he saw and he did – it was pretty gay. As a matter of fact it was very gay. Finally I asked him though: "After all of that was over, and the man stood up and you saw him from the front... Were you still interested?"

And he said no.

I asked him: "Have you ever imagined, or could you ever imagine holding hands with another guy? Kissing another guy?"

Again, he said no.

In the end I said: "Son, I don't think you're gay. I think you're horny. I think that you are a horny teenage boy, and that you saw porn – a form of material that is specifically designed to elicit a physical response – and your body physically responded. It sounds to me like the moment that this man, or these men that you watched stopped being an object – stopped being erotica, and started to become people – you immediately felt disengaged from the situation."

Let me tell you, when I think of the genuine relief on that young man's face – the look of a guy who wasn't being told what he had to be – who was able to have somebody just stop and listen to him and talk to him, instead of making assumptions on his behalf and pressuring him into something that he wasn't. I felt a sense of pride, I really did.

Young people are getting twisted up like corkscrews over all of the sexual politics in place today. It's being force-fed to them through every form of media imaginable, and the idea that everybody has to go and label themselves like a product – and that they have to commit to living their life based on those labels – has caught on like a social wildfire.

And that's sort of the unspoken problem with labeling everything. It's that human beings are stupid – we all know it. How many times have you met the "lesbian" who dated her high school boyfriend, didn't feel any pleasure from it because he was a dumb high school boy – went off to college and got drunk, fooled around with another girl and said "Oh wow! I must actually be gay!" Only to then ten or twenty years later end up with an older man who actually knew what he was doing and realize "Oh wow! I'm actually straight!"

I personally know three different women who went through that and I live in the middle of nowhere. It happens all the goddamn time. People are dumb – that doesn't mean that she suddenly up and changed sexualities – it just means that she's an idiot.

And again for the record - most people are idiots.

I knew a guy once who swore up and down that he was bisexual. I asked if he had ever dated another man, and he said no. I asked if he *would* date another man – and he said no. Finally I asked if he had ever even *thought* about dating another man – and he said no.

That's because he wasn't bisexual. He just claimed to be because it was more "interesting" than being straight. It's just a fad to most of them – right now it's "in" to be "out."

It's like when you meet somebody who swears they're a Catholic, but then proceeds to explain how they don't believe in or even agree with *anything* about Catholicism. They aren't *actually* Catholic, no matter how much they insist that they are.

Saying that you're "something" doesn't make you that "something."

Every aspect of human life is now viewed from beneath a collective microscope. We are splitting hairs across all facets of everyday life. Romantic inclination and sexual attraction are being forced apart into two separate categories, along with personal preferences and sexual identities.

A person who is naturally attracted towards people with strong, masculine personalities and characteristics, regardless of sex, is now termed "pansexual." In reality they are simply a person who is bisexual, with a particular taste in partners.

In order to combat this, the definition of pansexual has recently been changed to include a sexual attraction to people that display these same masculine characteristics – but do not identify as either male or female – meaning to say that they are equally attracted to strong personalities found in people that are male, female or otherwise none-conforming individuals.

The problem here, of course, is that there are only two sexes. A person's ideological belief does not alter the reality of their situation. Gender is not a social construct – and you have to be aware of that when applying the label of sexuality.

A person who experiences a low or otherwise none-existent libido – a sex drive – is now automatically labeled as "asexual" regardless of whether or not that person is actively interested in pursuing a romantic relationship with partners of the opposite sex.

This is another issue, because there's currently two simultaneous arguments for sexuality – and they're both coming from the same side of the political isle. The first argument is the classic stance that sexuality is static. You are what you are, because you were born that way. The second argument however, is that sexuality is fluid, and it can change over time. That a man who's been heterosexual for the past thirty years can suddenly wake up one day and be homosexual.

Most of the social movements surrounding sexuality began with the first argument – but now those same voices are crying out for the second argument.

Well by that definition, we are now inferring that the vast majority of men throughout history and across the globe, have spontaneously changed their sexuality once their libido dropped off and they started getting over the age of 50.

I would say that a person who is "asexual," but still has an active interest in finding a husband or a wife – finding a partner of the opposite sex – is just heterosexual but with a non-existent sex drive. If you actually go looking I think you will find quite a lot of people have a low or none-existent sex drive. Just look back at Japan again – look back at Victorian England or the pioneer days of America.

Human nature dictates that sexual attraction and feelings of emotional intimacy are intrinsically bound to one another – and yet now we seem hell bent on unraveling the tapestry of our own genetic makeup and natural instinct.

I've heard the argument that because man is descended from apes, we're somehow inclined to just carelessly rut on any partner we can get our hands on – but humans are creatures of companionship. We're creatures of emotion. You can suppress your emotions – you can ignore them – but a functional person still has them. Even the most casual one-night stand usually has some kind of emotional attachment connected to it – some kind of subtle, intimate feelings – regardless of whether you intend to ever act on those feelings or not.

I see a lot of people now claiming to be "aromantic" meaning that they experience little or no feelings of romantic attraction towards another person. Again, there are some pretty glaring issues with this – because while yes, many people do go through "crushes" and fall in and out of love – there is equally a massive number of people out there who don't. People like myself – people waiting for that "magic spark," that certain something – waiting for Mr. or Mrs. "right" to come along. I've known a few women over the years who I wondered: "Could it be...?" But in the end, I said "No." They weren't the "right one" and I never felt that connection.

Just to make things even more complicated you also have the people claiming to be aromantic and asexual. Claiming to feel absolutely no intimate attraction towards another person – though still perfectly capable of platonic love with their friends and families.

Honestly, I feel that my same points from above still stand.

Let's just say for the sake of argument, that you are in fact an aromantic-asexual. What happens if one day you're walking along and bump straight into "Mr. Right?" Suddenly you're filled to the brim with physical and emotional attraction to this person – you've fallen just head over heels in love with this person. Does that mean that the argument of sexual fluidity is correct? That people can just spontaneously change their emotions and sexuality at the drop of a hat?

Or could it possibly mean that you simply hadn't found the *right* person yet?

I think considering how lonely the world has gotten, how far apart that people have drifted – and how isolated our societies have become – that it's a much simpler answer to say that you've just been waiting for something "more." That instead of labeling yourself as "this" thing or "that," we should stop putting so much emphasis and pressure on people to split every single hair in life – just to try and fit the mold.

Life… is complicated. Believe me, I know that it's complicated – and oh what a poetic expression of man it is to take an already complex thing and to make it even more so.

Maybe there really are people who truly, genuinely experience no feelings of sexual or emotional interest in other people – but I don't think that there's half as many of them as we are being led to believe – and I also think that the conversation about "why" a person isn't experiencing those feelings is a topic for a different discussion.

I think that it stands to very good reason that so much of the numbers are being inflated by people that are confused, uncertain or just hopping on the bandwagon.

My ultimate point however is that these games we're playing with people's lives are dangerous. This modern Left-wing push for Marcusean politics has done nothing but cause utter chaos in our nation and in our world.

By attempting to subvert the intrinsic nature and the bonds of sexual attraction and romantic interest, certain political parties are able to punch holes in the greater majority and pick apart their opposition one by one.

These carefully constructed terminologies of asexual, pansexual, demisexual, omnisexual and so forth, are nothing more than tools which are used to divide and separate. To break apart a collective whole, like a hammer on stone.

It truly baffles me the way in which political tactics and stratagems such as these can be used so openly and in broad daylight – with such overwhelmingly heavy handed force – yet can somehow manage to go completely ignored by the vast majority of the public.

In many ways, the conversation surrounding sexual identities can be compared to similar tactics used to sow division among various Christian denominations.

All heterosexual men intrinsically share a common interest: women. Some like tall women, some like short women, some like plump women or like skinny women – but they all feel attracted and inclined towards the female sex.

This is no different than in Christianity, where by virtue of being Christian – regardless of denomination – all practitioners share a common interest and faith in Jesus Christ.

However if you were to take a group of representatives from each respective denomination, and place them together in a room – you could attempt to subvert their unified interest by making an off-handed remark about some part of their religious theology. The Virgin Mary, for instance. The Catholic in the room would say: "Now wait just a minute..." but the Baptist might turn around and say "Oh no I think he's right..." and thus, you have reduced the group into a frenzy of bickering, infighting and debate.

Sexuality is no different. If you begin to make up an argument that sexual identities are subjective – then you can break the ties that bind.

If you manufacture terminologies which target certain individuals who are not particularly sexually charged – or at the very least questioning their own personal feelings – then you can pick them off from the larger herd and corral them into a separate pen. If you were to follow through and do the same thing for feelings of personal preference or romantic inclination, you could pick those people off as well.

When you convince a person with an under-active libido, who also struggles with feelings of intimacy, or has otherwise failed to find love in their life that they are somehow inherently different, you make them believe they are different. When you saddling that person with a label such as aromantic-asexual – what you have done is not only thinned the overall "herd" as a collective obstacle – but you have also successfully cornered a small targeted minority, and opened up easier avenues of direct communication with them. Thus, you have lowered the chance for any opposing voices to stand in your way.

It is an ingenious, if not outright insidious way of conducting business and pushing a political agenda – compounded all the more by how terrifyingly effective it is.

The problem is that you don't actually care about these people – you're just using them as pawns. How do I know this? Because the modern basis of sexual theory lacks any and all grounds in reality. When you have to jump through hoops and perform outstanding feats of mental-gymnastics in order to explain yourself – it's simply not true.

I hear them in the streets and I see them on the television, demanding to be taken seriously – to be accepted for who they are – and every time I hear their arguments it sounds more and more like they're trying to convince themselves as much as they're trying to convince me. Because they're grasping for something that isn't there – and I think that most of them know it.

The ones who truly buy in to all of the socio-political pandering are the ones I feel the worst for. They'll make outlandish claims like "Homosexuality was acceptable in Ancient Greece!" Well it was, to an extent – but not only is "Ancient Greece" an incredibly broad and umbrella term – the fact of the matter is that not all of the Greek cities shared the same culture, and the ones that did were not viewing homosexuality in the way that we're viewing it today.

Spartans, for example, are probably the most famous Greeks in terms of male-on-male relations – but in their society they viewed those relationships as the ultimate form of male bonding. We know this, because they wrote about it. Spartan men loved their wives – they loved their women – but in a militaristic culture like theirs, your best friend could die for you on the battlefield tomorrow. If you were a Spartan man walking through the war-camp and saw your buddy in his tent and he was hard-up – the least you could do would be to go in there and help him out.

You can say you disagree with it, but those are the simple facts. I'm not going to pretend to understand it – I love my best friend – but not that much.

They'll say that "Ancient Rome was accepting of same-sex relations!" Well, again, this is partly true. Ancient Rome was pretty accepting of same sex relationships – assuming that the people involved in those relationships originally came from a culture that was cool with it – that's part of being a cosmopolitan society. Romans themselves however, were not particularly favorable towards the idea of homosexuality. Except for when they were… it actually gets a little more complicated than you'd think.

For the Romans, it was perfectly acceptable for a man to sleep with another man, though preferably a less masculine one, or even a young boy for that matter – so long as he was the one on top. If you were on the "receiving" end however, it was considered a pretty serious taboo. This doesn't really make a whole lot of sense to me if you think about it from a logical standpoint, because obviously it takes two to tango – but then again, I'm also not an ancient Roman.

I've heard some people say that Emperor Nero married himself to another man, and even went so far as to do so while wearing a traditional woman's gown – but it's very important to note that not only was same-sex marriage expressly forbidden in Greek and Roman society – but that Nero was also the Emperor who probably had an incestuous affair with his own mother, and absolutely set his own city on fire in order to attack the fledgling Christians.

I just don't think that this is the guy you want to hold up for your argument.

There's a popular argument right now for why polyamourous relationships shouldn't be taboo – for why they should be considered normal and acceptable. They use the example of Wonder Woman, who was based off of a girl that was involved in a three-way relationship.

All it took was five minutes worth of research to see what a tragic and atrocious life that woman lived. It was like reading a penny-dreadful, you couldn't make it up. She came from a broken and abusive home; clearly suffered from mental health and abandonment issues. Her college professor used to go back to her sorority house and make the girls dress up in baby clothes and crawl around for him – and then he took her home where he and his wife abused her. It's the most clear-cut case of Stockholm Syndrome and the abuse of an authoritative power-dynamic that I've ever seen in my life.

Just like Nero, this story is not the one you want to hold up as a standard for your argument.

Everything in our society has gone so far off the rails, I don't honestly know if we can get things back on track. Like a genie in a bottle, once that cork has been removed it's very difficult to put it back in. As I said at the top of this chapter – sex is everywhere and you can't really get away from it. Each new television program that comes out has to push themes of sexuality or sexual politics. Each new book or movie or video game has to do the same thing. Always pushing, always pandering – always further ingraining the issue.

Acclaimed English anthropologist J. D. Unwin famously wrote the 1934 book, "Sex and Culture" where he discusses his findings and research on human civilizations throughout history – and makes the argument that most of the great major civilizations in the world ultimately fell apart due to a societal shift towards sexual liberation. Ancient Rome of course is the classic example – as eventually the Romans became notoriously debauched and hedonistic in their society – but he discusses the rise and fall of many other cultures and civilizations as well.

The conclusion he drew is that as a nation is just starting out, it develops a society which depends upon the concepts of monogamy and premarital chastity. That cultures adhering to stricter sexual conventions such as abstinence, allows the population to focus their sexual energy into other means of productivity – art, science, exploration and expansionism to name a few examples. He also asserts that as a society grows and develops, it becomes more sexually liberal – which in turn accelerates a sense of social-entropy within the nation – thus ultimately diminishing its creative and expansive energy.

Essentially, Unwin concluded that after a nation becomes prosperous, it also becomes increasingly liberal when concerning sexual morality – and ultimately it loses its cohesion, impetus and purpose.

I don't know about you, but that sounds like a pretty accurate description of the modern day to me. Apparently it also sounded pretty good to the English philosopher Aldous Huxley, who in a 1958 interview with Mike Wallace, expressed his grim apprehension for the future, and outline several of his concerns such as: the difficulties and dangers of world overpopulation, the tendency towards distinctly hierarchical social organization – the crucial importance of evaluating the use of technology in mass societies susceptible to persuasion – and the tendency to promote modern politicians to a naive public as well-marketed commodities. I think those apprehensions were astoundingly relevant.

Listen, at the end of the day and when it's all said and done – whatever preferences, inclinations or tendencies that a person has is their business, not mine. Whatever it is that people get up to behind closed doors and in private, it is not my concern.

I should not have power over anybody else – and they shouldn't have any power over me.

The problem is that we have kicked down the doors and removed the notion of privacy. We've pushed everything into the public view – and once something is in the public view – it becomes my concern. Because I am part of the public.

I don't really care if you want to dress yourself up as a leather-clad horse or a dog and explore your latest kink-fetish, but when you have people doing that sort of thing in public parks in front of children, it's gone too far. They throw the gay pride parade because it's supposed to "normalize" being gay – except that it isn't trying to normalize it, because normal people don't walk down the street wearing assless chaps and showing their cocks to minors.

We keep pushing these concepts and pushing these ideas – and all that we're actually doing is just tearing ourselves apart in the process. We use sex to incentivize calamity, we use politics to twist people up inside – we treat human beings as if life is nothing more than a goddamn flesh market.

This is not how things should be.

Look, I know it might not seem like this after everything that I've just written, but I swear to you that I'm not just some stick in the mud. The fact that on I Love Lucy, Lucille Ball and Desi Arnaz had two separate beds in their own bedroom despite the fact that they were married, was asinine – and when it comes to things like music, one of my all-time favorite bands is the Bloodhound Gang – which if you've ever listened to their material, you know that it's more than just a little bit "raunchy."

But this overbearing infatuation – this unhinged *obsession* with sex and sexuality – it's *not* healthy.

Human life cannot sustain itself under the weight of this ever-increasing and constantly scrutinizing train of thought. We're not built for it. We're not designed for it. Every single one of these practices and beliefs flies in the face of our basic biological nature – and sooner or later it will prove to be our downfall.

Chapter XIV: Sheep's Clothing

I've been doing a lot of thinking lately. I've been thinking about language and our use of language – and how we often use it to try and confuse and belittle and degrade ourselves and the people around us. In all of my thinking, there's been one word that kept sticking out in my mind...

It's the "N" Word:

Normality.

Normal has become the newest insult. It's the greatest offense of our time.

As the malformed ideological practices of "transgenderism" and this post-modernist sense of liberal-progressivist indoctrination continues to gain more traction in society – a new language has steadily been constructed to further their own self-righteous cause.

The term "cis-gendered," for example, has been created in order to describe a perfectly healthy and sound individual who does not – or at the very least has not – bought into the growing rhetoric and blind ignorance of "gender theory."

A person who is normal – meaning to be average – can no longer be referred to as such, for in doing so you would also be implying that other people who do not necessarily fit that description are somehow inherently abnormal in the process.

Normality – as well as the mere concept of it – has been made into a dirty word.

But that of course is the great irony of all of this. Social movements such as the LGBT are inherently flawed, because its very existence is predicated on the ideology of celebrating their differences – by attempting to normalize them. All of the parades, all of the month-long celebrations of "pride" and the mass-media marketing of products and corporate pandering – it isn't normal.

Normal people don't get parades. Normal people don't get entire months dedicated to them – those things make them stand out. It makes them *special.*

A thing can't be "special" and "normal" at the same time. It's an oxymoron, a catch-22.

Something can be "unique" and still be normal. As individuals, we're all unique – each one of us has something that somebody else doesn't have. Each one of us has our own quirks and personalities – but that's not the same thing as being "special."

To remove the human element, let's talk about manufacturing. I'll use kitchen knives for example: Each one cut, each one pressed, each one prepared in the factories and sent down the assembly line to be packaged and shipped – but despite being mass-produced – each knife will inevitably have something just ever-so-slightly different about it than the others. It might hold an edge longer, or have just a fraction of difference in its balance. The handle might take more or less time than its identical counterparts before coming loose. Those are qualities which make each knife unique.

To be special, you have to order a knife from a craftsman. He will draw a custom design, and personally pick out the steel for the blade. He'll choose the wood for the handle and carve it himself – sanding and shaping every aspect of it by hand. In its final stages, he may apply a personal message or perhaps etch in an intricate pattern – but regardless of these things, it will have been given a personal touch.

The finished knife, a tool, an instrument, will be unlike anything else ever created – it will be singularly unique in the world – but the creation of this knife took a very specific series of steps in order to be made. The interest of the buyer, the effort of the craftsman – these things make this knife special – make it stand out from everything else.

The problem is that not everything can be special. If everything's special, then nothing is special – which is not the same as being normal. If nothing gets to be special, then no one is ever allowed to shine. There's so much pressure in the world today to be different, to stand out from the crowd – it's not realistic. They say that: "Being different is the new normal."

That's one hell of a burden to put on someone, let alone the human race.

Dexter Holland of The Offspring once wrote "The Kids Aren't Alright", and I think we can all see how this sentiment is just as true now – if not even more so – than when he first wrote it.

Depression, anxiety, loneliness, self-loathing, mental-illness, addiction and substance abuse have become a staple in the youth of America. Young people taking their first steps into the world of adulthood and buckling under the weight of social expectation.

There is a palpable misery which hangs in the air around us like a bad odor – and more and more kids are becoming lost in the noise with each passing day.

There are countless scores of people out there right now who are sick and hurting. Constantly seeking an outlet for the pain that they're experiencing. Some sense of validation for the chaos in their lives – and instead of helping them – we have created a society which takes advantage of them.

A society which abuses their vulnerability, and twists them up into corkscrews while gratifying some sick and self-serving agenda of human experimentation.

Approximately 0.14% of the global population – male and female – legitimately suffer from the very real condition of Gender Dysphoria. Several sources however, including the United States Census Bureau, are now reporting that anywhere from 1.6 to 2.0% of the entire U.S. population specifically identifies as being transgender – with another 1-2% self identifying as any number of variations of gender non-conforming.

That's almost a whopping 4% of the country that cannot recognize the differences between male and female.

Not to mention that these same census records are showing that an unprecedented 20-30% of the Millennial generation identifies as some form of LGBT – with 12% of that identifying as transgender. These same numbers are even higher in regards to Generation Z, though as of right now the generation as a whole is still too young to effectively lock in the census data.

Still, the very existence of these numbers is nothing short of ridiculous.

I would personally be willing to believe that some of these people are genuine. Real individuals who are really suffering in a way that I could not possibly begin to understand, and certainly could never relate to – but how many of them *aren't*?

How many of these men and women are simply wounded and looking for an out? How many of these poor, injured souls are simply seeking help and searching for an answer – becoming lost, misguided and confused by all the voices in their head? Voices that do not care about them, and do not have their best interest at heart? How many of them are simply caving to peer-pressure or going along with the fad – hell, how many of them are simply trying to get ahead in life by taking advantage of the culture?

I mean for Heaven's sake, at the time of writing this there is a public listing of over 107 *different* genders for people to pick from, and that number seems to be going up every couple of months.

It's sheer madness.

I think back to that conversation I mentioned in the previous chapter – about the kid I worked with that was being pressured to come out as something that he wasn't. I think about that conversation a lot, because I've experienced something similar to it myself.

When I was in my early teens I saw some gay porn by accident, and I got my rocks off to it. My head was spinning for weeks – I didn't know what to do.

Was I suddenly gay now? Or at the very least, was I bisexual? I had no clue – I didn't know what any of this meant. After days of tearing myself apart over the issue I decided that the only way to know for certain would be to go and watch some gay porn – and boy let me tell you, that was a different kind of experience.

I saw bears, I saw twinks, I saw weird shit done with leather masks and unicorn horns – and I can honestly say with no hint of confusion whatsoever – that I realized I was *not* gay. I was *very* not gay.

But what if I didn't make the decision to try and figure it out for myself? What if I had kept chewing myself up over the issue for weeks and months and years? What if I had the kind of people around me that didn't listen to what I was telling them? The kind of people that pushed me into a pen like some kind of cattle? That told me the only way for me to live my life now is to fully commit to this "thing" that I wasn't even terribly sure of?

That would have been awful. It would have been agonizing.

I cannot help but wonder just how many people are experiencing that same kind of agony right now – right this very moment as my fingers stroke the keys. I wish that I could help them – I wish that someone could help them.

But it's hard to talk about these things because anybody that says anything to the contrary of this narrative is automatically shouted down as being "homophobic."

Supposedly I am homophobic, though I think my gay friends might disagree with that sentiment. I know my family has been called homophobic – even though none of them have ever said anything to ever support that theory.

In fact I recall a story that my Nanny told me once, that back when she was growing up – I suppose in her early or mid teen during the 1950s, there was a man she'd see around Farmville from time to time. He was an older gentleman by her recollection – and he used to carry a billfold out in front of himself like a lady would carry a purse – with both of his hands together and pointed down very effeminately. He wore very nice looking high-dollar suits – always clean and sharply pressed – but he kept his fingernails very long like a woman's and he kind of walked with a bit of a sway.

Nanny said that she, her brother and sisters – and everyone else she knew for that matter – never really paid it much mind. They thought of him as being a little different, but according to her he was a nice and polite man. Nobody seemed to really give him any trouble or treat him any differently at all.

I don't know about you, but that doesn't sound terribly "homophobic" to me.

I remember when I was a kid, y'know, we used to watch all of those old programs that'd be rerun on television. I got to see Bewitched! and The Munsters and all sorts of shows from before my time – and a lot of them featured an actor named Paul Lynde. I grew up adoring Lynde – it didn't matter what show he was on or, if I could hear his distinctive voice for a cartoon or something – I'd stand up and say "I know him! I know him!"

He was always so upbeat and chipper, it just made my day. I suppose there was a part of me that realized he was somehow "different" from the other guys on screen, but it didn't matter to me any. I was just excited to see him whenever I could.

On Saturday nights we used to get access to some BBC programming through the PBS station – and there was this one show called Are You Being Served? which I absolutely adored as a kid. My favorite character on the show was Mr. Humphreys – who while I'm sure all the adults knew he was gay, to me he was just clever and witty. I didn't know why I liked him so much – he made me laugh I suppose – he always had a snappy comeback or stared humorously into the camera.

There were even a few episodes of All in the Family where that featured a transvestite character named Beverly. Nobody moaned or groaned that this dude was on TV in a dress – everybody laughed and thought it was some of the funniest episodes, seeing Archie have to deal with the fact that he gave mouth-to-mouth to a man.

I can still remember the episode where Beverly dies. Obviously the show had ended long before I was ever a thought in anyone's mind – but that episode was new to me. Beverly didn't die of some natural death somewhere. He was murdered. Beaten down on the street with lead pipes during Christmas.

I remember how much I cried. I couldn't understand it. He was such a nice man, and he was so funny – I couldn't understand why anybody would kill him. That episode has stuck with me for my entire life.

As I got older and grew to understand exactly what some of these things were, y'know, I may have realized that I do not agree with the concept of homosexuality – of going off and acting on those impulses and taking a lover or trying to have some kind of fake wedding ceremony – but I have never hated anybody over the simple fact that they are homosexual.

I have never gone out saying that somebody who's gay needs to live their life as a lie, pretending to be straight – or even worse being openly gay but still getting married to a woman – that's ridiculous.

I've certainly never told anybody that they need to try and "fix" themselves with some kind of goddamn conversion therapy. These poor people being injected, being electrocuted – being basically tortured by all kinds of madness.

I think that's deplorable.

But I also think that it's deplorable that a lot of people are being condemned as bigots just because they disagree with something. Especially when they have a very good reason to disagree with it, or are capable of articulating exactly why they disagree with it.

GLAAD wrote an article a few years ago noting that the coming generation seemed to be the most openly "Anti-LGBT" they had seen in decades. I find it no small wonder. I was not shocked by this revelation then – and I am less shocked by it now.

Never before has any group of people been so openly combative, instigative, hostile and irrational as the modern "LGBTQ".

This is a group of people so blinded by their own greed and avaricious nature that they constantly tear each other apart. Their entire statement of being – along with any factions and coalitions which make up the "WOKE" mentality – is to bully and suppress any and all other groups of people into complete obedience of their views and demands.

They force their beliefs onto children. Openly threaten violence against Christians and people of other religious practices. They belittle and berate any opposing view, and constantly heap themselves into the forefront of every social and political issue.

Rock n' Roll icon Dee Snider – a longtime advocate of Gay Rights and open activist for LGBT issues – has recently been hung out to dry by this movement. He has been denounced and demonized by this group of people and their followers as every manner of "ist", "ism" and "phobe" for the simple offense of stating that parents should have rights over their children's education, and that children should not be subject to gender reassignment surgeries.

Some years ago now, TV star Phil Robertson gave a straightforward and honest answer to the question of his beliefs pertaining to homosexuality – citing that as a Christian he believed it to be wrong, and stating that while he holds no ill-will towards anybody, he believes that those who engage in that sort of lifestyle will be held accountable come their time of judgment. This simple statement of his own personal opinion – which moreover was just the literal reading of scripture from the Bible – led to his removal from the television program surrounding his family, the removal and in some cases banning of his merchandise from stores and ultimately cancellation of his show.

I remember in the wake of this, one Gay Rights activist and blogger stood up to defend him and pointed out the hypocrisy of screaming and demanding acceptance when you are unwilling to accept someone who believes anything differently than you do.

Now I want to make it clear that there are many, many individuals that follow a certain bent, or fall into the category of alternative-lifestyles that I know and I love and I recognize as some of the finest, most honest, caring, sincere and upstanding people that I have ever had the privilege to know in my life.

Know that what I say is not directed towards you as a person or individual – but rather it is directed above you to the organizations, think-tanks and echo-chambers of the world. To the proponents of outrage-culture and professional victimhood.

In the most brusque words possible: People don't hate you because of what you put up your asshole. They hate you *because* you're an asshole.

They hate you because you are self-righteous and self-absorbed. They hate you, because you do not care about the problems that you're causing – about the pain that you're inflicting on the world.

They hate you because at this point in time, literally anybody who even so much as *slightly* disagrees with you, is automatically demonized to the highest degree imaginable – complete with being threatened with physical violence against themselves or their families. Complete with being threatened financially – of having their careers taken away or their businesses impacted.

At this point in time, literally anybody who so much as shows an ounce of question within themselves, or shows a momentary sign of self-doubt or lack of self-confidence – gets scooped up and pinned against a wall of social expectations – being bullied and being gang-pressed to turn around and upend their entire life on the whims of someone else without even getting the chance to voice their own concerns.

People hate you, because frankly, at this point in time you have become... I don't even know what to call it. "Psychological Terrorists" for lack of a better term.

I remember once sitting in genuine horror, as I watched a video released online by a beautiful young girl whom I imagine to be around seventeen or eighteen – who was weeping her eyes out. She was crying desperately, because one of her alternate personalities – one of her "head-mates" – identified as transgender, and in order to make her "head-mate" happy, she would have to give up the body that she loved. The body that she was born in, felt comfortable in. The body that she herself recognized as natural and normal.

I do not know this girl. I know absolutely nothing about her beyond the heartbreaking confession that she made – but she struck me as a genuinely sweet-natured person. Something about the way she spoke and the way she kept herself, suggested to me that she was a kind and caring individual, with a sensitive soul.

This beautiful, young, sweet looking girl that still has her whole life ahead of her, intended to undergo gender reassignment surgery in order to placate a fucking voice inside her head.

When a person suffers from multiple personalities, or becomes schizophrenic, we recognize it as a disorder of the mind – but when a person claims to be a woman trapped inside a man's body, or to be indistinguishable, non-binary or fluid – we hoist them up as brave and offer them affirmation. Further enabling their disconnection from reality – and harming them in the process.

Who was there for that young girl, or for the countless others like her? Who took the time to sit down and hold their hands, and tell them it would be alright? To tell them that they're just confused and that it's okay to be scared and to be uncertain and to be in pain. To be with them and to help them get the help that they need – the help that they genuinely need – without pushing them further over the edge? Without lying to them and telling them that this is what they're supposed to do – and that this wild and radical thing is going to solve all of their problems?

More and more we see them – first in dozens, then the hundreds and soon to be the thousands – these poor abandoned people that are "detransitioning" and being forced to live out the rest of their lives with the irreparable damage that has been caused by the negligent and uncaring nature of those around them. Those same voices that once egged them on, pushing them to take the plunge from which they can never return.

Anyone who offers any form of resistance or criticism whatsoever to this horrible and disgusting way of thinking, is quickly shouted down as a "bigot" and a "transphobe" when in reality, it is these voices – drowned out as they may be – that are offering a chance at logic and reason. That are offering a semblance of hope for the hopeless – and ultimately trying to save them from their own self-destruction, and the predators that they have surrounded themselves with.

Most people don't even know where the practice of "gender theory" comes from. They don't know the history of human experimentation, sexual abuse and mutilation that gave rise to this ideology.

This disgusting, unnatural and malignant train of thought is the brainchild of a cruel and unforgivable "man" by the name of John Money – who pushed this ideological cancer onto the world stage at the expense of David Reimer.

In the mid-1960s a young Canadian family by the name of Reimer had two sons, Bruce and his twin brother Brian. Something went wrong during the procedure for Bruce's circumcision and the majority of his penis was ultimately destroyed. The family was devastated, they didn't know what to do – and again with this being the 60s, reconstructive surgery on that level, with the complexity and intricacy of the nerve endings required to return functionality – it really wasn't an option like we might have today.

Uncertain about what to do in order to help their son, the family was taken in by a man on TV. "Doctor" John Money – a psychologist that proposed the idea of human gender as being "malleable" and that children could be effectively raised as either male or female, regardless of their biology. Not knowing what else to do, the Reimers came to America and met with the "doctor," who had just found his first test subject.

Money convinced the Reimers to change Bruce's name to Brenda and raise him as a girl. Money oversaw the performance of several "surgeries" which finished the removal of Bruce's penis, his scrotum, his testicles, and then carved a rudimentary form of "female" genitalia into his body. All of this took place on a child that would still have been wearing diapers at the time.

The Reimer family was instructed to make him wear dresses and play with dolls, and under absolutely no circumstances were they allowed to tell him the truth that he was a boy. So that's what they did, they raised him as a girl. They taught him to pee sitting down and they taught him to emulate his mother doing housework and baking, and they took their children down to see the "doctor" at Johns Hopkins every year, so that he could see the progress they were making.

John Money went public with his experiment, giving lectures on his subject which he referred to as "Joan."

He spoke of how "happy" she was and how "well" she was adjusting to the changes in her body. About how many "friends" she had and of how "popular" she was – and the worlds of science and academia gave him critical acclaim and praised Money for his "resounding success."

Later we would learn that Bruce actually preferred to pee standing up, in spite of everything he had been taught and of never having a penis. That he always felt an innate compulsion to urinate while standing – as if instinctually, biologically, he knew that sitting down wasn't normal for him.

Later we would learn a great many things, because as Bruce got older he changed his name to David – and then he told the real story about what happened to him.

In the decades before that however, John Money's theory became an ideological doctrine for the progressive left. They embraced it without question – and any time that another psychologist, geneticist or endocrinologist came forward with even a hint of skepticism – Money had their papers silenced. He leveraged his influence to stop editors from publishing works that might otherwise raise questions about his theories – and so his theories went unopposed. These practices took root in modern medicine on the basis that Money had "proven" how "successful" this approach to biology could be – and so countless thousands of boys across the world, if they were born with any form of genital ambiguity, were pushed into being raised as girls.

Money capitalized further on his academic approval in the 1970s by writing a book in which he doubled-down on the idea that his now-famous "twin study" had been so successful.

Jump to 1998, David Reimer came forward to tell his side of the story. He had grown up, he had gotten married and adopted three children – and ironically he was working as a janitor in a slaughterhouse. When he came forward with what happened, David opened up about the entire experience and called it a "hoax." He opened up about the fact that for over fourteen years of his life he was told that he had to be a "girl," but that the entire time he felt like he was a boy.

He said that during all of those "successful" and "popular" years of his life – he was not happy. That he was not popular. That he didn't have a lot of friends, and that he never liked to wear dresses or play with dolls. That he always wanted to play with his brother's toys, that he wanted to pee standing up.

That he was rough and he was masculine and that the other kids at school called him "cave-woman" and that he was lonely and miserable as a child – that the whole family was miserable.

He also spoke at length about what really happened during those visits to see the "doctor." That John Money sexually abused both him and his brother – taking them into his private offices away from their parents, and humiliated them. Starting at the age of six, Money forced them to strip naked – forced them to mimic sexual intercourse with each other. He would show them pictures, show them pornography and he would tell them that "This is what men and women do with each other."

He called it "sexual rehearsal play."

John Money made David assume the "female" position on all fours, and then forced Brian to thrust against him from behind. He also forced David into other positions, such as on his back with his legs spread, and made Brian lay on top of him.

The good "doctor" was also rather fond of photographing the two boys during these sessions.

When either of the boys showed signs of resistance towards these activities, Money would scream and berate them. Threatening them.

This abuse went unnoticed inside the halls of Johns Hopkins for years until another yearly "checkup" rolled around, and the boys refused to go. They wouldn't do it – and the parents couldn't understand why, because they never knew.

In the end, David's brother, Brian, died from a lethal overdose at the age of 36. Their mother attempted suicide, and their father spiraled into alcoholism.

Ultimately David committed suicide in the parking lot of a Winnipeg grocery store by shooting himself in the head with a sawed-off shotgun. He was 38 years old.

And what happened to John Money? Absolutely nothing.

He died rich and famous at the age of 84. The Prime Minister of New Zealand dedicated the wing of an art gallery in his honor – and he never once commented on the atrocities that he committed to those two boys, or their family.

What happened to the Reimers was a tragedy – but I think the even bigger tragedy is the fact that nobody seems to care. The fact that this abhorrent travesty was not only allowed to take place, but that the criminals and monsters responsible for it never had to face any form of justice for their actions. Never reprimanded, never penalized – but instead the opposite – they were praised and idolized for it.

It makes me sick – and what's even worse is that these practices and ideals are further perpetuated today by millions of people that have flocked to the idolatry of a madman with religious fervor.

The World Professional Association of Transgender Health, or WPATH, is the current leading world "authority" on transgender-healthcare. This organization holds so much political influence that in a recent court-battle taking place in Tennessee – in which the state voted to institute a ban on the chemical castration of children – the ACLU argued that WPATH should possess the concrete authority to overturn individual state rulings and legislatures at will.

Thankfully the court upheld its decision, citing that WPATH's incomprehensive amounts of data supplied limited information on the quote: "long-term physical, psychological and neurodevelopmental outcomes that result from administering hormones and puberty-blockers to minors." A great victory for Tennessee indeed.

The unfortunate truth however is that due to a security breach, we now know that WPATH is actually in possession of extensive documentation on the resoundingly negative effects of "gender affirming care" on children and minors – and that despite claiming to have only "limited data" on the subject – these documents prove that WPATH is not only fully aware of the severity of their actions, but that they have been intentionally covering it up.

Included in the leaked files is one document citing the communications of one of the "doctors" concerning a 16-year-old girl who developed large liver tumors as a direct result of receiving hormone-therapy and testosterone alongside drugs to forcibly stop her menstruation. Quote: "The patient was found to have two liver masses, and the oncologist and surgeon both indicated that the likely offending agents are the hormones." Another "doctor" responding to this report cited that his own colleague had suffered from severe liver failure due to testosterone injections over the course of a decade, and died.

It should also be noted that at absolutely no point in these documents does WPATH express any interest whatsoever in going public with these concerns. Instead they press forward with their mutilation of this tumor-ridden-girl, stating quote: "We're prepared to support the patient in any way we can, E.G. top-surgery when medically stable, etc."

Yes, that's right, after concluding that their procedures have been the direct cause of tumors in this underage girl, their only interest is to remove her breasts as quickly as possible.

Further examination of the documents show that WPATH's preferred method of treatment is to rush these kinds of procedures in general, before the patient can reach adulthood – with one "doctor" openly boasting that she has performed over a dozen "vaginoplasties" on patients under the age of 18. For those unaware of what exactly a vaginoplasty is – it is the removal of a child's penis, scrotum and testicles in order to replace them with a non-functioning open wound.

It is exactly what they did to David Reimer almost sixty years ago.

One surgeon in these documents also went on record regarding vaginoplasty by stating, quote: "I feel the best time for surgery in the U.S. is the summer before their last year of high school." This same "person" also stated that numerous other surgeons in their practice agreed with her.

To make things even worse, during a video conference WPATH members were captured on film admitting to the fact that children are unable to provide proper informed consent to these kinds of procedures – but that they also openly encourage these children, as well as their parents to follow-through regardless of that fact.

To quote one member he said: "I think the thing you have to remember about kids is that we're often explaining these sorts of things to people who haven't even had biology in high school yet... We try to talk about it but most kids are nowhere in any kind of a 'brain space' to really, really, really talk about it in a serious way. That's always bothered me, but y'know, we still want the kids to be happier in the moment."

Happier... in... the moment... that's the major take away from this. It has nothing to do with the life of these patients. It's only about the *moment*. It's only about the instant gratification of self-accolades and social approval, with absolutely no care or concern for the future and well-being of these people getting carved up like a Frankenstein's monster.

If you or anybody that you know actually considers yourself to be an "ally" of this movement, then you should know that it is an unprecedented statistical fact that individuals identifying as "transgender" suffer from the highest suicide rate of any minority that the world has ever known. Public data from the Williams Institute, and the National Institute of Health in 2022, indicates that over 82% of "transgender" individuals have seriously contemplated suicide – with 42% having actively attempted it and 56% having been engaged in otherwise self-harmful behavior.

These numbers often fluctuate higher, as I have seen more recent numbers suggesting suicidal tendencies as high as 90% among "transgender" teens and adults.

The common argument for this is that suicide rates are so high because of a lack of public acceptance. They claim that gender-affirming care, hormone-injection therapy and chemical castration in minors not only significantly decreases the rates of suicide, but also provides long-term positive psychological feedback.

There's one glaring issue with this argument however, namely that we haven't been doing this long enough to know. These claims are entirely baseless, simply on the fact that we haven't been engaging in this wide-spread medical experiment for more than the past few years. We've never seen anything like this before in history.

You cannot possibly claim to know the long-term effects of these studies, because there hasn't been any long-term studies.

This modern practice of chopping up children only began around sixty years ago, and you know how that turned out. Not to mention that once the general idea began to gain traction, it was nowhere near the size and scale in which we're doing it today.

Multiple radicalized far-Left organizations such as WPATH have commissioned their own studies in an attempt to prove that the treatments of hormones and puberty-blockers show a decreased rate of suicide in transgender youth – and even they couldn't find any conclusive evidence for it – because it doesn't fucking exist.

The sheer number of young people that are suddenly identifying as transgender has absolutely skyrocketed over the past couple of years. You can look at the numbers, some of which I listed at the start of this chapter – it's an exponential growth that is utterly disproportionate to anything we have ever seen before.

Pro-Trans activists will often argue that it's not a "social contagion" and that "there's always been this many trans-people." That they simply didn't exist in an open-minded and affirming society and so they couldn't come out into the open.

What an absolute joke.

If that truly were the case, and there has always been these millions upon millions of "trans" people hiding themselves from the world – living in fear, living a lie – and that the only reason they would ever have to kill themselves is the utter lack of social affirmation, then historically we should have seen an inexplicably high rate of suicide among children.

As Matt Walsh once stated before the Tennessee State House Health Committee: "We should be able to look back at history and find just this unbroken, incredible epidemic of children mysteriously killing themselves, because they weren't being 'affirmed as trans.'"

This entire narrative is a lie. It is absolutely a social contagion. These monstrous ideas get pushed onto children at every single turn. It's forced on them at home, where every television show, every cartoon, has to push an overtly sexual character onto its audience. Where even shows like Blue's Clues, a program designed for children ages 2-6, featured a goddamn transvestite that sang an alternate LGBT re-imagining of "Johnny Comes Marching Home Again."

It is forced on them in public schools where extremely graphic transgender and homoerotic literature is distributed to students of all ages. Where kids are instructed by their teachers to ignore their parents and not tell them about what's happening at the school – and where young children are exposed live strip-teases and sex-shows being performed in the fucking cafeteria.

And that's not even talking about the internet. The social influences on children across the internet are absolutely insane. There's channels on YouTube labeled as "for kids" where people sing "Toucha, Toucha, Touch Me" from the Rocky Horror Picture. Where there's videos that feature iconic characters such as Mickey Mouse telling kids that their parents don't love them, that they need to change themselves.

I've sat there and watched a video of a fully grown man wearing makeup on TikTok, telling children that they have to go "no contact" with their parents – completely cut them off – and that he was the only adult they could turn to. That he would always be there for them.

You want to tell me that this isn't a social contagion?

You want to tell me that this isn't the predatory targeting of children?

Everything about this movement is predatory. For fuck's sake, even their main flag that everyone rallies around is a goddamn rainbow – it's something specifically *designed* to be alluring to kids.

This entire ideology is predicated on the targeting of children – that's the purpose of the original study – it's the foundational principles of gender theory. Nothing about this ideological practice even comes into existence without the specific intention to target and harm children.

It is true that prior to these experiments we have seen other attempts at sex-changes and the transitioning of male to female or female to male – but the key difference in these cases is that the people involved were adults. They were fully grown and fully capable of making an informed decision about what it is that they wanted to do with their lives.

Ignoring the fact that almost all of the earliest transsexuals ended up either killing themselves, getting strung out on drugs or otherwise dying due to some horrific medical complications as a result of their surgeries – I have no problem with an adult making their own decision about their body. If they know the risks, and they're willing to take them – that's their choice.

That's my stance on it.

But this? What we have today? It's a wildfire that's burning throughout society at the highest peak in history. It's a baseless theory that has no foundation to stand on. Sex and gender are the exact same thing. They are two words for the same exact thing. Just because some uppity feminist decided that she had the arbitrary power to change the definition of a word – doesn't actually change the definition of that word.

If I asked you what the defining characteristic of a rock would be, you would almost certainly say that it's "hard." If I then say that I'm changing the definition of hard to being soft – do you think that rocks are now soft? Do you think that if I picked up a rock from my driveway and threw it at the window, that the glass wouldn't break? No, you don't – at least I hope you don't – because if you do, then you're a fucking idiot.

You cannot argue that gender is a social construct. You can argue that traditional gender-roles *inside* of society are a social construct – because by definition, they are – but you cannot say that sex is biological and that gender is subjective. It doesn't work that way.

The roles that we play within society are the only things that are a construct about the definitions of male and female. That is why you have seen various patriarchal, matriarchal and egalitarian societies throughout history – because they constructed their roles within those societies differently to one another.

I've heard some morons recently trying to argue that transgenderism is "natural," because certain species of amphibious and aquatic lifeforms are able to alter their sex in a single sex environments. That this was the solid proof that all conservatives were just ignorant-minded bigots. I suppose these people were just too busy being high on themselves to understand that those are the biological characteristics of those species – not ours. That it's perfectly natural for them to do that – because that is their biological nature.

Humans cannot do that. Humans cannot "will" themselves into a different sex any more than those frogs or fish can swim over to an underwater hospital and have surgery.

At the end of the day a man is still a man and a woman is a woman – no amount of cosmetic surgery, regardless of how detrimental and invasive it may be, is going to change that. You can take all of the puberty-blockers and hormone injections that you want. You can have your body carved up from head-to-toe like a Thanksgiving turkey – but if they take your blood sample, your DNA will still be that of whatever it is you're trying to get away from.

That is called *reality*.

That is the thing we live in. Life is not a fantasy – it doesn't bend and shape to the whims of our desires, no matter how much the hubris of man may wish to think it otherwise.

You cannot change biology. You cannot change reality. There is no such thing as non-binary and there's no such thing as gender-fluid. A person is either male or they are female – end of story – and as for the rest of those supposed 105 genders? They don't exist – and neither do any of the numerous "sexualities" that are specifically predicated on them.

What I am willing to agree to is that any person who is at least 21-years-old and has been screened, in my opinion, by no less than three psychiatrists – and is found to be mentally stable – can do whatever the hell they want. I don't care, it's not my life.

What I am not willing to agree to is this deranged expectation that I am supposed to placate you based on the decisions that you make. That I am supposed to refer to you as a woman, when clearly you're a man. That I'm supposed to enable your delusions, and rewrite my entire language just to suit your needs.

That I am supposed to sit idly by while the whole world teaches young girls that the only way for them to succeed is to be men, because grown men keep entering women's sport and brutalizing them. Entering women's bathrooms, locker-rooms or changing areas and harassing them, molesting them and assaulting them.

That somehow when a little boy plays with his mothers makeup, or when a little girl plays with her fathers tool belt – it actually means that I have to swoop in and destroy their entire lives instead of just letting them be curious like most children are.

That I have to surrender my rights as a parent over to the state, just to satisfy your goddamn greed for human test subjects.

I'm not going to do it. I'm not going to placate you. I'm not going to enable you. I'm not going to sit back and hold my mouth while a single side – one single side of the political system – tries to force its ideological ambitions onto the rest of the world.

I will not do it.

The entire sordid history of this perverted system of thought can be traced back from one genuinely terrible human being to another, and another before them in a completely unbroken chain of events.

That is nearly unheard of in all of human history – I mean even Nazi Germany had General Rommel for God's sake.

Whether you are talking about the eternally self-destructive Rita Ericson, her theory-perpetuating friend Zelda Suplee, their bankrolling and partnering of Harry Benjamin and ultimately the formation of the EEF – to the organization's fundraising and financial backing of John Money, who himself served as a board member at the time – to the EEF's closure and re-branding as the Janus Information Facility with the further addition of Paul Walker, and so on down the line.

It's just one horrible story after another with these "people."

At one point Harry Benjamin even wrote a book admitting to the fact that fake vaginas are quote: "Wounds," and that these organs will typically degrade to the point of being quote: "obliterated and useless."

He also acknowledges that the majority of interest in these procedures are socially motivated, as opposed to being medically motivated. One example he cites is a mother who was "embarrassed" to be seen with her son in public, and would not become proud of him until the boy started to identify as a girl. To add yet another layer of unpleasantness, the mother herself had stated that she found her new "daughter's" appearance to be quote: "Attractive," and even Benjamin added his two cents by stating that he could "verify the attractiveness" of this child.

I will never understand the minds of these people – or rather, the minds of these *monsters* – who seek only to benefit from the harvest and harm of those pitiful souls crying out for help.

What is worse, is that so many of them have become convinced that what they're doing is righteous and just.

These people are a blight upon the world. They are the enemy of civilization. They are a manifestation of everything wrong with society, and their only goal is misery. Their only mission, their only objective, is the downfall of mankind.

It is these groups of "people" that are the biblical plagues of the modern era. They are the scourge of civil liberty, the death of free-thinking, and I can no longer sit idly by and accept it.

In the 1980s a study conducted by researches at Yale and the University of Kentucky found that over half of post-operative complicated included quote: "Breast cancer in hormonally-treated males; the need for surgical reduction of bloated limbs resulting from hormones; repeated construction of vaginal opening; infections of the urinary tract and rectum; hemorrhaging; loss of skin grafts; post-operative suicides and suicide attempts; persistent post-operative economic dependency; patient demands to reverse surgery; chronic post-operative depression, psychosis, and phobia; and pre-and post-operative prostitution, often necessitated by by the high cost of treatment."

The study also noted that the majority of patients seeking or receiving sex-reassignment surgery exhibited signs of addiction to cosmetic surgery – or as they put it, a "polysurgical attitude."

It is so alarming to me just how many of these complications are the same ones that we see today. It might be easy to hand-wave this kind of information and say that "Oh well you know, it was the 80s and they didn't have the kinds of technology that we do, so of course people weren't as happy." But that's not the case. Medical complications as a result of these operations are vast and extensive, with post-operative depression and a desire for surgical reversal being at the fore-front of this issue.

The problem is that not only does this sort of thing often bankrupt the average person – which does push them towards those tendencies for prostitution which I spoke about in the previous chapter – but it's also irreversible. You can never go back after doing this, it is a one-way street.

Those double-mastectomies and hysterectomies and chemical castrations – they're permanent. You might get some fake breast implants, but you'll never have your breasts again. You may get some fake neuticles, but you'll never get your testicles back.

What's even more is that the common trend now is to not only engage in the medical procedure itself, but to also seek post-transitional facial surgeries – surgeries where they break your nose and eye-sockets in order to rearrange them. Where they shave the bone of your jaw to re-shape it into being more feminine. Not only does shaving down a layer of bone expose people to an increased risk of infection – but much like the other surgeries, you can't get those layers back again. They're gone.

The sad truth of this entire thing is that every single one of these procedures are entirely cosmetic. A sixty-something year old man or woman who gets a face-lift and a tummy-tuck, is still sixty-something years old.

Whatever problems, whatever issues and depressions that a person has to deal with prior to these surgeries, doesn't magically go away just because you cut off your penis. They're still going to be there – and you're still going to have to deal with them. The only difference is that now you have to deal with all of the issues that you already had – plus all of the news issues that you've just created for yourself.

Eventually the Harry Benjamin Association, which was built after Janus became defunct, paid for symposiums and lectures by Anne Lawrence who spoke rather openly about the fact that he was a self-described "autogynephile," which is a man who becomes sexually aroused at the prospect of being a female. Lawrence also further defends this fetish by calling it an "under appreciated" paraphilia.

In 1999, Lawrence made a very graphic update update to his website, in which he writes in no small amount of detail about his own personal experiences with genital mutilation, and his first encounters with a dilator. Quote: "Grinning with insane delight, I pick up my hand mirror and take a good look. There it is, thick as a closet rod, inserted six inches into me. For so many years I have longed to be penetrable, to be a vessel, a receptacle, and now I am."

What a very specific choice of words. A vessel. A receptacle.

I think that the word Anne Lawrence was looking for, is "woman."

I have been accused many times in my life of being sexist or male-chauvinistic – but I have never viewed women with such disregard, as to consider them little more than a walking orifice – as a "receptacle," just waiting for me to come along and make use of them.

That is disgusting.

That is the sort of abhorrent mentality which permeates the so-called "transgendered vocabularies" of today. The frequent references towards women as nothing more than "birthing people" or "menstruating people" that you hear everywhere. It is sickening to me. It's completely disrespectful.

This is exactly the kind of backwards mentality towards women that saw Riley Gaines, as well as several other young ladies, forced to strip naked and expose themselves in front of a man inside an all-girls locker room. Which sees countless female athletes – true masters of their respective professions – being pushed to the back burner and replaced by men who view them as nothing more than objects and inconveniences.

It's what leads to grown adult men referring to their assholes as "pussies" and their penises as "clities," and then dressing up in the most garishly barbie-doll-esque clothing they can find and go skipping back and forth saying "Now I know what it's like to be a woman!"

No, you don't. You don't know what it's like to be a woman. You will never know what it's like to be a woman – because you are never going to be a woman. How dare you – how dare you boil down the entirety of the fairer-sex into some superficial state of being, to the point that you think this gives you the right to say that you know "what it means" to be a woman?

In a world that is currently so intolerant of all things men, we're also seeing the complete erasure of women. The fact that this movement is built on the back of Feminism is ironic, to say the least – but I find it no less sad.

Before moving on to my final thoughts on this subject, I'd like to add that Anne Lawrence – in spite of his many accolades and honors in the field of furthering human rights – is a rapist. He was once let go from a hospital for a quote: "lapse in judgement." That lapse in judgement was going to a medical ward, entering the room of an unconscious female patient and being caught fondling and inspecting her genitalia in what he referred to as a "non-consensual genital examination."

I don't know about you, but I would say that finding a medically sedated woman that was currently unconscious and unprotected – and then sticking your fingers inside of her – counts as rape is most courts of law. But what do I know, because he wasn't charged or arrested for this. He didn't even get his license revoked.

All they gave him was a slap on the wrist, and a dismissal from his position.

I suppose I should be surprised, considering that the *vast* majority of this movement is now insisting that asking a person about their original sex at birth should be considered a hate crime – which means that anyone engaging in any form of sexual activity with these "people" would ideally be unable to give any kind of informed consent. It's a literal attempt at legalizing rape – if you're straight and you do not want to sleep with a man, but you are not allowed to ask if a person is *actually* a woman or not – you are unable to consent.

The fact that this is even a talking point or issue is just insane. Considering the rate at which medical science is advancing in this field, there are eventually going to be people who, at least on a superficial level, will be able to semi-believably appear be male or to be female – and if you're not allowed to confirm their biology through the potential of the law or the guilt of a social pressgang – that's rape. The support of this is the support of rape.

I mean I really cannot believe that we're having to even talk about it.

I have to close this whole thing out soon, because it's taken such a toll on my nerves just to write it.

Somebody asked me once if I could put into words what I found wrong with the LGBT – and I told them. It's a social movement based on three sexualities and an ideology, not to mention whatever else that they've tacked on to their alphabet-soup of an organization.

They use made-up words and terminologies to twist and confuse people that are scared, people that are hurting and uncertain about life. They target vulnerable people with ideas that sexuality and intimacy aren't related. That sex and gender are subjective. They feed off of the growing sense of social uncertainty and leverage peer-pressure to extort depression and anxiety.

That's why we're seeing this sort of... I don't even know what you'd call it. "Gay Washing" of historical facts. Printed art in the style of classic Americana depicting same-sex couples in the 30s, 40s and 50s as if it were the most normal and natural thing ever. Famous comic book characters re-written to suddenly be gay, or usually bisexual. Video games and television programming which depicts ancient cultures as being highly tolerant and accepting of homosexual relationships.

This forced narrative that every culture in the world was always "gay-positive" prior to the rise of Christianity – and that Christians are the sole reason behind anti-homosexual prejudice.

I've got news for you, it doesn't matter how many Iron Age viking shows and games you produce, they weren't "cool with it." It was considered to be a pretty major taboo in Norse society and culture – that is the purpose of the Argr – and in fact it was so intolerable that if you called another man "gay" he needed to defend his honor in a duel to the death.

It doesn't matter how many times you try to dig up that one story of a Hermaphrodite in the Roman Legion and cite the Ancient Romans as being "trans inclusive" – they weren't.

If you actually bother to read about him, you will find that he was so hated and so reviled by his fellow legionnaires and commanding officers – that his name became synonymous with negativity. Writings of him described his foul body odor – with special attention given to his "reeking" genitalia – and generally about how lazy and useless he was. In fact it wasn't uncommon for a Roman Decanus to address soldiers that weren't pulling their weight by some variation of this guy's name, in the same manner that modern Sergeants might call new recruits "worthless maggots."

And don't even get me started on the "gay caveman" frenzy that everyone latched onto like starving animals. As the story goes, archaeologists discovered a "caveman" burial outside of Prague in which a male skeleton was found to be facing in the traditional female position. They found no identifying items buried with the body – no pottery, no weapons – and so everyone said "Look! See? Gay cavemen!"

First and foremost, the skeleton is not a caveman, it's from the pre Bronze Age – and secondly, holy men and spiritualists – such as Shaman – were always buried in the female position despite being male. We have no conclusive evidence of who this person was. There hasn't been any DNA testing on the skeleton to the best of my knowledge – and without any burial effects, we have no real way of ever understanding how he ended up in the position he was in.

If it is in fact a man, could he have been a Shaman? Could he have simply been tossed in a hole in an impromptu burial? Could it have been an intentional insult by whoever buried him? We'll never know – but the media scramble to definitively label and validate this find as "gay" is fucking pathetic.

Like I said, who are you trying to convince? Me or yourself?

Now I've said it before and I'll say it again: I don't care what people do in their private lives. It's not my place to tell you what you need to think or feel or do. My support for "gay rights" both begins and ends with the general sentiment that people have the right to be left the hell alone.

That as wrong as it is for somebody to come marching down my street, telling me that I'm a bigot – or suing and harassing some bakery because they refused to bake them a cake – that it's it's equally wrong for religious organization to go around belittling people just because of who they go to bed with.

I have several gay friends and none of them like what this movement stands for. None of them like that they get lumped in and associated with it *just* because they're gay. If you think that anything I've said here has been harsh, then you ought to listen to some of them talk about it – they'll burn your fucking ears off, because they're directly connected to it in a way that I can't be.

They get so angry about it and it makes them so sad. They see the fact that it's political. It's a movement of division – designed to separate everybody from each other into their own little pens. To treat humans like cattle and to abuse the ones who don't know how to stand up for themselves.

One of my friends asked me what I thought about gay marriage and I told him. I said that gay marriage is wrong, but that civil unions were unfair. That if you wanted real equality you should have adhered to the separation of church and state, and simply made them equal in all legal aspects aside from the name. He said to me: "Well it still wouldn't be 'equal' because it wouldn't be called a marriage." To which I told him: "Yeah, but you don't give a Superbowl ring to a baseball player."

They're both sporting events – they're both equal – they're just *different*.

If you look at a Dodge and then you look at a Chevy, you'd say they're both cars wouldn't you? You wouldn't say that they're the same though, because they aren't. They're similar, but they're different.

I don't think there's anything inherently wrong with somebody being different. I think that each and every one of us is a little different in our own way – but somewhere we seem to have lost that. Somewhere we seem to have developed this idea that the only way to stand out is to be different – and that there's no reason to ever have a similarity.

I recently read an article discussing a fairly well known guy on YouTube who makes videos about historical food, and the article described him as, quote: "A gay YouTuber." What the hell is a "gay YouTuber?" The man makes cooking videos. That's all. The fact that he's gay has *nothing* to do with his business or his talent. He's just a guy – who happens to be gay. Why should his sexuality matter?

This constant need to label everything is so frustrating – it's so infuriating – it's driving me crazy.

I said before in the previous chapter that I really just do not believe that so many people are suffering from this sudden onset of... I guess you would call it a sense of sexual dysmorphia or sexual disconnection, for lack of a better term. That I wondered how many people claiming to be aromantic and asexual were really just confused, or really just unlucky in their lives and turned to this idea of definitively labeling themselves in order to gain some kind of comfort for themselves.

I also mentioned that maybe there really are people who legitimately experience a complete lack of arousal or emotional connection – but that we aren't really asking the question of "why?"

We know that the male Y-chromosome is changing shape. We know that medically speaking, alternative sexualities are the result of genetic imbalances within the DNA. We know that modern society is growing more and more isolated and we know that mental health problems are on the rise.

It just seems so dishonest to me, that we hear somebody say something that clearly doesn't sound quite "right" and then we just run with it instead of asking them "why?"

Instead of taking an actual interest in them as a person – or an interest in what's affecting them. What's causing them to be in this place where they feel the need to label themselves and get taken advantage of by predatory people in the world.

I don't know, I'm not sure that anybody has ever accused me of being particularly "humanitarian" but to me, this whole thing just seems so… uncaring.

But like that girl – that poor girl who gave her testimonial on video – I hope that somebody was able to step in and help her. To be there and talk to her and listen to her problems and try to get her the help that she needed, before some butcher got his hands on her and started carving her up.

I just wish I could be sure. I wish that nobody had to go through that.

They say the road to Hell is paved with good intentions – well I guess we're living in the fast lane.

This is how you end up with families like that one who took a grown adult man and "adopted" him as a little girl – only for him to then molest and rape their actual child. Families like the ones who make their daughter eat and drink out of dog bowls and go to the bathroom in a litter box because she "self-identifies" as an animal.

None of this is an act of bravery. It's an act of abuse on the part of those individuals who play along with it.

We can see the effect that these social movements are having on people. There's a growing movement right now of people – particularly young people – actively taking elective surgeries to amputate parts of their body in order to "become disabled." Expressing a sense of dissatisfaction with the fact that they don't suffer from a physical disability, and so they go out and get one on purpose.

"Disabled by choice, not by chance."

It's all a cry for help.

Every single thing that we're seeing is nothing more than a simple human plea, and yet we're ignoring it. We're consciously making an effort to re-affirm self harm.

I can't just sit back and take this anymore.

It's come down to that moment when I have to make a judgment call – and if you're a person who supports this agenda, then I think you're a goddamn monster.

Even the ones who just support it from the sidelines – let me tell you that as far as I'm concerned – you are just as *guilty* as any one of these butchers who have put their hands on a child.

You may want to think about that the next time you decide to hang up a bunch of flags or go marching down the street as a walking endorsement of this kind of predatory emotional-fearmongering and socio-political barbarism.

Chapter X: American Dreams

I find that the older I get, the more I seem to struggle with a sense of self-identity. I wouldn't call it an "identity-crisis" or anything like that, but I mean, the fundamental understanding of who I am and what I am – and specifically of who and what I am proud to be – those are the things I find myself struggling with the most lately.

For example, I'm proud to be a Southerner. My culture and heritage hearkens all the way back to the British – with a huge influence from both Scotland and Ireland mixed in for good measure. I love where I come from, and I love the "Southern" approach to life – even if our culture is admittedly dwindling – I still love it. I'm still proud of it. I'm proud of being from a group of people who are chock-full of rich histories, storied traditions and hard honest values.

I'm proud to be Catholic. I wrote in one of the earliest chapters that "pride" wasn't the word I wanted to use – and in that context it wasn't – but that word is absolutely applicable here and now. Catholicism can trace its roots all the way back to before the fall of the ancient world, and while the church has not always been perfect – because nothing is ever perfect – it has persisted throughout the ages and managed to touch the hearts and minds of countless people the world over. I am proud to be a part of that, even in my own small way.

But when the question comes up of whether or not I am proud to be an American... I find that lately It's been getting harder and harder to give a solid and definitive answer.

I *used* to be proud of being an American – I certainly grew up being proud to be American – but at some point I think I have lost that sense of pride and self-worth. That sense of deep-seeded national identity and patriotism.

I mean don't get me wrong, I still rise for the National Anthem, salute the American Flag and I can probably recite the Pledge of Allegiance in my sleep. Hell I can probably recite the Georgia *state* pledge in my sleep – but even with all of that said, I cannot help but feel as though somewhere along the way I have "lost" a certain part of myself when it comes to taking pride in my country.

I look around at my homeland and I see something that *should* be great – something that *should* be wonderful – and instead I see something that has become malformed and decrepit. Something that has lost its own sense of self-identity, just as much as I have.

I suppose that is probably why I struggle with being proud – because the United States itself is no longer proud. It's angry, bitter and resentful – it's given up on its dream.

It's given up on the *American Dream...* and that is a *very* sad reality to live in.

But I suppose that does beg the question of what exactly *is* the American Dream? What is it supposed to be and what is it supposed to represent?

A lot of people would tell you that it represents freedom – but that's not entirely the case. Freedom is more like... The dream *of* America, as opposed to the American Dream itself. It certainly plays a very large role in fulfilling that dream – but it's not the main focal point. No, the key focus of the American Dream is the idea of *opportunity*.

It's the golden promise that anyone can come into this county and have an equal shot at building a life for themselves – at securing a future for their family – regardless of where they come from.

The idea, at least in principle, is that it doesn't matter if your skin is black, white, brown or yellow – it doesn't matter if you're a man or woman. It doesn't matter if you were born native to this country or have immigrated here from somewhere else – you will be guaranteed the opportunity to try and create something for yourself.

But there's a keyword in that theory – *try* – it's a devilishly tricky little word and it is completely reliant upon that other aspect I mention. The aspect of freedom.

It's sort of a funny concept if you think about it: "Freedom."

It's the ability to go wherever you want and to do whatever you want. When someone has freedom, they can listen to any kind of music and wear any kind of clothing – they're free to eat any kind of food – and they're completely free to say and think and feel anything that they want to.

It's a very beautiful thing – but it's also a very terrible thing.

Freedom is not terrible in a "typical" sort of sense, but rather in a more cosmic one. For everything that freedom allows to one person – it also allows to another. It's a two-way street, a double-edged sword. That's why freedom is such a fragile concept because it gives *anyone* the ability to live freely – which means that it also gives anyone the ability to do something terrible.

I think that growing up as an American, one of the hardest pills to swallow is the fundamental understanding that we do not have "true" freedom in this country. What we have is a great deal of civil liberties that are afforded to us by the Constitution and the Bill of Rights – but "freedom" in its most literal interpretation, is *not* something that we really have.

In America, the concept of freedom gets thrown around a lot and frankly it's become more of a slogan than anything else. In fact as it stands right now, I would be willing to argue that the term has become so synonymous with the United States that anyone who hears it probably thinks of the old Red, White and Blue whether they actively want to or not.

The term "freedom" is as American as apple pie and baseball – and it's also a lie.

Freedom is a facade. It's an illusion, like a magic show, and it's become a sort of "safety-blanket" that we wrap around ourselves to feel better.

I don't think that that's necessarily a bad thing though, at least not on a surface level – but I'm trying to think of how I could explain it...

Imagine, if you would, a beautiful old house with a *huge* backyard. There's a fence running around the edges of that yard – but it stretches on for miles and miles and miles to the point that you can't actually see the fence anymore.

That fence is our "freedom." It *is* there – which means that we aren't *actually* free – but it's so far out of view that nobody really thinks too much about it. That's sort of the system that we have – or at least it's the system we're supposed to have – and it is a good system, I think, because on the other side of that fence is *true* freedom.

The fence represents law and order, and it's the only thing separating us from pure anarchy. Nobody *really* wants anarchy – even most people who claim to be "anarchists" don't *really* want it – because what anarchy means is the complete loss of comfort and security.

Out there beyond that fence, a man can walk down the street, pull out a gun and shoot another man in the head for absolutely no reason at all – and the only way that he would face any form of repercussion for his actions is if a *third* person decided that they didn't like what he just did – and so they shoot him in retaliation.

That's the freedom that exists beyond the fence.

It's a beautiful, glorious, breathtaking, invigorating, violating, penetrating, horrifying thing that can do so much good – and so much harm – just by its very nature.

That's why you *want* to have the fence. You want to know that you can go and run and play as much as you'd like – but that you are also ultimately insulated, protected and safe inside of it at the same time.

The problem is that lately, the size of that great big American "backyard" is getting smaller. Every new rule, every new regulation, every new law and social expectation causes that beautiful fence to shrink just a little bit more – and now we're getting to the point where we can actually *see* it. It's not so far out there in the distance anymore. Now it's here, it's closing in and we can feel it restricting us like a collar.

It's claustrophobic.

It affects everything from our industries and economy, to our society and its culture. It's like a serpent coiling around the nation – constricting every part of our body – and you can see the reflection of that in modern day life.

Everyone is bitter, everyone is agitated – nobody is happy – they're all chafing under the strain of it.

The people of this country have become a reflection of the nation – or perhaps a better way to say it is that the nation has become a reflection of the people.

Folks used to be able to drive their car without a seat belt, or ride a motorcycle without a helmet – but they can't do that any more. You could argue that it's a stupid idea to do those things, and I suppose you'd be correct – but that doesn't mean that it shouldn't be their personal *choice*.

People used to be able to buy cigarettes and alcohol at eighteen. When my mother was growing up the legal drinking age was eighteen, and by the time I came along it was twenty one. I think I was around twenty five or twenty six when purchasing tobacco was *also* raised to twenty one.

Now you might argue that those things are bad for a person, and again I suppose you'd be right – but we also let people enlist into our military at eighteen. Let them vote at eighteen. If someone is old enough to have a say in the political leadership of this country – old enough to fight and *die* for this country – then by God they are old enough to buy some beer and a pack of smokes.

Almost nobody can work a job in the United States without having to deal with OSHA, MSHA, the OFCCP or any number of other Labor Department agencies. OSHA alone has around 1,000 different standards and rules for businesses to comply with – and that's not even mentioning states that have to put up with all of the rules and regulations brought on by the various Labor Unions.

I'm sure we can all agree that smoking a cigarette near flammable substances is a *bad* idea, and that properly labeling all of your chemicals is the smart thing to do – but over regulating *everything* to the point that both employers *and* employees have to walk on eggshells just to do their job is *stifling*.

There's a reason that America's industrial sector is a laughing stock. Milton Friedman understood what happens when governments enforce unnecessary regulations onto businesses. It strangulates industry and has a direct negative impact on the economy.

Now I know these are some fairly minor examples, and if you were to read them out of context it really sounds more like whining: "Oh I want to be able to drive without a seat belt, and I wanna be able to smoke my cancer sticks at work!" But that's not the point. The point is that each of these *little* things do add up into something bigger.

Like a tower of toothpicks.

You start with one little toothpick and it's nothing, it's insignificant – and then you add another, and another and another – until you have this massive tower that's wiggling, wobbling and unstable. It's the classic example of the straw that broke the camel's back – all sorts of little things adding up over time to cause a very serious problem – and once you mix the big issues in with the little ones, you begin to *expedite* that problem ten times over.

I could sit here and say that all of these minor issues cause life to be "un-fun" and that people need a break – but you'd probably say that life isn't supposed to *be* fun and that every rule exists for the common good. While that might be partially true, nobody said that life shouldn't be enjoyable either – and while yes many of these things do exist for the common good – how many of them don't?

At this point in time there are approximately 50,000 individual laws in the United States, not counting state and local laws either – that's just from the federal government. There's also something like 89,000 federal regulations in place.

That's a lot. That is a *lot* for people to have to deal with, be consciously aware of, or otherwise navigate around in order to go about their daily lives.

You might say that it's "stupid" for a person not to buckle their seat belt while driving – but just having that choice, without the threat of breaking the law, gives them some tiny little bit of personal freedom.

It gives them that small sense of liberty – and ridiculous as this might sound – it makes them feel *better* just by knowing that they have the *option*, and that feeling goes a long way in a person's life.

So many laws, so many rules that we have in this country have been enacted on behalf of the "common good," but how many of them were really ever thought out?

People used to be able to go buy a gun and keep it with them – but now there's new laws and regulations coming into some states that say you can't even keep a gun in your own house, unless you keep it unloaded and locked inside of a safe. You may argue that it's a responsible approach to owning a firearm, and on the surface you aren't wrong – but what happens when an intruder breaks in? Are you supposed to ask him to kindly wait patiently while you remember your combination in a high-stress environment, take the time to carefully load your weapon and *then* go deal with him?

Not to mention all of the laws which keep penalizing the *victim* of a robbery, instead of the robber himself. Where the homeowner who fired in self-defense is charged with assault while the guy who came to rape, murder and rob is set free.

We used to have public school systems that encouraged activity, competition, critical thinking and creative problem solving – but as education became entrenched with bureaucracy and moved away from local control in favor of more regulated Union control – we've seen the removal of recess, the removal of shop and home economics. We've seen the *dumbing-down* of school curriculum and academic expectations.

Not to mention the fact that so many parents are terrified of even *sending* their children to public school now, because the schools have proven to be actively antagonistic towards parental control and will often outright *punish* students based on the beliefs of their parents.

We've got laws and even a constitutional amendment which protects the "Freedom of the Press", and essentially grants power to journalists to go around harassing private citizens for their own personal gain, without any real thought or consideration for a person's right to privacy. Sure, we do have laws that are supposed to protect our privacy rights – but whenever a journalist comes sniffing around those rights get overlooked in an instant.

You have federal entities such as Social Services and their many branches, who hound and accost the general public at every turn, because they are agencies *specifically* made up of people that feel as though they have some God given right to assert control over the lives of others.

I had one jump on me while I was in the hospital recovering from a surgery – I'm doped out of my mind on painkillers and she just comes into my room and starts asking for personal information such as my social security number. My Great Uncle had a stroke because some "social worker" decided that she had the right to call him, unprompted, and begin grilling an elderly retired man about his personal finances.

My friend's son took a soccer ball to the face at soccer practice and got a black eye. A few days later, someone from Child Services came banging on their door, trying to speak with his son without his permission, and even threatened to have the boy taken away.

Countless stories like this are common, because we deliberately created a job industry built on deputizing narcissists.

We've got the "Risk Laws" in place right now, where if you think a person might be at-risk for suicide or self-harm, you can call in a "Wellness Check" and take control over their entire life – but nobody stopped to consider the reality of that law. That most people who are suicidal, are feeling that way because they no longer feel like they have any sense of control.

Like they don't control their money, or their job or their family or their relationships – like their spiraling and have no anchor. If you're dealing with somebody who feels that way, and they send you a text message saying they're going to "end it all" and suddenly you've got cops banging on their front door – that person is going to panic. They're going to pull that trigger, because that's the last shred of control they have in their life.

Now I'm not saying you ignore somebody whose suicidal – quite the opposite – but laws like this that infringe on a person's rights were created by people who clearly have no idea how to talk to somebody whose in that much pain. Somebody who's *that* scared.

I mean for God's sake, I have sat there and listened to a licensed counselor telling a suicidal person that he's "selfish" for wanting to die – that doesn't make him want to live, it just makes him feel like *shit*.

There's always a time to take a hard stance and give some good old fashioned "tough love" to somebody – but people view these things at face value and never put any more thought or consideration into them at all.

Would you like a less morbid example? Modern headlights: Somebody thought it was a good idea to standardize the installation of LED headlights onto all modern vehicles because it offers better vision for the driver – which is true, it really does – but do you know what else it does? It blinds oncoming traffic. I haven't met a single person who hasn't experienced an oncoming car late at night with those LED bulbs and didn't suffer diminished vision while they were passing.

That's what I'm talking about.

There's so many "things," so many rules, systems, laws and regulations in place that nobody bothered to think through – from the big to the small and everywhere in between.

It's too much.

I've talked a lot in this overarching section about the things that are happening in our society. About the changes taking place in our culture – from the reduction of individual worth to the over-reliance on electricity and technological dependence, to the active effects of chemical exposure, drug addiction and mental health – all the way down to propagated racism, indoctrinated education and radicalized political ideologies.

So much of these things all tie in together. They fold over each other like dough, or weave in and out like fabric.

The dream of America is that you're supposed to be free – or at the very least, you're supposed to *feel* free – but instead, nobody can even breathe. Our "freedom" often gets used against us for the express purpose of strangulating everything that we do and it's excruciating.

That old fence of ours has gotten so close now that everybody's bumping elbows.

And as for the "American Dream" itself? It was supposed to be the promise of opportunity and freedom. A place where you could come to build a future for yourself, even if you had nothing – but that's not what we have anymore.

People don't want to accept that the "freedom of opportunity" is not a "guarantee of success." It's a gamble that we all have to take.

A person is always free to *try* and succeed, but they are equally free to fall flat on their face and fail.

I remember when Donald Trump first ran for President back in 2016, the media mocked him relentlessly over an interview he had back in the 80s where he said that his father gave him a "small loan of a million dollars." They talked so much about him being "out-of-touch" with people, and that anybody who would vote for him must simply be out of their minds.

There was this one girl I knew at the time who was so adamantly against the man that she practically foamed at the mouth over the mere idea of anyone voting for him. She couldn't understand it.

Finally I had to explain it to her – that in the world of big business and construction, a million dollars, even back then – is *nothing*.

Fortunes can be made and lost in the blink of an eye on Wall Street. When Trump said that he had a "small loan" he wasn't bragging about the money – he was saying that his father gave him an *opportunity*. That he gave him a *chance*.

I tried my best to explain to her that if somebody came up and offered me a hammer and some nails, and then said to go build them a barn – that that was the exact same thing. That was my opportunity, my chance. That hammer and those nails were my "million dollars."

That's what the American Dream is *supposed* to be.

It's supposed to be this living idea that anyone can come over here to this country and have an equal opportunity to make something of themselves. That everyone has a chance to build a better life and a better future.

The thing is, you just can't find that much anymore.

The problem is that people only want the first half of the equation. They want the success part – but they don't want the failure. I can't really say that I blame them – nobody likes to fail, nobody *wants* to be a failure – but when you are unwilling to accept the risks associated with "playing the game" so to speak, your choices are either to go play a different game or to stay and change the rules.

And they did start changing the rules.

In an effort to try and "guarantee" that anyone and everyone is going to somehow always be successful, they implemented more and more requirements, restrictions, expectations and general prerequisites to the job market. Now everything is regulated, everything is monitored and has to follow some form of protocol.

Most of the time when you're applying to some place you'll get turned down and told that you "need more experience." Well how the hell are you supposed to *get* that experience if nobody is willing to hire you? Nobody really wants to take on apprentices anymore, you have to go out and pay to get "experience" by attending classes at a college.

I've known guys with fifteen-plus years of on the job experience as mechanics, plumbers and electricians, getting passed over for teenagers fresh out of a "crash course" at Central Georgia Tech, just because they had a flimsy little certification that proves they hadn't fallen asleep in class.

Of course you'll often face the same issue when applying for positions like being a bouncer – I'm pretty sure there's no bounce school... yet. I wouldn't be shocked if in another few years you needed to have a certification that says you know how to toss drunks out of a bar.

I mean for the love of Christ, you can't even flip burgers at McDonalds or hang off the back of a garbage truck anymore without having a high school diploma or a GED.

Assuming that you do manage to get a job somewhere, and also assuming that it's not some local "Mom & Pop" shop – God forbid you do one little thing that doesn't comply with the overwhelming mountain of rules set in place because your ass will be canned in a heartbeat.

Did you have the *audacity* to witness somebody shoplifting items from the shelf at Walmart and confront them about it? Well I have news for you – you've just lost your job.

The simple fact of the matter is that as the year rolled by, there became less and less opportunities for employment – and when you drastically reduce the opportunity for employment, people begin to struggle.

And I don't just mean they struggle financially – I mean they struggle with a sense of *purpose*.

Young people – especially young men – *need* to have a sense of purpose. A sense of obligation. They need to be able to reliably have access to the opportunities in life which can occupy their time in both a meaningful and productive manner – because if they don't, things always start to go sideways. It's just like that old adage about "idle hands".

You end up with a generation of people where they have no sense of purpose, no sense of self-worth, they become depressed, restless, agitated, irritable and eventually bitter. They turn to drugs, they turn to crime – their mental health deteriorates and they continue to spiral.

In short, it's how you end up where we are today.

People need to have "stuff" that they can reasonably go and do without excessive barriers to entry.

And we don't have to go back into the 1800s to find examples of this, we can look right back at the 1920s, the 30s or 40s. If you were a kid and you didn't have a good home life, or you didn't know what to do with yourself – you could take yourself down to the coast, pick a direction and follow the water. Eventually you'd find a harbor town and you could find some easy work as a deckhand on a ship. The labor would be intense, but the opportunities were everywhere.

Same thing with working on the railroad. Get yourself to a train station, find a railroad office and try to get hired on – you didn't used to need a five-mile long resume filled to the brim with certifications and degrees just to be considered for a position.

Lighthouse keepers. Lighthouse keeping was a great job for young men, because you'd get the chance to work with some older fellows who knew the business. If you were good at your job, then you were pretty much guaranteed two weeks of good solid pay at a time – and it also let you get out of the house and grow a sense of independence.

The problem is that as technology advanced and introduced automation into the workforce, and we erected more and more barriers of entry, all of those opportunities which people used to reliably have started to go away.

Which is not to say that all technology is a bad thing, or that automation doesn't have its benefits. When the first automated systems started coming into use, they actually created *more* jobs than ever before. If you worked at a printing press, either printing papers or pressing metals, etc, you had the guy that operated the press itself and you had the assembly workers. Well, when the first hydraulic presses were coming in, the operator got to keep his job because someone still needed to push the button – but the assembly process sped up and the line needed more workers. That's growth.

I think a good visual example of this is the 1957 Desk Set starring Spencer Tracey and Katherine Hepburn.

The film centers around the issue of the very first computers coming into the workplace, and most of the characters are deeply concerned about losing their jobs and being replaced by machinery – but as the film comes to a close it turns out that it's actually the exact opposite. Now that the work can be done faster, more people are going to be hired and thus more opportunities for employment are going to open up.

But the movie does have the incredible foresight to commentate on the future of technology, with several hard-hitting and insightfully prophetic lines being given throughout the film – such as the exchange between Tracey and Hepburn during their rooftop scene where they are discussing EMERAC, the electronic-brain.

In the scene, Tracey asks the question: "Did you see it translate Russian into Chinese?"

To which Hepburn replies: "Yeah, I saw it do everything. Frightening. Gave me the feeling that maybe, just *maybe*, people were a little bit outmoded."

With Tracey closing the scene by remarking: "Mmm, wouldn't surprise me a bit if they stopped making them."

I do think that those lines were incredibly prophetic because look at where we are today. Fewer and fewer jobs are available and more and more places are becoming automated. I don't remember the last time that I had to make a business call and actually got to speak to a real human being – or at least be able to speak with one without having to waste ten minutes arguing with an automated speech system.

We're even seeing it take over the food service industry. More and more restaurants are introducing automated systems for placing your orders – which is perfectly understandable if you're ordering from home – but a lot of places are beginning to switch over to touch-screen computers inside of the restaurants themselves so that the customer never has to speak to an employee.

We're not in the days of the toughest jobs like being a lighthouse keeper going off the market – pretty soon your average teenager won't even have the chance to stand behind a counter at the burger joint. Hell, pretty soon we'll have machines working the grill.

You've got the big grocery stores with all of those unmanned checkout lines because it's easier and cheaper just to run the automated ones. I complained a few paragraphs up about riding on the back of trash trucks, but realistically that's already gone with so many of them switching over to using those mechanical arms.

Everything's just going away.

It's no wonder that our society is completely falling apart.

Look, I'm not going to pretend that my country's perfect – because no country ever is – but it used to be better than this. People used to be allowed to actually "live" their lives. They used to be allowed to go around and develop skills or earn opportunities without having to fit and conform to all of these preconceived notions of what their "value" is.

We talk so much today about "progress" and yet all of us are just being put inside a box. A little tiny box covered in red, white and blue wrapping paper.

I don't know how much more I can take.

I don't know how much longer I can stand the confines of this place.

There's so many rules in place today that people aren't even allowed to *talk* anymore. We're told that we just have to accept everything, and validate everything, and be compliant with everything – unless the things we're compliant with go against the grain – in which case we're demonized, shouted down and often face severe repercussions.

Sometimes you're punished even if you *do* play by the rules.

I remember the story of some news media executive a few years ago, who caught his young daughter singing along to a rap song. Whoever was singing the song said the "N" word – and so the daughter repeated it. When the man explained to his daughter that you aren't supposed to say the word "nigger," he got fired for it.

This man lost his job, because he told his daughter *not* to use a racial slur.

About a decade ago now, one of the big things to do was to burn the American flag. That became the big social display of rebellion – any kind of public gathering had to have a live demonstration of destroying or otherwise defacing the flag.

One of the great debates around that time was the question of a person's right to do such a thing – and ultimately the consensus was that yes, they did. That the freedoms of America gave people the right to cripple the icon of those freedoms.

And that's why I said freedom, or at least the ideals of freedom, is a very fragile thing – because it does afford the ability to destroy itself.

It's a lot like fire in a way – fire needs material to burn in order to sustain itself – but it is fully capable of eating up everything around it until the flame dies out.

It can rage out of control, but if it's going to be maintained, it has to have someone there to maintain it.

We don't really seem to have that anymore.

All I've ever wanted to do is be proud of my country, but lately I feel like my country doesn't even want me to *live*. I feel like it doesn't want *anyone* to live anymore.

The *American Dream* is dying...

We have this idea now where everyone has to conform to every single label under the sun. That we have to split hairs on every issue and jump through hoops in order to "justify" the creation of those labels, and then jump through even *more* hoops in order to justify the *justification* of the labels. It's insane.

Every one of us wants something different. Each one of us needs something different. We're all individuals who make a nation – but the one thing we should all be able to share in common is the desire to just let people breathe.

When I think about America now – and more specifically when I think about America in the future – I'm reminded of this movie I saw a long time ago called Idiocracy. It wasn't terribly well-received at the time of its release – but considering that it came out in 2006, I think that looking back it did a very good job of commentating on the issues of our country.

The film depicts a dystopian future in the year 2505, where landfills as tall as mountain ranges cast shadows over the country. Where farming and agriculture have become fables of lost sciences and technology. Where the English language has devolved into nothing more than muddled grunting, disjointed sentences and excessive profanity. Where the inflation of the economy is so outlandish and extreme, that it costs thousands upon thousands of dollars just to order a single box of french fries.

A future where materialism, consumerism and commercialism have grown so prevalent that 80% of your television screen is taken up by over twenty different advertisements while the other 20% is allotted to whatever mind-numbing show that you're watching. Where corporate mergers and monopolies had turned into such a travesty that Costco was a several-mile wide, multi-leveled mega structure – and long-distances phone services were now brought to you by companies such as "AOL-TimeWarner-TacoBell-USGovernment."

In fact the only industry that hadn't been negatively impacted by the collapse of society was pornography. The "adult" industry is going strong – with most recognizable franchises from the real world offering some form of sexual services.

The film even touched on things such as the institutions of the American electoral system becoming little more than a popularity contest – an open stage for showboating and pageantry. That all citizens must receive a government mandated bar-code on their wrist for identification – and that the government, despite becoming so laughably incapable – possessed the power to remotely deactivate your vehicle and track your every movement.

And I think that one of the most poignant and striking is that this dystopic future wasn't brought about by some "doomsday" event – it wasn't the result of nuclear fallout – it was just... *us*.

We did it to ourselves.

I remember not thinking too much about the movie when it first came out, but having just gone back and re-watched it – it's startling just how "prophetic" I think a lot of the messaging in the film seems to be.

While I don't know if I would call it a classic under any stretch of the imagination – the predictions and commentary that it makes on the current trajectory of the United States is incredibly thought-provoking. I'd put it right up there with Wall-E and it's disturbingly apt commentary on modern-day western society and where it's going to lead us in the future.

You hear the old-timers talk about how "all the good-times are gone." Well they are gone – and I'd like to see them come back.

Nobody needs this nation to become the wild west again – but I just wanna be able to *breathe*. I'm *desperate* to be able to breathe.

I often hear people mock or ridicule this sort of idealistic view of the 1950s. They'll say "oh yeah, it was *such* a 'better time' before Civil Rights." Nobody's saying they want to go back to a time before Civil Rights. Nobody's saying they want to get back to an American where women and minorities don't have the right to vote.

They're saying they want to go back to a time when this nation actually had a sense of identity.

A time when fathers were in the home; when families ate together at the dinner table. When "crazy" teenagers spent their Saturday nights cruising around the malt shops and going to cheap rock concerts.

When some of the worst things you saw on Halloween was a guy's house getting egged and tee-peed, not mass-shootings and drug overdoses.

A time when Globalization hadn't taken over and whole cultures hadn't been diluted. When a minimum wage family could still make ends meet, and inflation hadn't completely destroyed the American economy.

A time when the nation seemed to have a much healthier sense of respect for authority – but authority also seemed to have a much healthier sense of respect for the individual.

My uncle Billy was a Prince Edward County Sheriff's Deputy for over thirty years, and he never once had to shoot anybody. Could he have just been incredibly lucky? Maybe – or maybe it was because he served at a time when people used to walk down the street and call the officer's by name – and when officer's themselves hadn't lost the plot, and forgotten that their job was to serve and protect.

There's no reason that we couldn't try to build ourselves back to that way of life and bring with us all of the good things and growth that we have developed over the years – but nobody wants to.

They want to keep pushing forward without ever looking back and realizing that maybe, not "everything" was bad. Not everything was perfect – but not everything was *bad* either.

I wasn't born in the 40s or 50s, I got here in the mid 90s – but even compared to just a few short decades ago, I can't even *recognize* this country anymore. I'd be happy if we could just get back to the 80s or 90s again.

If we could just get back to a time when people were able to eat at a fast-food joint and still keep a flat stomach. When technology hadn't completely taken control of every facet of our lives. When every single conversation didn't have to somehow get political. When education wasn't withheld from students because it made them "uncomfortable," and laws didn't exist to protect "your truth" as compared to factual realities.

I said it before and I'll say it again – the country wasn't perfect but goddamn – it was a whole lot better than *this*.

I really do want to be proud to be an American... but I'm not. I try every day but I just can't seem to find it anymore.

Maybe I am just an idealistic fool. Perhaps it is as they said in I, Claudius, when Thallus the usher spoke to Aristarchus the orator and said: "It isn't what it once was" and Aristarchus replied: "It never was, what it was."

Maybe there's some deep-seeded truth to that sentiment, but regardless, *whatever* it was that we used to have is now gone...

In the end... maybe that's why they call it a *dream*.

Blood is Thicker

Chapter XVI: Fathers and Sons

I've said before that I had never experienced any form of racial discrimination as a child, and would not begin to experience such things until my early teens – but I did experience discrimination, of a sort – and have felt the lasting sting of it ever since.

Growing up without a father is a difficult burden to bear – especially for a boy. There were no hunting trips or baseball games. No camping in the woods or weekends fishing on the lake. No throwing the pig-skin with the old man or even just getting to those father and son heart-to-heart talks.

There was simply... nothing.

I'm very open and honest about being the only child of a single mother. She brought me down to Georgia from Virginia to live with my grandparents when I was two, so that she could go to college and get a better education. My mother worked very hard to make sure that she provided me with a good future – a level of effort which I am ashamed to say I did not appreciate until I was considerably older.

In many ways it was almost a blessing, those times when I did not know or understand the truth. My mother never lied or hid the facts from me – but as a child, I did not ever think to ask. I saw the fathers in my classroom and saw the fathers on TV – and I knew it was a "thing". I knew it was a concept of normality, to have a father in your life – but I never sought to question it. I never sought to ponder.

As a boy I simply took it at face value and never stopped to wonder "Why?".

Why was it that I didn't have one? Why was it that I hadn't ever heard of him or been told about him? These just weren't questions that were on my mind. I had a family, I knew who they were – and to me, at least at the time, his absence didn't strike me as odd or abnormal.

There simply wasn't a dad in the house – I just didn't have one. That truth alone seemed to make sense to me.

But the delicate veneer of that truth would inevitably begin to crack and peel as time went on.

My Grandfather, in particular, often made comments that I never understood. Sideways remarks or expressions of frustration – mostly verbal – but sometimes physical, and always in a very heavy-handed fashion – about my father or the nature of my birth.

I would often spend time with my grandfather – who I called Pa – because I was told to go and do it. Told to help him and whatnot. He was the only other man around, so I suppose it makes sense that they'd send me to hang around with him.

I just never understood why he always seemed so unhappy that I was there.

Like I said, he'd usually say things to me that I didn't quite understand. He once said I was a "mark on the family name" etc. Sometimes he'd pull the door open real fast to hit me, or slam it real hard behind him when he knew that I was following so that it would either hit my face or I'd get caught in it.

Sometimes he'd just shove me into the door when he wanted me out of his way – and the basement door was a pretty solid and heavy kind of thing.

One time I remember being told to stay down in the basement with him – which is where his workshop and tools were – but he was in such a foul mood I just tried to keep to myself. I was playing with the wheel of a metal-grinder. It wasn't turned on or anything, I was just sticking my hand under the shield to make it spin around.

I guess that bothered him or something, because he came up behind me, grabbed my hand and shoved it up under that grind stone. Again, it wasn't turned on – I'm not missing a hand or something – but there wasn't but so much space between the stone and the base of that grinder shelf. It crimped my hand all up and I still have a slight tremble in my right hand to this day.

Maybe it's some nerve damage or something, I don't really know.

The bruises he left have long since faded, but the scars he made will live on inside of me until the day that I die. I never really understood why he hated me so much, when all I wanted was to love him.

His was the first voice that ever called me a "Bastard". I can still remember it so clearly – and the words have rung in the back of my ears ever since.

Looking back on it tonight, I suppose that it is possible, in some small way, that he did not really hate me – at least not for the sake of hating me, myself – but rather that he hated the "idea" of me. The living reminder of his daughter's failure. The indiscretion which I represented whenever he looked at me.

I suppose it doesn't really matter, and the truth is that I'll never really know for sure.

I can so vividly remember the other children in the classroom asking me why my father never came to class for Parent-Teacher day. Why they never saw him picking me up from school, or heard me tell stories about him when I would talk so openly about the other members of my family.

I can remember the way they looked at me when I would tell them that I didn't have a father. I can remember trying to explain to one boy that you didn't "need" a father in order to be born – because at that time I didn't know any better. I remember the way the other kids would tease me – and the way their parents would look at me – turning away and whispering between themselves as they glanced in my direction.

Oh yes it may seem like a rather silly thing to most of you reading this, but there are parts of the world and even America where being a bastard is still looked down upon – and certainly *was* looked down upon even in the late 90s.

Born and raised a Presbyterian, my mother turned away from the church after they expressed what some might call a certain... sense of disapproval, shall we say, over the nature of my existence. After moving down to Georgia and doing a little research into the local schools – she settled on St. Joseph's Catholic School in Macon. Being a Protestant by nature, she was concerned about the idea of sending me to a Catholic school – but the Principle Nun assured her that Father Cuddy would never turn away a child or refuse to baptize him over something so petty as the legitimacy of his birth.

And so it was that my mother began attending Mass and learning the Catholic faith. She converted, and I was baptized not long after.

This did not stop the other parents from judging, and I suspect that seeing as St. Joseph's was considered to be a rather "well to do" school, and the fact that I was one of – if not the only child from a lower-income family – had something to do with their standoffishness.

No, I had never known the ugliness of racial prejudice – but I knew well enough what it meant to be looked down on and judged by others for things which I could not control.

Their leering faces and side-long glances. Their hushed whispers and condemnation for being something "lesser" is an image I shall carry with me for the rest of my life – and I am genuinely glad for it.

I am glad to know the difference between the righteous and the imposter. The honest and the dishonest – the true and the false.

I think I must have been about ten or so when I finally asked my mother for the truth. I'm sorry to disappoint you, but it was not an epic affair – nor a grand and dramatic one. If memory serves, I do believe that I caught her entirely off-guard with the asking.

We were in the upstairs hallway of my Nanny's house, and the hallway light was on. I remember that because it was a very rare occurrence. I asked her quite plainly why I didn't have a father – and she answered me. Truthfully, and honestly, she answered me.

Maybe it would have been better if she had come up with some sort of lie. If she had told me that he was a soldier – which he was – and that he had died in the war – which he didn't – the whole thing could have been wrapped up neatly into a nice little bow and forgotten about. An unfortunate ending to a man I'd never known and, maybe even a little jolt of boyish pride in the process. But that's not what she did.

I remember that she told me how she had sent him some of my photographs – which I did not like – but otherwise, I asked a question and it had been answered; that was all I needed to know.

It wouldn't be until I was around twelve or thirteen that we'd have this conversation again, and that was a horse of an entirely different color.

More details were given, more questions were answered – and that is when it truly began to bother me. To become a thing which hung over me like a shroud, and constantly stabbed at me from the back of my mind.

That is the first time my father ever came into my life. Not as a man, not as a memory – but as a vaguely understood idea, and comprehended reality.

I remember having a conversation once with a friend of mine who had never really been on good terms with his own father, wherein he expressed no small amount of jealousy over the fact that I had never known mine – and wished that we could trade places.

I told him that I'd make that trade, and do it in a heartbeat.

I told him that he should be grateful for what he has. That no matter how wicked or rotten a person may be – if they are actually in your life, at least you have a reason to be angry.

My father never wrote me letters. He never sent me postcards or photographs – he never even called to talk to me on the phone. I didn't know what he looked or sounded like. All I had of him was… that I knew his name.

I remember asking my friend: "Don't you know how lucky you are?" It doesn't matter how often he beats you or how many times he's abused your mother – you have something to hate that is tangible and real. You have a true and genuine thing – no matter how bad it is – at which to direct your feelings. At which to understand.

Can you even begin to imagine what it feels like to have all that anger, all that resentment, all that bitterness and rage and guilt and sorrow and misery upon misery and have absolutely nothing to point it at? Not an image, not a memory – just a thing – a vague concept, like a shadow hanging over you.

Can you imagine the self-loathing and stupidity you would feel to be so utterly tormented by something that may as well not even exist? To have so many questions, and so many doubts – and so many "What ifs…" and "But whys…" and having no way to find an explanation for it? Nothing to show you and nothing to help you understand?

It's like being angry at the wall. A blank, unwavering *thing* – for nothing more than the simple reason that it exists.

It is an empty feeling. A hollow feeling, from which there is no escape. An endless series of questions upon questions for which there are no answers. It's just rage. A bottomless chasm of hatred – and there is nothing you can do about it.

It's just, simply, there.

That's why I told him he was lucky, and in the end he did agree. I believe some time later he had told me that his relationship had actually started to improve – and I was happy for him – truly.

There is no reason that any person – man or woman, boy or girl – should be made to feel that way. There is no justice in it, no rhyme, no reason. Only bitterness and contempt. Spite and malice. A consumption of the heart and a corruption of the soul.

It is a dangerous road to tread – and if we are not careful, it is one from which we can never return.

In the end I never met my father. I never had the opportunity to sit down with him and talk. To see who he was and what he was and hear what he had to say. I never had the chance to ask him all the questions I had burning in my heart. I never had the chance to break down crying or wind up screaming or sock him in the mouth or get drunk together. I never had the chance for closure. I never had the chance to do anything.

I did manage to track him down when I was eighteen and called him. It took a disturbingly long time to convince him of who I was, and to explain why I had called.

I'll never forget the first thing he said to me:

"...What's your political opinion?"

Eighteen years, and that was the very first thing he said after learning recognizing who I was.

I told him to go fuck himself – and we never spoke again.

He died a few years later and, at the time, what struck me the most was that I didn't even care. I wasn't happy and I wasn't sad. I didn't feel relief and I didn't feel regret – I simply felt nothing. Not a single, goddamn, thing.

That realization upset me. It upset me more than the news of his passing. Hearing that your father's dead should normally be a once-in-a-lifetime moment that elicits *some* kind of reaction, either for good or ill – and all I felt was nothing.

This thing which should have been a momentous occasion in anybody's life – a monumental happening that would cause a person to reflect or contemplate all the things that have happened – all their thoughts and all their feelings, was met with total indifference.

Like hearing the news of a total stranger in some foreign country that you've never met, suddenly dying in a car crash – the only response it provoked was a simple "Huh, well alright." and that was it.

These unfortunate truths of my life are just some of the core, fundamental reasons that I despise the modern world and the culture we have created. A social structure built on the idea of breaking up the nuclear family and driving men away from their wives and children.

This ongoing narrative that men aren't necessary in life. That they aren't worth anything and that we should look down upon them and spit on them when the only thing they want to do is what's right and actually be somebody worth looking up to. Somebody worth admiring.

I know first-hand what the impact that the absence of a father can have on a child – and it's not pretty.

I spent roughly the first nine years of my life not knowing him. Roughly the next nine hating him – and at the time – the next nine after that, just not caring. Still not caring.

It is a sad thing in the end, when fathers and sons cannot love each other. When families are broken, and trying to pick up the pieces only ever leaves you cut and bleeding.

This isn't to say that I learned nothing from him, however.

I never learned how to be a good father, and I never learned how to be a good man. Not from him – and not from my Grandfather for that matter – but what I did learn from these men, is what *not* to do.

I learned what a boy needed when he didn't have love. I learned what he needed when he didn't have a man to show him. I learned what a boy needs, because I never got it – and I know now what to give, when it is my time to give it.

Chapter XVII: A Mother's Love

Growing up in a single-parent household with just my mother has not been easy. As a child, I viewed her as an angel – a guardian sentinel with golden wings, who was always there to protect me. Watching over me and keeping me safe from harm.

She was my whole world – and I adored her.

But something inside of her seems to have changed somehow. I cannot really point my finger at any one specific moment, or recall any particular incident as the pivotal turning point – it just sort of seems to have happened as the years went by.

She became more reclusive and standoffish. The warmth of her heart turned cold – and the once roaring fire of her spirit reduced to nothing more than smothered embers. She grew increasingly lazy and inactive. Paranoid, arrogant and distant – and I've watched as a peculiar and twisted cruel streak began to run through her like a line of black ink in a pool of white paint.

The past twenty or so years of my life have been spent enduring her wicked barbs and callous remarks. Constantly fighting with her to be reasonable about things. To be reasonable about... Anything. Anything at all. Whether it be her own health or our relationship with each other or the welfare of family members or... Anything.

And now, as I write this, I am afraid for her life. Her health has recently taken a very bad turn, and I am not entirely convinced that she is going to make it out the other side.

I am terrified that at the age of twenty nine, I am going to lose my mother.

Maybe writing and reflecting about her here can help walk me through some of the things that have gone so wrong. I don't really know – but I suppose I'll have to try.

I think it's safe to say that my mother has never exactly been a "neat-minded" person. I have never known her to be very tidy or particularly organized.

After moving down to Georgia to live with my Grandparents, we had to share a bed in the upstairs room and I cannot recall a single instance in my mind where I would have seen her actually *make* the bed. My Nanny – my grandmother – would turn down the linens for everybody once a week and I think that she would make the bed – but it wasn't something that my mother ever concerned herself with.

I remember this one time, I had seen one of those fancy canopy-top beds from an old movie and I wanted to know what it was like to sleep under one – so my mother took off the sheet and stretched it over the four-posts and we slept beneath it. Of course that also meant we were sleeping directly on the mattress – but it really didn't seem to bother her.

As a matter of fact, later in life she would just abandon the concept of bed sheets altogether and just sleep on top of the mattress.

We did eventually have to move out of my grandmother's house, as in the summer of 1999 – or maybe it was 2000 – my Nanny went away on a trip somewhere, leaving just my mother, my grandfather and myself at home. What happened is that I, being a child, accidentally walked onto the kitchen floor that my grandfather had been mopping – and so his natural instinct was to become completely unhinged, go ballistic and to attack me. He grabbed my arm and struck me, sending me toppling over a chair – and my mother came to my rescue – but we were ultimately forced to run away.

The next few nights were spent in a hotel room until she could find an apartment over in Macon. It was a small, humble place – but looking back, I think I quite liked it.

Even there she still wasn't much of a housekeeper. Never making up the bed and just dropping our laundry into a heap in the corner instead of folding them up and putting them away – but it wasn't until we moved here in 2001 – to the house I live in now, that she began hoarding.

I suppose that if I had to pick a time where it all started, that would be it. She's always had a fondness for Pepsi cola – and she would just have mountains of bottles and cans piling up in the corners of the house. This habit of hers would eventually grow into including grocery bags and takeout boxes. Drink cups and dirty plates. Heaps of garbage, filling up every room like a landfill.

By the time that I was fourteen our living room had become a dumpster. The entire room, save for a single narrow path from the front door through to the couch and bedroom – was a mound of trash so high that it came up to my waist... And she didn't even seem to be bothered by it.

I tried to clean it. I tried desperately to clean it – but whenever I did, she'd become furious. Not disgruntled or annoyed or even agitated – but angrily screaming at me in a blind rage because I had "moved her things" or "touched her stuff".

There was one particular occasion in my early twenties – by which point I had learned to put my foot down on certain issues – that I had spent the entire day and most of the evening cleaning a massive section of the house. I was relaxing that night on a computer-call with some friends of mine, when my mother came out from the bedroom where she'd been sleeping all day – and looked around at what I had done.

I said "Doesn't this look good Mama?" and she just silently looked around at all of the space, before saying "What did you get rid of?". I said something along the lines of "I picked up the trash, I got rid of the garbage."

to which she casually walked over to one of the trash bags that I would be taking to the dump in the morning – reached out with a finger and tore it open, spilling out all of the garbage inside just so she could see what was in it. Then she turned and walked away.

I was fuming. I said "Hey now, wait a minute aren't you going to pick that back up?" and she looked me dead in the eyes with the flattest expression I have ever seen, and said: "Well you picked it up once. You can do it again."

Then she walked back to the bedroom, leaving me to the murmurings of my friends that had overheard the entire interaction.

That's the kind of person she turned into.

The sort of person that would intentionally start an argument or a fight, and then blame the other person – usually me – for becoming angry and upset. She became overtly manipulative and utterly self-absorbed to an alarming degree.

You know I, I remember when my father passed – she never even called to ask how I was doing. I've already stated that I wasn't particularly distraught over the news – but you would think that as my mother she might at least… ask. She might at least want to know how her son was doing – but she didn't even seem to care. Not in the slightest.

When I did get to broach the subject with her a few days later, she even went so far as to make fun of me for expecting her to reach out about it.

I really found that whole situation to be quite… *unnerving*, if I'm honest.

One of the things which has always stuck out to me as being odd, is the way in which she seems so adept at picking her moments. Any high point in my life – any hard fought achievement or accomplishment of a goal – she would strike like a coiled serpent, ready to inject her venom and undermine the entire thing.

My moments were never allowed to be mine. They had to be hers, or they would be no ones.

I recall one instance where during the most casual of disagreements, she needlessly decided to go for the throat and accused me of being just like my father.

I think that hearing those words may well have been the lowest point in my entire life.

And the worst and most painful part is that, just when I think that my heart is finally spent – when the end of my rope has been reached and my final straw has been broken – I'll see it. A tiny glint and glimmer of the woman she used to be. The image of my beloved angel which I cherished so many years ago. Those are the worst times of it all, because that's when things will go back to being normal – for maybe a week, or two at best – and then she will grow cold again and the cycle repeats anew. Ever downward and ever spiraling into the endless black.

Maybe part of the reason that I'm writing this is to try and make my mother proud. To finally attain some small semblance of her approval which has always evaded me.

I think somewhere deep down, I know that that's a lie.

It is true, I think, that there was once a part of me that had hoped – but I knew that I would never again feel the gentle warmth of maternal affection.

Last night I asked if she would let me read to her my most recent pages – those being about my father – and after finishing, her only response was to feign an apology to me, for how much I "clearly hated" her.

I asked her what she meant, and I asked if she had not heard the part where I admitted to not appreciating her enough – I inquired if she mistakenly thought that my speculations over my grandfather's feelings were my own, which they weren't – and the only thing that she could say was that I must have hate for her, because otherwise I would not have "insisted" on reading this to her.

I had not "insisted" upon reading anything. I simply asked if I could narrate the most recently completed section of my book – and she obliged. I even told her what it was about beforehand, and she still wanted to hear it.

I said "Mama you... you can't really mean that?" and I was met with nothing but sheer, unadulterated silence.

I think last night was the moment when I truly realized that there is no hope in ever finding that woman again. The woman I had known and idolized had long since died – and had been replaced by some other creature wearing her skin.

Maybe there is some partial blame to be found on my part for not being more considerate of her – but I told her about it. She knows what this book is about, she knows that I am writing it and that I'm not pulling any punches – I just don't know what I'm supposed to do when I have to walk on eggshells in order to speak with my own mother.

She used to be the sort of person who would fly to your defense like some kind of lioness – and now she's become so reclusive and bitter towards everything. She actively tries to undermine *everything* around her – and I hate her for it.

No, I love her – and I hate myself for it – because to love a thing that does not feel is a fool's endeavor. One which only leads to misery and regret.

I remember when I was eighteen, I told her that I wanted to get a tattoo – and she agreed on the condition that my first one be a traditional "MOM" tattoo. I agreed, and never mentioned to her until after the fact, that that was the design I had wanted to get.

I always felt quite sly about that. Like I had pulled the wool over her eyes and gotten away with something for free.

I've asked her before – many, many times – that if I truly hated her, why would I have gotten this tattoo on my arm? Why is it then, if we weren't already bound by blood, would I have so willingly branded myself in homage to a woman that I supposedly despised?

But it did not matter, and does not matter to this day. She has become a pale shadow of a human being – and lost any reflection of her former self. I know for a fact that she suffers from a plethora of various health conditions – none of which are insurmountable on their own – but combined together, they have certainly taken a toll on her throughout the years.

But in spite of these issues, she doesn't really seem to care about them either.

For example, my mother is a diabetic and thus needs to take insulin and watch her sugar, but she won't. I've heard her tell me every excuse under the sun as to why she wouldn't take her insulin. She said she couldn't remember because of her memory issues – but she also refused to set notes or reminders for herself. She would not allow me to set an alarm on her phone – and when I would actually call her like clockwork to tell her it's time to take her medicine, she'd scream at me to leave her alone.

But of course, to hear her tell it, it was never her fault that she couldn't take her medicine.

I said earlier that she loved Pepsi, I mean she loved Pepsi. I forget the reason why I had to bring her some, but she asked me to pick her up a case one time – and even though I knew I shouldn't, it made her happy – so I got her one of those larger 15-cases because I assumed it would last her awhile.

She turned around and called me two days later to come bring her some more. She drank fifteen full-sized cans of Pepsi in forty-eight hours, and didn't seem to think there was anything wrong with that.

It infuriates me so much because, my whole life she has lectured me on the horrors of diabetes. It runs in our family – and she would have grown up seeing various relatives with blindness or amputated legs or any number of other problems caused by the disease, and yet she refused to take it seriously in regards to herself.

My mother has recently been in and out of the hospital because of complications due to her condition. At one point she was discharged and sent home and when I arrived at my grandmother's house to help her inside – she could not walk. Her legs had dwindled away to the size of forearms – and while normally rather plump – you could see and feel her ribs.

She was pitiful, in every sense of the word.

She could barely speak and, frankly, I'm not entirely sure that she even knew who I was. Even as I tried desperately to lift her inside the house, I don't think that she knew that I was her son.

The only thing she managed to ask for with any level of coherency, was a bottle of Pepsi.

I suppose I just never took her for a suicide.

In reality I recognize that I have not always been the greatest son to her. We're a lot alike, in a lot of ways – maybe too much alike if I'm honest. We've often fought like cats and dogs. We've often mixed like oil and water. We've always had a lot of matching interests – history, music, literature, food – but inside of those interests we differed so wildly. Like two sides of the same coin, we were always so very close and yet ultimately far apart.

She liked the early Beetles, I liked their later work. She liked William Alexander, I liked Bob Ross. She liked the songs that Stevie Nicks sang for Fleetwood Mac – I liked the ones sang by Christine McVie. And so on it went – like billiards in a game of pool, we both shared the same common table and always stayed so close in the pocket – but she was stripes and I was solids. We are the same, but not the same.

There was an incident, when I was thirteen or so, that we fought like never before. I don't remember what the fight was even about – I don't know if it was about my father, I don't know if it was about my grandfather, I don't know... anything. But I do know that it was that day, that I broke something inside of myself.

I struck my own mother.

I was so angry – I was so incredibly angry – and I don't even remember why. I know that she had been pushing my buttons but I don't know what it was about, only that I'd never been so mad a day in my life and that she just wouldn't stop. She wouldn't leave me alone or drop the issue.

I remember so distinctly how we were just screaming at each other – howling and hurling insults back and forth. It was bad. It had been bad before, but not like this. I remember we were in the living room and I backed her towards the front door. I barked so furiously at her – hounding her with a question, some kind of question that I don't even remember – and she just looked at me. She didn't answer, she only stared – starred with the eyes of a woman both terrified of the man in front of her, and heart broken over the pain and rage of her child.

That was it. That was the moment. Those eyes stared at me and I just froze. The moment of silence felt like it lasted forever, and that look in her eyes ate away at some part of me like a wild animal starting to feast on your body before you've fully passed away.

It horrified me, and I hit her.

I might have been only thirteen but I was bigger than her by then. Stronger than her by then.

I watched, almost like an out of body experience, as my right hand – this right hand which pens these words – pulled back and hit her, sending her reeling backwards into the door and left her crumpled on the ground in a heap.

That has been the single greatest shame of my entire life.

Anything I might have done before, or since, that could have ever made me feel ashamed of myself has always paled in comparison to that one, singular moment.

That one conscious decision to do something so vile – something so wrong.

It is a thing that, while I would not call it evil – not in itself – certainly knocked upon the door of evil. It is a thing that very easily could have led me down the path of evil – could have made it easier to strike my mother again. To strike other women and to treat them as I treated her.

To become a person who was violent and aggressive. To become a creature of nothing but hatred and venom. Like a gateway drug which takes you from one substance to another and another and another – it was the sort of dangerous thing that could have opened the very gates of hell and led me to become a criminal, lead me to become a rapist and lead me to become a murderer.

It is a thing that I never thought myself capable of until that moment. A thing that I thought only "bad" men were capable of. Men on TV and in movies only ever seemed to hit women – really *hit* women – if they were bad men. Angry men. Men who were drunk or on drugs, or men who were some kind of an outlaw in one way or another.

I might have struck my mother that day – but in doing so, the same hand that hit her also wrenched a gash across my heart that has never fully healed. I think I wounded myself more than I did her.

And I pray I never forget it – because I will never raise my hand against another woman for as long as I live.

But the worst pain of all is actually what came after.

As I stood there, blood boiling and dumbfounded – my mother stood up. She didn't hit me back. She didn't scream or cry or beg for me to leave. She didn't turn and run away to leave herself – she simply grabbed me, held me, and hugged me.

She embraced me, and loved me – and we *wept*.

My heart is aching to write this. No other thoughts or feelings that I have offered on these pages have made me hurt like this. I can feel it – with each and every word I can feel it – pulling down into the pit of my stomach like a stone into a sling, waiting to be released and come rocketing up into the back of my throat. The pain constricts me, it tightens in my chest. I feel so dizzyingly faint, as if every ounce of my energy were being strangled out of me by an invisible noose around my neck.

Tears flow from my eyes like twin-rivers of guilt, falling upon the keys of my typewriter in a torrential downpour of agony.

Oh God, what has become of me.

What is this pain which grips me to the core – when a mother's love is a dull and dying thing. Lost without ceremony or reverence.

When a woman who was once so full of life is reduced down to nothing more than a frail, withering creature that cannot see past her own self-destruction. That cannot and will not comprehend any possible alternative other than her own stubborn desires.

If there truly is a God then I beg of thee to mend my broken heart – for its shattered pieces cut so deeply – and the constant laceration is an anguishing pain that I can no longer stand to bear.

No, I choose instead to think that this tattoo represents a woman from my past. A woman whose memory will never fade – and whose grace and goodness will live on inside me forever.

I know, logically speaking, that the person she turned into is not really my mother. I know that it's not so much a question of her "losing her love" or "harboring contempt" for me in some manner or fashion. I know that it is more an issue of life taking its toll and crushing her under the weight of it. Of years spent trying and failing to secure a future for herself and for her child. Of nearly sixty years of trials and errors – mistakes and consequences – with very little triumphs or victories to show for it.

I know, in reality, that my mother is simply hurting – but whether she is hurting in her head or hurting in her heart, I could not say.

Wherever you are now, Mama, I want to tell you that I love you – from the bottom of my heart – I will always love you.

You are my shining star.

You are my beacon in the night.

You are the solid ground beneath my feet, and that very air which fills my lungs.

You are my angel and my everything.

I love you.

Chapter XVIII: Family Man

I wanted to write the above chapters – about my father, about my mother – because those are two very... I suppose very gut-wrenching chapters. Very deep-cutting and personal chapters for me to write – but it was important for me to write about them.

I wanted this chapter to come next so that I could use both of those experiences of not having a father and growing up in a single-parent home, in a broken home, to better emphasize the effects that this sort of thing has on a person. The trouble that it causes for little boys and little girls who have to grow up dealing with this sort of thing.

Right now, and especially in America – although I have gathered from my friends in other places that there's quite a bit of turmoil surrounding this issue in other nations – that there's this sort of "war" being waged against the idea of "family." Against the mere concepts of family and familial life as a whole.

I think it's all sort of wrapped up in this ongoing "Battle of the Sexes" that we have right now, which is quite prominent here in America.

Men are in a very awkward position right now. The entire male sex is in a very awkward position where, societally speaking, and culturally speaking – we're hated.

We're hated for existing and we're hated for being alive. In one of the earliest pages I had mentioned that there really isn't a single day that goes by where either online or on TV or even in person, whether directly or indirectly, that I haven't had to listen to this running theme of "patriarchy" and "male privilege" and it's really becoming an extreme and detrimental issue.

As a man in the modern day, if you think or say anything critical of feminism or a women's movement, then you're just instantly shut down as a pig or a chauvinist. You're told that you're a Nazi, that you're a complete piece of shit – that you're the problem.

There's a lot of recent upheaval to the law but certainly during the high-point of this issue, men didn't get to have a say on the matter of abortion. Father's having their children wrenched away from them without any ability to express their opinion or concern. Custody battles are decidedly one-sided, and when relationships end the father may want to take his child – but he gets tossed out on his ear.

There's countless cases of mother's that were in no fit state to keep the kids being ruled for instantly, because the alternative was – healthy and stable as they might have been – a man. It's very rare for a man to win custody battles.

It's heartbreaking.

Men get absolutely raked over the coals when it comes to things like child support payments – often ruining them financially for the rest of their lives if it happens when they're young enough. In an alarmingly large number of cases, men are even expected to provide child support for children that aren't his – there's even been court cases where anonymous sperm donors get tracked down via DNA testing and forced into child support.

There's a lot of laws and regulations and expectations that are stacked against men – even from just a very basic standpoint like car insurance. On average, the price for coverage of a teenage boy is radically different from the cost of a teenage girl.

It's tough out there for a guy. You have to deal with all these pressures and prejudices towards you on the basis of your sex while simultaneously dealing with the expectations of society – that even though you're a "problem" for doing all of the things that you're expected to do – you are still *expected* to do them.

You're expected to make a lot of money, you're expected to be very successful. You're expected to be a leader and you're expected to be a provider. You have to acrew various accolades and endorsements and always come out on top – otherwise you're just a loser. A failure. You're *worthless*.

I think it's because of this attitude that a lot of guys are sort of conditioned by society to view their sense of self worth at an almost exclusively numerical level – and I don't just mean by how much money they make – but in all aspects of their life.

How many women have they slept with? If they get married, how many years have they kept it together? If they own land, what is the total acreage? Do you have a 1,500 square foot home? How about 3,000? Is it only one story? Add a second floor and a basement and make it three stories instead. Does your neighbor have an enclosed garage? Build your own and make it a two-door garage.

This numerical fixation can easily get out of control and I think that when a guy doesn't have some sort of anchor in his life – he doesn't have a father figure around to help "ground" him in reality and say "hey, you're doing just fine" then he'll often get lost in the numbers.

And this isn't to say that girls don't possess a sense of numerical value – but I think that by and large women tend to look at things a little bit differently. They see a four acre plot of land and say "Oh my goodness honey, we have four whole acres for our home!" And the guy says "Yeah... we *only* have four acres..."

There's an intrinsic difference between the two viewpoints and it can be very difficult for a lot of guys because they carry this ingrained attitude that says: if you're just "puttering along" like most people are – you're not considered to be successful or valuable.

It's really like having to live out your entire life between a rock in a hard place. You know, a man – especially today – is expected to be emotionally available and emotionally vulnerable – and yet if you do show those emotions and you do open up, you're criticized for it. You get socially castrated, even by the people who asked you to do those things.

It's a lose-lose situation.

There's a lot of hatred and resentment and bitterness aimed at men today. There's a lot of handicapping of men – you can't be a good man anymore in the eyes of the general public, and still be considered "acceptable" or "tolerable" by modern standards.

A good man sees a woman being roughed up by somebody, and he rushes over to help her. Well if you do that today you're considered an icon of "toxic masculinity" you know, you're looked at as some kind of "barbarian" or "savage." You get treated like a knuckle-dragging brute and in spite of stepping in to save somebody's life, you'll probably end up being charged with assault. Instead you're told that what you "should" have done is call the cops and walk away, or maybe just stand there like a fence-post watching this thing take place.

A good man – a gentleman – if he was raised right, opens the door for women. He opens the car door or holds the door at the restaurant or wherever they're going – well now you're sexist if you do that. You're a product of the past, you're a product of the patriarchy – and you're looking down on women if you do that. If you don't do it however, you're thought of as rude and inconsiderate and frankly like you're a scumbag.

I was talking to someone I know recently who was complaining that there's "no good men left out there anymore." And now, this woman is exactly the sort of person who used to belittle and berate men for doing things like opening doors – I know this because I've heard her say it – and I had to explain to her that one of the greatest injustices of taking away this "idea" that a boy should hold the door for women, is that you are actively teaching him not to have respect towards women.

That just as it is important to teach a young girl how she can be independent, and how she can be able to protect herself so that she can grow up to be resilient and self-reliant – because the world can be a very scary place – boys also need to be taught how to be gentlemen. They need to know how to be careful and considerate and how to be mindful – because when you are taught how to be a gentleman, it helps to keep you from going off and doing things that you shouldn't be doing.

If a boy is taught how to open doors for ladies and how to pull out the chair for his girlfriend, and how to walk on the outside of the street so if anything happens it'll happen to him first – these sorts of things aren't there to teach a boy that a girl "can't" do those things for herself – they're there to teach a him respect towards women.

It's so ironic to me that in the modern day we have this social clamor and call for the dissolution of those teachings and ideas, while simultaneously saying that men need to have more respect for women. That is how you teach them respect – because a boy who grows up being taught those things, being shown those values, is not the boy who grows the kind of man who beats women. Who grows into the sort of man who abuses women – who rapes women.

He cherishes them instead, and we're losing that. We're losing that because society is taking it away from us.

And then of course, because boys and men have really had the wind taken out from under them – there has been a sort of "call and response" to that. That's why you see the rise of people like Andrew Tate or Myron Gaines – who preach a message of "men first" and self-appreciation and self-value and all of this other stuff – and it draws men, especially young men, like a moth to the flame.

It draws them in because nobody is telling them like they have any value. Nobody is telling them that they're good enough or important. The only thing that they're telling them is that they can't do anything right – and the only way to be good enough or important is to be a part of some "protected" minority – otherwise you're just an inconvenience.

So these guys go out there and they get drawn in by people like Gaines and Tate, who don't even know the first thing about being a "man." Those guys don't know what it means to be a man, they're just an empty front of "machismo."

I listened to Tate tell this one story about how he had a girl for so many months and every day he'd ask her to bring him two cups of coffee in the morning – but every day he'd only drink one of them. When she finally asked him why he asked for two but only drank one, he went on a tirade about how: "I provide for you. I pay for your pretty clothes. I pay for your hair and your makeup. I pay for all of your jewelry. I keep you in my house – I give you somewhere to live – I give you everything, and the only thing I ever ask you for is two cups of coffee, and so you had better be damn grateful and bring it to me."

That's not being a man, it's being an asshole. It's being a piece of shit is what it is.

Real men do not look at women like "property," and they don't look at women like they "owe" them something.

And conversely on the flip side of that coin, real women don't look at men like *they* owe *them* something either – but I'll come back to that thought in a minute.

It's so easy to see why young guys flock to people like Andrew Tate, because despite how completely backwards that way of thinking is – and frankly how asinine the logic is – when you don't have anybody to teach you what to do, you become attracted to strong personalities.

Now in my case, I obviously had my own head on my shoulders and I was a little more… well, I don't normally consider myself to be a terribly confident person, but I suppose I had the sense of self-confidence, or the sense of self-awareness to know who to emulate and who to learn from, and who not to.

But a lot of guys don't. A lot of guys question everything – you know, men are riddled with doubts. They are. You think of a man as this "stony" thing but, that's "older" men. I think it's a thing we all get to – but younger men are often full of doubts.

And I'm not articulated enough or eloquent enough to really say if that's just "boys" and how they develop with this need to find approval, and this drive to prove themselves – or if that's just something society has done to us over the years. I think it's a little bit of both, really. But it is a common struggle of men – and especially in today's world where the home, the family, and the traditional family unit has been so utterly dissolved in the commonality of its existence – there are a lot of men out there who will find that strong personality on their own.

Especially by a social media influencer – it's in the job title, to influence people – and they will latch onto them.

Somebody will say "Well this is the first guy in my entire life who has ever stood up for me. Who has ever said that he gives a shit about me. Who has ever said that it's okay for me to be who I am, and not feel ashamed of myself. That it's okay for me to feel confident in myself and to give me a sense of self-worth."

In a lot of ways it's very much like what I've talked about in other chapters. You have people out there who are hurting or who are struggling, and then somebody comes along who they'll just "attach" themselves to and then get led into a life where they're acting or behaving or believing in things that aren't "really" them. They turn into people they probably wouldn't turn into on their own, or if they had the right guidance around them.

With boys especially, you can see it like a sort of surrogate father situation. I was recently re-watching the Kill Bill films by Tarantino, and there's a line towards the end of the second film that really didn't register to me back when I had first watched them.

The line reads: "Like most men who never knew their father, Bill collected father figures."

It's such a powerful line, I mean thinking back on my own life it's absolutely true. It's extremely accurate – or at least it was for me. When I was growing up, even before I was aware of my own father – or lack thereof – and certainly knowing that I couldn't turn to my grandfather, I adored getting to go up home to Virginia and seeing my uncle Lloyd and my uncle Billy.

I idolized those men when I got to see them. And one of my best friends growing up, his father Mr. Jimmy, I idolized him too.

I mentioned working in a restaurant at one point with Mr. Kenny – I absolutely adored him. It was a lot of picking up different older men here or there and... I don't want to sound like I'm undercutting it or to downplay it but, really if I think about it, it was a lot like collecting G.I. Joes. It really was. Going out and getting ahold of these sort of "action figures" and putting them on my shelf in a collection as I tried to piece together a positive male role model for myself.

And it wasn't just "real" people of course, it was people on TV as well. Tim Allen on Home Improvement, for example. He was really sort of like my "TV dad" in a way. Matt Dillon and Festus on Gunsmoke, y'know, they were great examples for a young boy to emulate. To learn how to be a man, and how to stand up for what's right – and also how to have quirks and be fun, while still being good and honest.

Archie Bunker I think is a really great example of having such a powerful impact on me growing up. TV Land used to play all of those old reruns of shows, and so I got to see a lot of these things that just aren't around anymore.

Archie often gets criticized today as being a racist and a bigot and this thing and that – but nobody ever bothers to stop and talk about how much he loved his family.

It wasn't necessarily easy for him to be emotional, but no matter what he loved his family above all else.

There's a very powerful moment after the original show had finished airing, and the spin-off series had begun its second season, where the character of Edith, who is Archie's wife, dies. Archie, for all of his gruff and bristling exterior, has this moment where he's alone in their bedroom where he finds one of her slippers that had been left under the bed.

In this scene, he picks it up and stares at it – before slowly hunching forward, holding her slipper to his face – and he begins crying. He just breaks down and weeps.

I think that was one of the first times that I saw a man really crying. It was one of the most powerful moments for me growing up. To witness a man like Archie Bunker – a guy that nobody could ever accuse of not being a "man" you know, a man's man – he wasn't exactly what you might consider a "peak physical specimen" but he was burly and gruff, and he drank beer and smoked cigars and he swore and he shouted and he was the real King of the Castle so to speak – and here he is crying.

Here he is vulnerable.

It's such a truly, genuinely powerful moment.

A lot of what we do today, in what I think of as a grand twist of irony – is that we keep actively discouraging men from being in touch with their emotions, because we keep telling them that they "have" to be – and that we keep pushing all of these other things on to people that aren't necessarily applicable to their lives.

When Peter Jackson filmed his adaptation of The Lord of the Rings, there was a lot of male emotion on display, because there's a lot of male emotion in the books. A lot of positive male emotion I might add – because Tolkien was very grounded as an individual and he had certainly seen things and he had been through war and he knew what it was like. He understood those struggles.

And in the books and in the films, you see Frodo weep and you see Samwise weep, and you see Aragorn weep and be vulnerable and see the different characters become riddled with self-doubt and having to overcome fears.

There's a beautiful moment in the first film – I'm not going to dance around "spoiling" it because it's so incredibly famous – but another character, Boromir, dies. He dies in this moment of redemption – and Aragorn kneels beside his body, holding his hands and kisses his forehead as he passes away.

This beautiful, wonderful and emotional moment is often tarnished or ruined by people who – not necessarily with malicious intent – will typically try to bring matters of sexuality into it. They'll talk about how it's "progressive," "homonormative" or "gay-positive" and they'll end up drawing contrasts that don't exist, and place this sort of pseudo-homoerotic spin on what should otherwise be a very male-positive moment.

And what you end up doing by that is simply making people feel self-conscious.

If my best friend were laying in the hospital and dying, I would hold his hand. I would kiss his forehead – I would tell him that I love him. That he's been one of the greatest things in my entire life, and that I'm not going to leave him. I would weep for him – I would mourn him.

And I hope – and I would like to think – that he would do the same for me.

It's hard to do that when somebody keeps trying to push and prod this idea that there must be something "more." That there must be this underlying subtext of sexual or romantic involvement, which has nothing to do with how you feel, or the earnesty of your feelings or with the genuine nature of who you are.

So a lot of men will just swallow it down because they're afraid of being "accused" of these things – when these things have no right being brought up in the first place. What was once a natural interaction gets stifled because of somebody making an unnatural connection – forcing a crossover by skipping "B" and going straight from "A" to "C" and shoehorning a narrative or connection where it doesn't exist. And that's sad to me.

It's sad that people can't look past themselves and they can't look past their own agendas – and they can't understand that they're taking something away from somebody. They're taking man's ability to be emotionally vulnerable away from him, because if he does that, there's this accusation – or even if not presented in an accusatory way – there's this strange narrative that it has to be something more than just true friendship.

It's like I said further up, we're seeing a great deal of men struggling with this lack of respect towards women because they're having that "training" or that "discipline" taken away from them – because they're told that they're wrong for doing it. They're told that they're wrong for opening doors – and there's this very real negative consequence of that happening, which nobody seems to really care about.

I think another excellent example are two characters from my favorite book, which is Herman Melville's Moby Dick. In the story we get to explore the wonderful, beautiful and overwhelmingly loyal friendship of Ishmael and Queequeg – two characters who could not be more different from each other if they tried.

Ishmael was a school teacher, and wants to undertake his first ever whaling voyage. Queequeg was the son of a Chief, and has spent years of his life as a harpooneer. Ishmael is relatively young, Christian and white, with very little experiences to his name – while Queequeg is a "savage" Pagan cannibal from the Pacific Islands, who is also much older and has seen a great deal of the world.

Regardless of which version of Moby Dick you're looking at, whether it's the book, the 1956 film starring Gregory Peck, or the 1998 miniseries starring Patrick Stewart (which is my personal favorite), very early on in the story these two characters are forced to share a bed together in a tavern.

The scene always unfolds with the two men being very unsure of each other, and Queequeg threatening to outright kill Ishmael for being there – before finally coming to terms with the fact that they have to share the bed – and they even end up bonding over Queequeg's tobacco pipe before falling asleep.

As the next chapter and the next scene opens up, Queequeg's arm is slumped all over poor Ishmael and he's been snoring all night long, flopped out in the bed – and Ishmael always makes some remark that: "You had almost thought I had been his wife." Or in the miniseries he states: "He must be dreaming of his savage wife somewhere, from whatever savage home that he came from."

When the harpooner finally wakes up, Ishmael indignantly says good morning to him – to which Queequeg shouts something in Maori, causing Ishmael to fall out of bed, and then he laughs at him.

There is an extremely large amount of people who want to push for this relationship to be homosexual in nature, when it very clearly isn't.

There is no romance between Ishmael and Queequeg – there is however male bonding – as later on in the book Queequeg rests his forehead on Ishmael's; takes him by the waist, and says that he is now his "wife." Which in his own custom means they are now bonded. Specifically saying that they are "bosom friends."

These two men are boon companions, joined at the hip. They're the best of friends and never separated from each other. They openly rely on each other, and Queequeg watches out for Ishmael as he is trying to learn his way around the ship and deal with the rigors of an incredibly demanding life.

Not to mention of course all of the tragedies and hardships that the two of them will face together during their time aboard the Pequod.

People take these things at face value without ever attempting to contextualize the story, the writing or the meaning behind it – and so they force this narrative and interject their own agenda onto something that is completely unrelated – all the while ignoring the fact that Queequeg speaks very broken English.

That he only possesses a very rough grasp of the English language, and that it's a fairly substantial part of his character. It's what helps to set him apart and appear more initially alien – before bringing the true meaning full-circle once you realize that he is often far more considerate and thoughtful than the supposedly "civilized" white people.

Instead they'll say "well obviously there's this underlying gay romance going on" and in reality what Queequeg is saying, is that they are family. That he and Ishmael are bound together and that losing him would mean losing a part of himself – a feeling and an emotion which I think almost all men can relate to in terms of their best friends.

It's such a deeply emotional, meaningful and integral part of the book, and yet people often reduce it down to nothing more than this perverted sexual innuendo.

And thus of course you do produce men who are simply unable or otherwise unwilling to bunk with someone else – to share a bed or a sleeping bag with another man – because they're scared of this notion that they're going to be forced into this role of "well it has to be this" or "oh well it has to be that."

I've talked a lot in this book about this sort of recurring theme of not being able to breath and of having to go around walking on eggshells. Of generally not being able to catch a moment's peace. Well this is just another example of that. It's another example of walking on those eggshells – because a lot of people are going around being constantly scared of this.

Not even necessarily because you're scared of being "perceived" as gay – but just because you're scared of people forcing and pushing this idea onto you, because it's not who you really are. So you'll see a lot of guys going around putting up this front or this facade of being this incredibly "macho" or "dominant" kind of man – when it's really not who they are. It's an issue of over-correcting.

And there's this strange idea right now that it's a "modern invention," this idea of men getting in touch with their emotions. No it's not. As I just gave you the example of Melville and I gave you the example of Tolkien.

There's a story I heard once of these two guys in World War II who were the best of friends, not unlike Ishmael and Queequeg – not unlike Frodo and Sam – and they were constantly joined at the hip. One was tall and skinny while the other was short and kind of round, like characters from a comic strip.

Well they got shot up on those beaches at Normandy – and the rest of their squad couldn't get to them because they had to fall back. When they started advancing again to retake their position, a few men went off to try and find them – and what they had found was that one of them, who was completely torn to pieces, had crawled over to where the other one had been shot, and he laid his head on his friends chest so that they could die together.

That's friendship. That is loyalty and it is love.

It's the purest and most honest love – and there are people who will hear that, and they will make accusations or try to besmirch it – and they will warp it into some fetishistic "retelling" of the tale.

And it's simply not true.

And again it comes down to this issue of being stuck between a rock and a hard place because these same people will tell you that if you were "really" confident in yourself, or if you "really" have no prejudices, then you wouldn't "mind" if somebody says something that's not true. That you wouldn't "mind" those accusations – well I would mind. I would mind because I mind falsehood.

I mind dishonesty, and I mind somebody saying something about me that is not correct.

But if you stand up and rebuke those accusations or narratives – you get accused of being a bigot or being insecure or being closeted or homophobic or this, that and the other.

So it is hard out there right now for guys. It really is sort of a "tough gig" in a lot of ways – especially when you don't have anyone to look up to and be an example of how to deal with all the things you're struggling with. Somebody to teach you how to handle the stress of it and keep going.

And then of course you have just the... loneliness to deal with. I've talked a lot through the previous chapters about this sort of "loneliness epidemic" that the world is dealing with – which in that regard I wouldn't say is simply relegated to the United States. I see that issue going on in a lot of places – but things have gotten so bad here specifically – with being unable to find somebody who sees you for yourself. With being unable to find somebody who acknowledges you for your own worth, that a lot of guys are leaving.

They're going overseas to find a wife somewhere – or in a lot of cases they're just simply giving up on the idea.

You can go online right now and watch countless videos of countless women giving their opinion on what they find "valuable" in a man – and they'll be asked questions like: "What's the minimum it would take for a guy to date you?" And the answers are almost universally along the lines of requiring him to make a minimum of $100,000 a year, and that he has to drive a Lamborghini, and that he has to be at least 6'4" and that he has to have this and that he has to have that – which all just goes back to those expectations of success.

It's so shallow. It's so incredibly unrealistic.

When I was growing up, and we do still hear about it today but it was very prevalent in the mid 2000s – there was a lot of talk in the media and the culture about the unrealistic expectations of women, and about the very misogynistic and sexist "view" of women in the world and in works of fiction and so on.

The depictions of having to have a certain body type that was thinner than a pencil, and the expectation that all women need to act a certain way or behave a certain way and this, that and the other – and it was very one-sided. It's only ever been – at least so long as I have been alive – this running narrative of men objectifying women, and that women aren't objects to be objectified.

And it's also been a running theme that men are incapable of being objectified.

To that I'd like to reference back to Conan the Barbarian. I mentioned him somewhere quite awhile ago – but Conan is absolutely an objectification of men. Any of the artistic works from Boris Vallejo, Julie Bell, Frank Frazetta and so on are usually depicting an objectification of men. Famous fictional characters such as Batman, Superman, Wolverine – these are objectifications of men.

This idea that a man has to be some kind of "mogul" that he has to be some kind of "titan of industry" that he has to be rich and be wealthy and handsome – that he has to be brave, strong, fearless and mighty – these are objectifications.

And I'm not necessarily saying that I mind these things – quite the contrary I love the works of Vallejo, Bell and Frazetta. I love the characters of Batman and Superman. But to act like there is no such thing as an "objectification" of the male sex is asinine.

It's a lie that modern society has really sort of latched onto over the years.

There absolutely is this idea that in order for a man to be "desirable" he has to walk around looking like some kind of bronzed Adonis. He has to look like a wrestler from the WWF. That to be successful, a man has to wear Armani suits and bespoke shoes and flash his shiny Rolex – and it's simply not true.

What it is is hurtful, and frankly agonizing for a lot of people.

The balancing act of this, of having to manage the two realities of being constantly objectified by society, while also being simultaneously scorned as the objectifier – it's really a Sisyphean task to try and deal with. A task made all the more difficult, again, when you have so many guys out there that don't have anybody to help them.

Guys that don't have a good home to go back to where they can quiet out the noise – guys that don't have a father they can look up to and draw strength from. To gain confidence from or whose example they can use to really ground themselves.

I saw this one video that sort of made me laugh due to just how sad it was, where a woman was saying that: "If you were my man, you would never cheat on me, because you would be drained. You would get all of this, constantly, and you would be satisfied – but me? I would cheat on you all the time because I would be bored as fuck."

There's just this sort of very crass attitude right now towards dating and towards fidelity and towards monogamy, and so as I said, a lot of men are really hurting to find somebody.

I saw a statistic from a year or two ago that, if memory serves correctly, cited that approximately 41% of American men between roughly the ages of 21 and 40, who said that they would rather either: A: Go abroad and look for a none-Western wife overseas. B: Stop looking for relationships altogether and commit themselves to being alone. And C: An alarmingly large percentage of this study said that they would rather just give up on women entirely and simply "go gay."

I don't think I'm quite there myself yet boys, but best of luck to you.

If I'm being perfectly honest though, I can't really say that I blame them. I really can't.

I don't want to be mistaken in any context – I do not think that there's "no good women" left in America or left in Western civilization. I don't think that all women are some kind of "evil misandrists" or something to run away from like some guys seem to have gotten into their heads. I don't think that at all.

But I do think – or rather I know – that there is a culture here that is made up of all these things I have talked about. Between the obsession with the internet, between the warping of perspectives, between the sexualized nature of just every-day life and the ingrained biases towards men in general – that it has just become this incredibly difficult thing for guys.

And that number I said, that 41% or so, from everything I have seen or read or witnessed or experienced – I have to imagine that that number is getting bigger, not smaller – because it's just so hard in America these days to try and find that certain somebody.

As a matter of fact, frankly, it's hard everywhere in the modern day.

Even when you do manage to find that special someone, you often have to deal with being criticized or attacked for it. The concept of the "Nuclear Family" is becoming somewhat of a dying dream. It's turning into this sort of "unicorn" of an idea – where the father and the mother are married, and the husband goes out and provides for his family while the wife stays home and takes care of the house and kids. That whole "2.5 children and a dog" and all the rest that goes with it.

It's a dying dream.

And it's not because the dream is unrealistic, but because there's currently just so much animosity towards it. There's such a sense of active aggression and revilement just, hurled at the idea of the traditional family. Even just talking with a few people around my local area, the whole concept just gets mocked and ridiculed as the "trad" family - "dirty trads, filthy trads" etc.

There was a commercial that aired awhile back that was advertising for McDonald's of all things. It came out of Japan and was done in a sort of "anime" style I guess you would call it – and it was just this little thirty second clip of a mother, father and their daughter sitting in one of the more "cafe" style restaurants while soft piano music played in the background. There wasn't even any dialogue – just a family enjoying a meal at McDonald's.

This thing was met online with open disdain. I mean some of the things being said about it were so repugnant and vile over just a thirty second clip. I saw people saying things like: "This is fucking trad propaganda." "This is just pandering to goddamn traditionalists." "How fucking dare they show those stupid mother fuckers like they're special." "I'll eat McNuggets out of that little girl's ass and make the father watch, how's that for fucking traditional?" "This commercial would be better if they raped the mom in the bathroom – she should be used to it, fucking trad bitch."

Just the most putrid and hateful things – I mean what do you even say to that?

Some people tried to downplay this and, I don't know if I looked at a different upload of the video than they did and so it had a different comment section than they had, I really couldn't say – but from what I saw they were just so... angry.

They were just so incredibly angry at the mere thought of a man and a woman being married and raising a family.

And I spoke to someone I know about this when it happened and they tried to say "Well y'know, it's the internet and you know how people are on the internet." And I had to tell him, I said "No, it's not just the internet. This has gone beyond 'the internet' y'know? We've had an entire generation at this point who have been raised online – raised without any sense of repercussions for the things that they say – for the stances that they take.

An entire generation who has been stewing and embroiling themselves in this sort of vitriolic behavior, and you can see this attitude bleeding out into the general public. It's gone beyond cyberspace and it's here. It's real."

I don't live in some amazing or vast social mecca – I live out in the middle of nowhere. My closest town is Byron and beyond that is the city of Warner Robins. These aren't exactly "beacons of civilization" we're talking about – I mean for God's sake Warner Robins is just an Air Force base with a town growing off of it. This ain't no Macon and certainly no Atlanta or something.

But even out here in these rural areas and small towns, you can see those attitudes in person. You see it around the college campuses and the coffee shops and the malls and whatnot. I've overheard plenty of people talking like that whenever I had to drive into the city.

Hell I've heard shit like that out here in the county.

You can hear the sheer level of disdain in their voice for people who are straight, for people who want a home, for people who want a family – a nuclear family – it's horrible. I overheard one guy talking and he said: "Man this is 2022, the 'nuclear family' is a joke, it's a fucking lie. Ain't nobody need that shit."

You don't have to simply listen to all of my anecdotes. Look around at all the human pieces of shit like Katy Perry, who recently told a wonderfully talented young mother – on national television – that she was a slut.

For the full context, this lovely young lady went out to audition on American Idol, revealed that she was a 25 year old mother of three – and Perry said: "Honey, you've been laying on the table too much."

That's *disgusting*. It's disgusting and it's sad.

It's so very sad to me that this is where we've gotten to in society.

That this is where this ideological bowel movement of anti-familial propaganda has taken us.

Even in the cases of people who are happily married, I constantly see them undermining the sanctity and significance of their union these days. I'm not just talking about the extreme examples of all the swinging and "lending out" of spouses – but the casual nature that a lot of people use when referring to their husbands or wives.

The "work-husband" or the "game-wife", these terms might seem to be harmless on the surface, but the reality is that you're disregarding the status of your spouse by inferring that the only thing it takes for someone to hold that same position in your life, is to just share a few interests and exist in your general vicinity.

It's incredibly disrespectful whether you intend it to be or not.

Being a husband or being a wife is supposed to be this incredibly important thing – it's supposed to be an extreme honor for both parties involved – so to treat it as something so casual, insignificant and nonchalant, it's pretty heartbreaking.

Now, obviously some traditional families do still exist, and of course the idea behind them is not completely gone – but you also have to recognize that the amount of broken homes that exist, certainly in my country, do drastically outweigh the traditional functioning ones.

Single-parent households in America are at an all-time high, especially single mothers, with something like 14.3 million children in the U.S. living in a single-parent home with their mother as compared to only around 6 million having both parents.

This nation practically subsidizes single motherhood. There's numerous incentives for a person to have children, multiple children, and never get married. I was friends with a girl from Fort Valley back when I was around twenty or so, and her sister had around 12 kids from a few different men –

never married any of them – and she was making more money than some of our active-duty servicemen.

Each new baby was another new check from the government, as well as another new tax write-off. With all those children she "couldn't" work, so she got to have unemployment. She was able to get food stamps, she had Section-8 housing. She was benefiting from a few different aid-programs.

And of course she was also collecting child-support in addition to everything else.

So as far as this girl was concerned, she had it made. She was her own golden goose.

There's a very big push today that says men aren't "necessary" in the home – that a child doesn't need to have a father and a mother. That men aren't required, that men don't provide anything of value.

I said at the start of this that we're seeing attacks on women increasing, that we're seeing things go wrong – because men are required. Well, I won't say "required" because required is a very stringent term.

A man in the home is a good thing – if he is a good man.

Having a father and a mother who are married does not equal automatic success in life, either for the parents or the children – but it is the best possible chance of achieving that success. Being the child of a single-parent also isn't an automatic guarantee of failure – but you will often have to deal with additional struggles that you might otherwise not have had to.

I would have loved to have had a dad. I think part of me would have hated it, because I do have a bit of an issue with authority figures – but at the same time I may not have those issues if I had a good father around that I could look up to. I can't really say for certain one way or the other, because I never had the chance – but I do think my life would have been better if I had one. Certainly if I had a good one.

I do have a godfather, though I've never met him. To touch back on that "G.I. Joe" analogy – even though I've only ever spoken to him a handful of times in my life over the phone – it's really always meant the world to me, just to know that he existed. That he was out there somewhere.

I'm not sure if I'll actually ever get to meet him.

It would have been nice if he had lived closer. My mother knew him in college and she's friends with the lady that he married so, when she got pregnant with me she asked if he would be the godfather – but his work took him very far away to the other side of the country for a long time in my life. He was out in California for as long as I could remember – though I won't hold that against him. At least not too much anyway.

But just knowing that he existed has always been a huge comfort to me.

I'd like to add though, that I am eternally grateful that my mother never went out dating. She never had trysts or flings, she was always home. She never had a slew of 'boyfriends' coming in and out of my life – I never had to deal with an uncle Tom, Dick and Harry or whoever else. She never tried to get married and I never had to deal with some stepdad that – maybe he could have been great – but probably would have made my life a living hell.

I don't want that to sound overly harsh or overly negative – I don't want to discourage anybody from ever stepping in and finding love or becoming a caring and compassionate step-parent. It's just for me, for my part, I don't like it.

I've seen too many people get screwed over by somebody else coming into the family and treating them like shit. I just don't like it – it's a personal thing.

I think that if you're going to act adult enough to go off and have sex, then you ought to act adult enough to be a responsible parent – and a responsible parent always puts their children first.

Going back to the dating situation and just discussing why exactly it was so important to bring up my mother and my father and so on, is because I am the only son of a single mother, and I am the product of a broken home.

This chapter isn't meant to be the "Woe is Me" chapter, or the "Struggles of Men" chapter – it's meant to point out the things that people deal with in the world and the reasons why having a stable home is so important.

Obviously I am speaking to this point from a predominantly male perspective – because I'm a man. It is my perspective – but all of these issues that I've spoken about, or will continue to speak about, are just as damaging to young girls and women as they are to boys and men.

If a young boy needs a strong father figure in his life so that he can learn how to emulate and become a good man himself as he gets older – than a young girl needs one to understand what a good man is supposed to be. She needs a good father so that she can know what qualities to look for in a boyfriend, in a husband – hell even just her buddies that happen to be guys. She needs someone that she can turn to, that she can trust – that she can depend upon for protection, for security – for stability in her life.

And yes, again, a lot of my commentary here has centered around the idea of a family missing its father – because I did not have a father – but for the inverse of this, a boy needs to have his mother around while he is growing up so that he can learn how to be more nurturing, more caring and more gentle. He needs to have the first 'woman' in his life that he can, essentially, practice on while learning to become a gentleman. Someone to open doors for, someone to bring in the groceries for. Somebody to be protective of.

And girls need their mothers too, just like boys need a father to emulate – girls need that mature sense of femininity to be present within the household so that they can understand how to be more confident in themselves. So that they can understand how to hold their head up high and be successful – so that they can have an image in their mind of what it means to be a good woman, a good wife and good mother – and have an easier time aspiring to be those things in the future.

I'll also say here, that two parents in the home is, quite obviously, not a guarantee of success.

And coming from a single-parent home is likewise not a guarantee of failure.

But it is, statistically speaking – and with all due reverence to the omnipresent Law of Averages – the best possible way to try and assure a more positive life and outcome for your children. To try and lead them in the right direction so that they can grow up as happy, healthy boys and girls who know – no matter what happens – that they will always have a home to come back to.

I never really got to have that, and I often worry now that I never will.

My grandfather despised me for being a bastard – or perhaps for being a reminder of his daughter's failure – and my Aunt treated me with nothing short of cruelty and contempt when not enjoying her pleasures in *other* ways.

My mother worked very hard, and she went to school – so she usually wasn't around except for early in the mornings and very late in the evenings – and my grandmother, bless her, could only do so much.

It should come as no surprise then to know that I grew up wanting a family. A real family. My own family – one where none of these sad truths would ever take place – and I could right the wrongs of those who came before me... but now I'm not so sure.

A family of my own, in a house that is my own – and on land that is my own – is the only thing in life that I've ever truly wanted, but now I see the ways in which the world has become so warped and twisted that my deepest desires are now shrouded in a black veil of doubt.

I have endured so many temptations, and taken such careful steps and measures to ensure that I would never be responsible for fathering some poor, miserable and misbegotten child such as myself – how can I now in good conscience ever think to bring new life into a world like this one?

To grow up being scorned for having values, and being torn between the imaginary "Rights" and "Wrongs" that have been made up by modern society? To have a million voices in their head, each contradicting what the others have to say – and never having a chance to succeed when success is now viewed as a crime?

How can I have abstained for so long, and for the singular purpose of assuring that no child of mine ever be forced to endure even a modicum of the hell I have been through – only to turn around and bring that child into a literal Hell on Earth?

One by one, I sit and watch as the pieces of my broken heart slip away. My hopes, and my dreams, shattering upon the ground beside them.

I've heard it said that "Good times make weak men, and weak men make hard times. Hard times make strong men – and strong men make good times."

Maybe that's really sort of where we're at. That everything's been a pretty "easy ride" for such a long time that everyone's gone soft. That everything sort of spiraled out of control and became skewed. That nobody has done anything to stop it. That everyone has let this entire situation get out of hand.

I don't know.

I don't know if I'm a strong man and I don't know if I'm a weak man. I don't even know if I'm a good man – but I like to think that I'm a man who *tries* to be good.

All I know is that I am a man, and that I have been alone for pretty much all of my life – and I don't see that situation changing any time soon.

I can be stubborn, I can be hard-headed. I'm riddled with doubts and insecurities.

But I don't let those things stop me from trying to do whatever it is that I have to do at any given moment.

I know that in my mind, to be a man means that you have to be honest. That you have to be loyal. That you have to be forthright and speak your peace, always adhering to your own conscience.

That life is less about confidence and more about courage – and that it is a truer statement of character for someone to do the things that they're afraid of – rather than to say they have no fear at all.

That masculinity is a thing to be earned, and that femininity is a thing to be protected.

That women are something to be respected, and that wives are something to be honored.

That families are a thing to be cherished – and that children are the greatest gift we can receive.

The hands on the clock are slowly moving onward. Every time I glance down at the keys to begin composing my thoughts, it feels as if mere seconds were counting down in my moment of contemplation – only to look back up and see the hands have leapt forward – as if some unseen thing were playing tricks on me.

I almost wish that was the case – for if there were some form of ghostly spirit or apparition – I would not feel so alone.

The weather forecast did not call for rain, but I can hear the distant rolling of thunder. I can smell the water on the wind. I hope that it does rain – for I have always found a strange sort of comfort in storms. Maybe it's just that the sound of rain is enough to drown out all these noises in my head.

I could really use that about now.

I wish that I were not so alone.

I don't exactly have what you might call an "active social life" as I live quite far out in the county – but even with that in mind, the women around here are typically either quite homely, or unintelligent, or involved in drugs, or loose with men – or perhaps even worst of all they're simply too young.

I've met several very pretty young women with a good head on their shoulders and a sense of strong moral character – but not a one of them were over seventeen. I suspect that most of them move away the moment they can in order to break away from this miserable backwater – and I can't really blame them for it.

I'd like to find somebody, or at least I'd like to think that I could find somebody – but I have a lot of hangups about certain things – I have my own lines and stances that I'm unwilling to compromise on.

I've been told before that I'm "sexist" for wanting decent qualities in a woman. I've been told that I should not care what she looks like or how many men she's been with before me – but I say that that is not sexism.

Having standards is not a crime, and nor is it a slight against anyone. It is a thing which most people used to have and maintain – and I refuse to settle for somebody that I know will not make me happy.

That isn't fair to me – and it also isn't fair to her.

I've written several times throughout the book that I'm Catholic and I do have my own religious beliefs on not having sex before marriage, and I expect my wife, whoever she may be, to be a virgin on our wedding night – and that's very difficult today.

I suppose the other reason that I'm just so adamant on this, is that not only do I have my own religious stance on the issue – I also have a deeply personal one.

I am the product of adultery.

I am the product of a union outside marriage.

I've had to grow up dealing with the scars of that reality – and I know what kind of damage that it does to a kid.

I've never gone out looking for some "fast and loose" hookup or fling – because I am unwilling to ever put myself in a position where there might be a child out there with my eyes, or my hair, or my nose.

A child that I don't know, and don't know about, or don't care about.

I'm looking for somebody who feels the same way – maybe not necessarily for the same reasons – but somebody who understands that. Who respects that, who recognizes and acknowledges that.

Somebody who wants to have a family – who wants to be a family – the same way that I do.

I have settled for less with just about everything in my life – I will not settle for less when it comes to the women I want to marry.

I want to find a girl who is kind by nature. Who is loving and nurturing. Intelligent and strong. A woman that adores animals, and will transform our house into a home.

Someone who will kneel beside me in the dirt as we plant flowers together in the garden. Someone who will laugh and cry and sing and shout right along with me, instead of without me.

In short, I want a woman that I can give my heart to – utterly and completely – until the day that I die.

If that sounds like sexism to you, then you're an idiot – and you're part of the problem.

I know all too well what it is like to go through life alone, but if being alone is what is required of me – then I suppose I'll have to endure that burden until I can find my "Mrs. Right", or myself fade away – forever comforted in the knowledge that I have never forced an innocent child to experience even a modicum of the things which I have.

That I will have never raised a child in a broken home, or abandoned them when they no longer suited me.

I think in a lot of ways my feelings on this issue play into what I wrote about in the chapter on my father. That I never really had the chance to learn what to do – only that I had the opportunity of learning what not to do.

And first and foremost on my list of things not to do is to compromise my stances.

I do not come from a good home and nor do I come from a good family – but I intend someday to have both.

In other words, if I am to find a wife and build a family – it will be with the right woman, in the right place and at the right time – or it will simply not be at all.

The Theory of Conspiracy

Chapter XXI: Narrative Division

I've been very critical of liberalism and the Democrat "Left" throughout this book, but I suppose within these next few pages I had really ought to give a more in-depth look as to why I take such an extreme disliking to them – but in order to properly do that, I think that first I need to talk a little about myself.

At least in a minor capacity.

Contrary to what anyone might think upon reading this book – should it ever get finished – I actually dislike the subject of politics. I may have said that before somewhere else but I'll go ahead and say it again here.

I hate politics.

I find the subject distasteful. I find it cumbersome and exhausting. I think that more often than not it sort of bogs down or otherwise outright ruins any kind of decent conversation that two people might be having – and in general I just find the subject very boring. That last one may not be a terribly "good" reason to dislike something – but it's an honest one nonetheless.

Growing up I sort of viewed politics as… I don't know, a "foreign" concept somehow. It was something discussed by people on TV, or by adults that were discussing the people discussing it on TV. As I got older and I learned a little more about the topic I generally took a very "neutral" stance on it.

I've always leaned Right in regards to politics – meaning that I've always believed in traditional family values. I've always loved and admired the idea of country living and the Southern way of life. I've always believed in God and specifically adhered to the teachings of Catholicism. I've always been patriotic and proud to be an American – those sorts of things – but I never grew up having to worry so much about "politics" in the conventional sense.

As I said, it wasn't something that had much to do with me, at least not from what I could tell. Mama would talk to me about something if I ever had a question, but in general, politics just weren't "discussed" in my family –at least not openly.

From what I've gathered, essentially, my grandfather was a Democrat and my grandmother was a Republican – and in the first Presidential election after they were married he assumed that she would, naturally, vote for whoever he told her to – and she didn't. It was apparently quite a fight and so the subject was never brought up again. That was just the "rule" of the house I suppose, and that rule stayed in place from the 1960s all the way up until… well I guess around 2008 is when it sort of broke away.

In general though, I knew exactly what it was that I believed in and in a very vague sense, I imagine that I understood that what I believed in would be called "Conservative" or at the very least Republican – but since nobody immediately connected to me ever discussed the subject – I just didn't either.

I think the first time I was ever really aware of politics and the way they can divide people, was during the 2004 re-election campaign of President George W. Bush, my school held a "debate" which for some reason focused on the previous election of Bush vs Gore. Looking back at it now I have absolutely no idea why they made the class go through the debates of George Bush and Al Gore when in the current election he was fighting against John Kerry – but that's really besides the point. I didn't participate anyway, I just had to sit there and listen to everybody else.

The point is that, that was probably my very first time having to sit down and listen to people argue over something that – to me – seemed like a none issue. Bush was our President, so of course we should support him – that's all that mattered to me, though of course I was a child – but that's what made sense to me. As if it were an obvious answer. If that wasn't a good enough reason that we shouldn't be arguing about this, then my followup would have been something like "I've never met him and neither have you." I just wanted to go play at recess.

(To be perfectly honest here, despite being so young I can vividly remember the Bush vs Gore election – but until looking up the information just now to write about this section, I could not have told you who Bush ran against for re-election. That is how little of an impression Bush vs Kerry made on me.)

With all of that being said though, that's pretty much how I viewed politics. It was "weird" and seemed like a waste of time. People were yelling about stuff that didn't sound like they really understood, and complaining about people they had never met and probably never would meet.

I didn't understand it.

As I got even older I sort of kept that same general attitude. I knew what I liked, and I knew that some people liked the same things that I did and that some others didn't. It all seemed pretty simple to me.

I just sort of figured that Republicans and Democrats both wanted the same thing: they wanted what was best for America. The only difference, as far as I could tell, was that they wanted to achieve the same end result but by two different methods – and as far as I was concerned, I liked the Republican method.

That's what I mean by "neutral." I kind of viewed it like taking a trip – two guys both want to go to the same place, but one guy wants to drive on the interstate and the other guy wants to drive on the highway. Either way they're both going to the same location.

That all started to change in 2008 with the election of Barack Obama.

At first I didn't really care – I wouldn't be able to vote until the 2012 election – but I supported my mom and the rest of my family who, as I said, had started becoming more verbal about politics by this point. I was sort of disappointed that "our guy" didn't win, but realistically I kept the same general attitude towards politics and I sort of took it the same way someone would if their favorite sports team lost a game. Sort of an "Aw shucks, but we'll get 'em next time" kind of thing.

But as the Obama administration began cementing itself into office and the ripple effects of his policies and decision making started to take root in the country – I noticed a "change" in the air that didn't feel right to me. Things were starting to be... different.

People weren't talking to each other like they used to. Fingers kept being pointed and voices kept getting raised on the nightly news. The previous administration started getting verbally blamed for everything going wrong, and Bush's policies were being overturned left and right.

I grew up watching the wars in Iraq and Afghanistan – and specifically the conflicts taking place in and around the city of Baghdad made an incredible impression upon me. That blood soaked city seemed to be on the nightly news every single evening for the majority of the end of my childhood and early adolescence. President Bush laid out some pretty clear rules for how to properly withdraw from the war. How to properly train the Iraqi military and ensure that all of the progress we made had not been in vain.

Obama disregarded everything Bush had laid out, pulled US troops, and I watched as that entire region devolved into a war-zone as new Terrorist organizations grew and took power. As every grain of sand that our boys fought and died for was given back to the enemy – or new enemies – and made the whole thing "pointless."

I watched as this weird – seemingly "fringe" concept to me called racism began dominating every aspect of life – and how generally everything in the country seemed to just fall apart on a social and economic level.

I watched as every institution I had ever known came under fire. Everything from religion to patriotism. I watched as the folks on TV started saying that the viewers were the problem, that the bases were the issue – and maybe that sort of thing had happened before but it seemed different now. It seemed like things had escalated. That escalation is what took us from comments in 2008 about how working-class, small-town conservatives are nothing more than bible-thumping rednecks that are clinging to their "guns or religion"" all the way to being a "basket of deplorables."

Everything just sort of started going tits up – and I also witnessed, with no small amount of astonishment, how people kept saying that things were getting "better" as time went on.

It made no sense to me. I'd watch my mother struggle to pay for groceries each week, but the man on TV said the economy was great. Other people that I knew at the time said the economy was great – but the prices kept going up, and up and up.

I'd watch people break out into fights in the street – but supposedly we were all getting along just fine. That the nation was prospering due to unprecedented social progress and reforms – despite the fact that all of the local businesses were going under and everyone kept losing their jobs.

What really twisted me up inside like a corkscrew was that, not only was the country itself beginning to spiral out of control – but all the people in power kept selling this line that everything was perfect. Everything was fine.

It was like a real-life version of that running joke in Zoolander, where nobody except for Will Ferrell could tell that Ben Stiller only made a single face for every photo shoot that his character ever did.

The nation seemed to be slipping out of bounds in regards to reality – and it frightened me. It still frightens me.

This sort of ongoing narrative of divisionist rhetoric started pouring in as the years rolled by – only Democrats know what's right, Republicans are always wrong – but don't worry, because everything's fine.

It wasn't fine. It's still not fine.

I can't sit here and list every single news broadcast or political speech – but that's what started happening. It's still what's happening to this day.

That's why I began to take an "interest" in politics, although I use the term loosely. I'm not really interested in the subject, it's just that I realized how unhealthy it was to keep my head buried in the sand. That no matter how much I stood there and said "Well, it really doesn't affect me" didn't change the fact that it did affect me. That it *does* affect me.

I have friends who, even now, will actively hold on to this weird attitude of "hear no evil, see no evil" where if they just don't talk about politics, that somehow means that politics won't affect them. But it does affect them.

Refusing to look at something doesn't mean that it isn't standing right there in front of you.

I spoke with one of my friends not too long ago about the troubles happening in schools. About highly sexual and graphic material that is being pushed onto children in the American school system, and that since he's got a son of his own he should start taking a more active interest in these issues. He said to me: "Well I ain't gotta worry about it, 'cuz that sort of thing wouldn't ever happen down here."

There's been a slew of these books found all throughout numerous counties here in Georgia – and at least one teacher even made the news for reading a book on transgenderism to her fifth grade class. I told him, I said: "It is happening down here. You can't just say that it isn't and make these sorts of things magically disappear."

There's also a growing narrative surrounding these books that all Conservatives and Republicans are simply "ban happy" censor-machines that are trying to dictate what people have the right to read, which isn't remotely true It's an issue over what is and is not appropriate for school children, not for what their parents show them at home. Nobody at any school should ever wheel out the TV and show Caligula to their classroom – but if you want to show that to Little Timmy on your own time, have at it.

Because of this running theme that Conservatives are the only ones who want to censor anything – there's a parallel theme that Liberals would "never" try to dictate media that is available to the public. Well that's simply untrue, as we have seen Of Mice and Men, To Kill a Mockingbird, Catcher in the Rye, The Adventures of Tom Sawyer and Huckleberry Finn and many other additions to the classic "American Canon" being removed from classrooms and school curriculum. There's even been calls to have them removed from the libraries, though none of them have as far as I'm aware.

That's a pretty big leap of the imagination to suggest that Liberals never want to ban anything, and that it's only those "bigoted Conservatives and Right-wing nut jobs" that ever try to assert some form of censorship over reading material.

And it's an even bigger leap to suggest that there exists any comparison whatsoever between Conservatives being uncomfortable with books such as Jack of Hearts and Other Parts – a book which vividly describes a boy performing fellatio on his teacher and then going online to have sex with grown men – and something like To Kill a Mockingbird, which is a staunch example of why racism is wrong.

But that's the *narrative*.

I've heard people say that there's "no such thing" as indoctrination taking place in public schools, and that anybody who raises concerns over it are just "crazy conspiracy theorists." I don't know, when I see that sort of behavior taking place in regards to sexually explicit books being read to ten year-olds, I find it a *bit* disconcerting.

I find it very disconcerting that many schools insist that "political imagery" is not allowed inside the classroom – but then I've seen photographs and video recordings of entire classroom windows that are being blocked out by gay pride, trans pride and BLM flags – while the American "flag" is often nothing more than a small grainy picture on a piece of printer paper that it taped to the inside of the classroom door.

I do find it disconcerting that the modern American school-system is so preoccupied with telling kids that the Gadsden Flag is "racist" and that kids shouldn't tell their parents about what they saw in Lolita – that they have forgotten to teach them things like basic math and science. When eighth graders are only functioning at a second or third grade level – maybe, just maybe – the school has been a little too busy teaching the kids something else that they weren't supposed to.

But no, I'm the crazy one. Me, and all the people like me – we're the conspiracy theorists. Right.

You see this same narrative trend with just about everything these days. Systemic racism of course is a big one – according to the political Left – all white-European colonists and settlers were basically just the physical manifestation of pure evil that raped and pillaged their way across the entire continent. Massacring indiscriminately anything and everything that looked different than they did – and ruthlessly enslaving anybody that they didn't outright slaughter.

Conservatives are all racists. White people are especially racist. Republicans want to reinstate slavery and chain all the minorities under the iron heel of White Supremacy.

What a fucking joke – but people believe it.

According to Liberals, we're the ones who went out hunting down free Africans in the jungle and bound them into slavery. Never mind the fact that European trading ships bought slaves from other Africans that had already enslaved them.

There's this fictitious image of white men running through the jungle catching slaves, when in reality they just sat on a beach and traded for them. Does that make it right? No, but it also doesn't mean that white men are somehow this great "white devil" that came out of the ocean to enslave a group of innocent tribal people that were living in perfect harmony either – but that's what happens when you read Roots and think that it's factual – and that's what happens when an entire side of the political isle convinces you that it is factual.

To quote Thomas Sowell: "Contrary to the "myths to live by" created by Alex Haley and others, Africans were by no means the innocents portrayed in Roots, baffled as to why white men were coming in and taking their people away in chains. On the contrary, the region of West Africa from which Kunte Kinte supposedly came was one of the great slave-trading regions of the continent—before, during, and after the white man arrived. It was the Africans who enslaved their fellow Africans, selling some of these slaves to Europeans or to Arabs and keeping others for themselves. Even at the peak of the Atlantic slave trade, Africans retained more slaves for themselves than they sent to the Western Hemisphere."

But no, ignore all of that. Thomas Sowell, along with numerous other historians and basic historical facts, are all inaccurate. White people are actually the greatest enemy to minorities everywhere – and they've also "never" been enslaved themselves.

Forget that the word "slave" comes from "Slav" and refers to the Slavic peoples being enslaved by Muslims – forget that slavery had existed within human civilizations for well over the 9,000 years, dating back to the Neolithic period and for people at the time, it would have been considered perfectly normal – forget that throughout the history of slavery in America there were over 3,700 black plantation owners with more than 12,000 slaves of their own.

Forget all of that, and remember – white men are all wrong and they should be ashamed of themselves. Oppression is their invention. It is unique to the Anglo-European white and no one else.

This is what I mean by a narrative of division. This is what I mean by the constant running of lies and falsehood.

You can tell me that racism still existed in the 80s, in the 90s, in the early 2000s, and I wouldn't argue with you – there's always going to be someone whose heart is full of hate – but this idea that it's perfectly normal and acceptable to just fabricate history in order to shame an entire ethnicity is on a completely different level.

There is no comparison between "those assholes over there" and an entire political body attacking people over the color of their skin. Those numbers do not add up to the same thing.

This same narrative extends to issues of violence. Conservatives don't have the right to be violent – they're "hateful bigots" that only want to threaten, extort and abuse anyone around them in order to get their way. They're nothing more than inbred, knuckle-dragging, redneck, hillbillies with no education and no capacity for thought.

Liberals though? Oh well that's different, Liberals can hurt anybody who offends them because it's some form of "attack" against their person whenever anybody disagrees with them on an issue – so their violence is always justified – while the violence of others is always condemned.

Just look at the summer of 2020 and the riots which shook the nation that year. The "BLM Riots" broke out across the country in the aftermath of the George Floyd incident in Minneapolis, Minnesota. Democrats used this as a mechanism to spur on the mass rioting, mass looting and mass destruction which lasted for months and totaled over two billion dollars in damages – not to mention the deaths and serious injuries of over a thousand people – law enforcement officers and civilians included. I watched the news each night as smug Left-wing anchors touted the riots as "peaceful acts of civil protest."

I watched the footage of Democrat leaders and civil activists standing in the streets, calling the rioters "soldiers" and telling them to "keep on marching and keep on burning."

The carnage and chaos hearkened back to the Los Angeles riots of 1992, and they justified this devastation by calling it "righteous" while they used it to denounce the principles of law and order. Liberals utilized this as a platform for continued racial division and a destabilizing of the American government. They called for a mass "defunding" of the police and pushed this narrative that officers of the law were not people – and that they were an institution designed to shackle and oppress minorities.

In the upcoming elections of that same year in 2020, the nation sat back and watched as clear signs of election interference took place across the country. Mass ballot harvesting, double and triple ballot entries from multiple municipalities. Mass ballots addressed to vacant lots, empty fields or abandoned buildings. Boarding of windows at ballot centers and additional ballots brought in backpacks and suitcases. Thousands of ballots were missing, only to turn up in ditches after the election. The unprecedented hold on counting ballots during the night before starting up again within hours. Broken water pipes that never malfunctioned and the use of electronic voting machines with a high concern for compromised integrity.

You don't have to believe that Donald Trump somehow secretly won the election – but the narrative dictated that this was, and I quote: "The safest and most secure election in American history."

They ran warnings on Twitter, Facebook, YouTube and the nightly news – everywhere you looked there was a big fat message insisting that there could never be any issue whatsoever with the voting process or the counting of ballots involved in the 2020 election. Anyone who so much as asked a question had their videos removed from social media platforms and were censored online – even today those disclaimer messages still appear on anything questioning the events which took place.

They denounced Republicans and Conservatives as conspiracy theorists and as fascists who sought an end to democracy. They vilified us on the news and in Congress, saying that we wanted to overthrow the U.S. government in a hostile takeover.

They used the truly unfortunate events of January 6th to incite violence against whites and Conservatives. They used it to persecute Donald Trump as some kind of third-world dictator – in spite of the fact that he called for "peaceful protests" and in spite of the fact that his office held every legal right granted to him by the Constitution to question the integrity of the election.

They called the storming of the U.S. Capitol Building a "siege" and an "open insurrection." They had the audacity to compare what happened on the 6th of January to Nazi Germany and the infamous atrocity of the Night of Broken Glass.

Liberals have leveraged this incident to persecute, harass and criminally charge peaceful protesters that had arrived earlier in the day and attended the rally, but left and gone home before all of the chaos broke out.

No I am not in favor of those assholes who stormed into the Capitol and broke the law – but to hear a Democrat say it you would think that there were tanks and missiles and artillery fire taking place in the streets of Washington. Some Democrats even took to social media to tell of their daring exploits in surviving the "attempted coup" with one mentioning that she was trapped inside of a bathroom with a man who tried to rape and kill her – except that she wasn't actually anywhere near the rioting and that never happened because she was caught on security tapes in a different location at the time.

If they do something outlandishly wicked, it's justified. If we do something wrong at all, it's the rise of the Fourth Reich.

That's the narrative.

Total and complete control over the minds and bodies of U.S. citizens. They used this tactic during the pandemic too, and everybody fell right into it.

Towards the end of 2019 and the beginning of 2020 I watched as the entire world started flipping on its axis over the prospect of COVID-19; and as the year went on just about every single person that I knew, watched or listened to had completely lost their minds due to CoronaVirus.

Media corporations whipped themselves into an absolute frenzy over it – and both sides of the political aisle dug their heels in and waged a propaganda war over the issue.

The whole thing was a complete shit-show.

Somebody on the Left dug up a "doctor" by the name of Anthony Fauci, a man with so little medical knowledge that he wouldn't know an elbow from a big toe – and there he was on TV every night, telling us just how bad this virus was. Just how bad the effects were going to be, how basically it was the end of the world – and that all we had to do was surrender our independence over to the government in order to survive it.

At first he suggested that we all wear masks to protect ourselves from airborne contagions, and that everyone adhere to the 6-foot rule of "social distancing." Then he suggested wearing two masks, just to be safe. Finally the man suggested wearing three masks – even in your car while driving. Before the end he had gone so far as to suggest wearing masks at all times, including in your own home.

News reports flooded in daily with reports of an ever increasing death toll due to the virus. That this new and never-before-seen thing was truly the herald of the end times, as numbers ranged into the hundreds, then the thousands and tens of thousands, the hundreds of thousands – even into the millions – and then back down into the thousands again.

Republicans wanted to issue a fifteen day shutdown in order to properly deal with the pandemic. "Fifteen days to flatten the curve!" They said – but the Democrats said "No, that's not good enough." And so the nation began shutting down, and before anybody knew it, fifteen days had come and gone.

Business after business closed its doors and laid off employees. Those who could work from home started doing so – but the others were simply out of a job. Everything came to a complete stand still as the great national lock-down set in. We were now in quarantine.

Of course nobody seemed to truly grasp the concept that if no one is able to go out and work, then eventually you run out of food and water and toilet paper – so people still had to go and work. I had to go and work – in fact the entire thing basically didn't affect me at all, except that I didn't have to deal with as many people during my day so if anything it was a bonus.

Republicans kept trying to say that we need to get things back to normal, but the Democrats kept insisting that we maintain the lock-down for the "common good."

No more going out in public without wearing a mask – in fact several states introduced a mask mandate policy that penalized anyone seen in public without one. Except for Democrat politicians who frequently went out without wearing masks, such as Dianne Feinstein, a woman who actively lobbied to block relief aid for non-mandated states, and also went to the airport and then in fact to Congress without wearing a mask.

No more social gatherings of any kind during the pandemic – except for Democrat elites in California, such as Gavin Newsom and prominent Left-wing lobbyists, who were repeatedly caught on camera either at fine-dining restaurants or jet-setting off to other parts of the country to host fundraisers. Eric Garcetti threatened "none-essential" California businesses that refused to close their doors during the pandemic with legal action against them by the state – and to have their water and power forcibly shut off if they did not comply – but it didn't stop him from attending Black Lives Matter rallies, and going maskless at that.

Chris Cuomo called the citizens of New York "fools" for having the sheer audacity to go out in public without masks, calling into question their sense of public duty as well as their general intelligence. He of course was free to go from vacation home to vacation home at will, and ignore his state's "Shelter in Place Order." Of course when he did ultimately contract COVID, he said that nobody else had the right to criticize him or his decisions.

You even had Lori Lightfoot caught going out to the hair salon, which she then defended as an "essential service." Not to mention Nancy Pelosi and literally any of the things that she did during the "pandemic." She also went maskless to a hair salon – and I even remember one time that she stood there eating expensive ice cream in front of what looked like a five-figure refrigerator and basically said that other people really didn't need COVID relief funds from the government.

Either way, the list of hypocrisies goes on.

"Rules for Thee, but not for me" became a common slogan as the general "Do as I say, not as I do" behavior set in on the Left.

But what about on the Right? Oh you were demonized if you went out in public without a mask as a Conservative. Republicans were frequently referred to as "murderers" and "terrorists" whenever they didn't wear masks or adhere to social distancing. They were also called "racists" for doing it, which I never understood – but at one point during the "pandemic" high ranking health officials in the White House did say that racism was a greater social health crisis than COVID so, who am I to really say.

Public shaming became a huge part of the "pandemic" that actual city officials across multiple countries instituted a "Snitching Hotline." I'll reference back to Eric Garcetti who famously said: "Snitches get... Rewards!"

Talk about a fiasco.

Of course I also witnessed a lot of Republicans play into this bullshit. As the Left overreached and oppressed the masses, some Conservatives on the Right took to this stupid idea of "course correction" by implying that COVID didn't actually exist. That it was some kind of elaborate hoax.

I always viewed COVID as this: If you wanted to get the vaccination, then get it. If you didn't want to get it, then don't. I've never been vaccinated for COVID-19 and I don't ever intend to be. I have never contracted it, but all of my vaccinated friends have come down with it multiple times.

I felt the same way about masks. I never wore one, unless it was the policy of whatever building I went into – but I never made fun of anybody else who wanted to wear one. Except maybe the people who wore the masks in their own cars or in their house – that was moronic.

The point being that COVID-19 isn't "fake" and it's certainly not a "hoax." It's very real – but it's also not the literal "end of the world." These two things can be true at the same time – they aren't mutually exclusive to one another.

The entire thing reminded me of a Fox News anchor – I can't recall his name – but he spoke up about the idiocy of political narratives during the Ebola crisis. I can't remember the exact quote that he made, but essentially what he said is that: "The people in power want Ebola to be mundane. They want it to be considered a non-issue so that it doesn't make their administration look weak. The people who aren't in power want everyone to go crazy and be scared out of their minds so that they lose faith in the current government. Both of these are stupid and they're wrong – Ebola is not the end of the world, but it is also a very serious issue."

I wish I could remember his name because that took some balls and he deserves credit for it. But that's what I think frustrates me so much about modern politics and my own side of the isle. They're not used to playing the games that Democrats play, and so whenever they do – they do it badly.

They make a knee-jerk reaction and just jump to the opposite extreme and it never really works. It doesn't work because they don't have the media narrative – and so Democrats are always able to spin those bad decisions into a new narrative that denounces everything Republicans do. It's infuriating.

Getting away from politicians and tackling the issue of the public during COVID, you also have the political narrative of the social elite. Celebrities and rock stars shaming the "little man" into cooperating with unjust civil policies and trying desperately to draw "connections" between their plight and ours.

Imagine how little self-awareness someone has to have in order to sit there as a Hollywood actor and stream yourself "crying" to the masses of people about loneliness while everybody else is being shamed into staying home. Imagine being a multi-millionaire platinum album pop star sitting in your bathtub and telling people that we're all "equal" now.

Imagine recording yourself and others singing fucking Imagine in your fancy mansions and surrounded by money while all of the little people are out their losing their parents and grandparents because of political mismanagement of hospitals and care facilities by your side of the political isle.

The entire thing turned into this far-Left "poor me" affair in regards to the social elite, at the complete expense of all the regular people that were just trying to survive in a world gone mad. It made me sick to my stomach – I'm still sick just thinking about it. The complete and total disconnection from reality which took place and is still taking place just baffles me to no end.

Democrats continued to capitalize on the aftermath of COVID by asserting that Joe Biden had created more jobs than any other president in history. People returning to their old jobs that you forced them to leave is not the same as creating "new" jobs and lowering unemployment – but much like Obama blamed Bush for everything that went wrong in his administration, Biden took credit for everything that Trump succeeded in during his.

They touted his "booming" economy and wasted no time in telling everyone what a great job he was doing – except that the economy was in shambles and it's still in shambles to this day. You can't break away from it. Emergency tax cuts have been called in numerous states because the price of gas with full taxes still in place is sitting at almost $6 a gallon. Even with the tax cuts it's nearly $4 a gallon.

Grocery stores are almost always running on empty and whenever they do have items for sale they are massively overpriced because of just how bad everything has gotten. Half of the people I know don't even shop at grocery stores anymore, they go to dollar stores and live off of potted meats and off-brand breads – and it's still too expensive – but don't let that stop CNN from listing articles about how "strong Biden's economy actually is!"

Speaking of Biden, of course, you cannot talk about political narratives without mentioning the countless and continued controversies surrounding his family – and especially his son Hunter – who has been hidden and protected by every Left-wing media outlet, big or small that you could possibly name.

They covered up the "Hunter Biden Laptop" prior to the 2020 election and only allowed the news to really circulate just after the inauguration of Biden into the White House. Hunter received millions of dollars from Russia while his father was the Vice-President. Biden leveraged his political clout with the Ukraine to have the man investigating him fired in exchange for payments to the country. Biden and Hunter have been caught receiving tens of millions from China both during his tenure as Vice-President and even now as the current "President." The investigations however, keep getting held up by the Senate.

Seemingly nobody wants to talk about it like it's a real issue. There is serious corruption in Washington, and the masses just turn a blind eye to it – because that's what the narrative tells them to do. It tells them that everything's fine, that nothing is going wrong. There is no corruption, there is no economic crisis.

Life is "perfect."

I have news for you – life isn't perfect. It's miserable.

Every day feels like waking up inside of an M. C. Escher painting where everything's been flipped upside down and makes no sense.

These lies and changing of attitudes even trickle down to a re-defining of the fundamental building blocks of American life. The Christians and Jews and other institutions of religion are somehow "hate mongers" and "extremists." This idea that America is not a spiritual nation – not a Christian nation – and that it was not founded on Judeo-Christian values.

I hear more and more people saying that these ideas of morality have no place in America – that they have never had a place in America – as the political Left continues to assault and assail the idea of worship and spirituality. They'll say that the Founding Fathers weren't Christians and that our nation has none of these things baked into its DNA.

While it is true that our Founding Fathers were mostly secular, with only a few of them being Christians themselves – their sense of moral compass is that of the Judeo-Christian.

All of those things which tell us in society that rape and murder are wrong – those are ideas built on Jewish and Christian morality. You can't claim "moral relativism" when you have been raised in a society which believed in those sets of morals.

Look back at civilizations throughout history. Theft? Almost universally condemned – rape? Not so much. Murder? If the guy wasn't important, it often didn't matter.

There's still societies in the world to this day that don't have an issue with rape or sexual assault. These things became "bad" within the context of a moral compass, only once the Jews and Christians started showing up. That isn't to say that there's never been another society outside the influences of Judaism and Christianity that held values similar to these – but our values specifically come from these influences.

All of those things that tell you that you shouldn't lie and you shouldn't cheat and you shouldn't harm others – those are Judeo-Christian ethics and you do not have to be a practitioner or believer in order to recognize them – so this growing narrative that our nation was not built on these principles is outlandish and terrifying.

It's terrifying because these narratives – these accepted trains of thought – they only work to undermine the structure of our nation and they're spreading like a plague.

I've been told by some of the more "liberal-minded" acquaintances of mine, that all of these things I'm complaining about aren't real. That it's just smoke – it's just "noise" stemming from a very vocal minority of the Liberal demographic.

They've told me that all of these things which I am addressing in this book are a product of the "fringe" and that the vast majority of Liberals and Democrats don't buy into this radical line of thinking or rhetoric.

To that I would like to ask you – to ask anyone who feels this same way – at what point does this stop being part of the fringe?

What exactly does it take for you to consider all of the things that are happening – and all of the things that have already happened – and realize that it is no longer the "fringe?" What is specifically required to take place in order for you to see these stances and actions that your party is taking as the main-stay instead of the outlier?

What more has to be done before you to realize that this "fringe" is actually the majority of your party?

That's the question I'd like to ask.

I'd like to ask it, because this stance is something that I am seeing quite a lot these days – life-long Democrats who will throw their full support behind all of these horrible and atrocious choices in the name of "Progressivism" and then turn around once the milk's gone sour and say that "Oh, well, it's not me – it's just them."

I call that cowardice. I call that being disingenuous – and worst of all I'd call it blind.

When Bill Clinton was first elected President back in 1992, he was considered to be a pretty Liberal figure in the political world. If Clinton was running for election today – he'd be considered a Moderate, if not outright viewed as a Left-leaning Republican.

That's how much your party has changed over the past three decades alone.

So don't tell me that everything happening today isn't real, and that all of this chaos and discord is only caused by some radical "fringe" movement – because it isn't. This is your party, and it is your party because you and the people like you have allowed it to become this way.

George Takei wrote a book in which he describes exactly why he has supported the Democrat party for his entire life – despite all of the terrible things that they've done – and as much as I admire the man it truly made me so sad to read the things he had to say. They way he defended every action in the name of Liberalism – they way he insisted that somehow all of it was worth it – because by continuing to vote for them he was in reality fighting for change from the inside. Fighting for things to be better.

He touted the powers and virtues of the American vote – which is true and to be respected – but he pleaded for all of his readers to continuously vote for the Democrats, no matter what, because that would be the only way to bring change.

That's not how you use your vote to bring about change – you turn away from the things that are wrong and stop supporting them if you want change. True change – positive change – not the deepening of power and corruption, or the entrenching of radicalized ideologies.

I admire Takei's passion, and I admire the elegance in which he wrote – because the man is far more eloquent and well-spoken than I could ever be – but his blind faith and naivety on the matter speaks a lot for itself.

Everything that he wrote on the matter reminded me of someone else I know, who once preached to me about the virtues of optimism – of always looking for the optimistic view in regards to everything.

The problem with his logic, I told him, is that: "There's a very fine line between blind optimism and naivety – and an even finer line between naivety and ignorance."

Case in point – one of the best pieces of advice that I was ever given growing up came from an old black man that worked in mining. We were all sitting around on break, shooting the shit – when the topic of politics came up. The old man didn't flinch, didn't shudder a single hair on his bushy white beard. He said: "I love the Republican party. I've loved 'em for the past fifty years of my life."

Down here most black folks are staunch Democrats, and the younger guys all laughed at him. I was one of only two white boys there, and I was kind of shocked to see him being so openly Conservative – so I asked him: "Why?"

He told me this: "The Democrat party has always been the party of the poor, and the Republican party has always been the party of the rich. It seems to make sense to me, that if the Republicans really are the Rich-Man's party – then it is in their best interest to make you money. Conversely, if the Democrats really are the Poor-Man's party – then it is in their best interest to keep you broke.

I wouldn't say that the Republicans have ever made me into a rich, rich man – I'm never going to be a millionaire – but the Democrats, for as long as I've lived, have always worked their hardest to make me poor. At some point I realized that I was just a number to them – and that every time a Republican made it into that big White House, I was able to do just a little bit better than I ever did before."

That's what he told me – and went on to say that he'd saved enough to retire in the next year or so. I hope he was able to, I'm not too sure what's happened to him in all of this economic strife.

That's why blind optimism is so dangerous. That's why buying into your own rhetoric is so destructive. It's basically akin to "getting high on your own supply." It makes you totally ignorant to everything going on around you – and before you know it, you're just another sheep who is following the herd.

But nobody cares – or at least nobody seems to care – because they've been told not to. They've been told a narrative, fed a line – and they believe it. Even if they don't completely believe it, I think a lot of people are simply too tired, too hungry and too worn down to try and say anything.

I could sit here and try to list everything that's ever been said until my fingers fall off – but the chapter would never end, and I'd never be able to move on to other things.

I will however close out with this...

I've watched Republicans and Democrats – Conservatives and Liberals – sit down at the table and try to talk to one another. I've watched a lot of them, from professional political actors all the way down to the average, every-day citizen – and the results are almost universally the same. People on the Right understand Liberal talking points – but people on the Left have no idea what a Conservative stands for.

They can't describe the party, or the person, their general or individual beliefs, without ever resorting to petty insults, misdirection and question-dodging.

They'll either lock up and freeze, throw a fit and have a temper tantrum – or simply make a wild and outlandish claim. It's very rare to hear one openly admit that they have no idea what a Republican stands for – because the vast majority of them have never been taught what Republicans stand for.

I understand what Leftists believe in – I disagree with it - but I understand it. Liberals on the other hand cannot say the same. They have no idea what Conservatives believe in – and they do not care.

Look at Donald Trump, I mean… just look at him. In the 80s he was sort of a "Media Darling" in his own way. Liberals adored Trump – they thought he was fantastic. They used to ask him "When are you going to be running for President? Do you think that you'll ever be running for President?" They loved the man. When he finally announced that he'd be running on the Republican ticket however – everything suddenly changed.

Seemingly overnight Trump became known as a "racist" and a "bigot" and a "misogynist." He went from being an "Outstanding Titan of Industry" to being a "Filthy Capitalist Oligarch."

I don't think a man who is racist goes out of his way to help up and coming black artists in the music industry with their personal finances, or achieve the lowest unemployment rate for minorities in the history of our country.

In spite of being a bit of a playboy, I don't think that a misogynist goes out of his way to try and save an underage girl from people like Jeffry Epstein. In fact I'd argue that any man who fits the bill of misogyny wouldn't take extra precautions to assure the safety of their female employees at all.

I don't think a man who is xenophobic becomes the first American President in history to step into North Korea. To recognize Jerusalem as the capital of Israel, or to go and pray at the Western Wall.

Liberals will scream out their condemnation and hatred for President Trump, denouncing him as this thing or that thing until they're blue in the face – but when you ask them to give you a single example of one thing he did, or one thing he said – they can't. They can't answer the question because they do not have an answer.

They hate him… just because they hate him.

You can say that he's vulgar or you can call him loud, you can call him crass. You can just flat out say that you don't like the man's attitude – but nobody seems to have an actual reason for hating him.

They just "do."

It's the literal manifestation of "orange man bad!" They spurn him and have nothing but contempt for him – but none of them can give you a legitimate reason as to "why." None of them can actually point to anything specific that he's done – because there isn't anything specific that he's done. There isn't any actual reasoning that they have – only a narrative that they follow because they have all been told to follow it.

I'm not trying to convince anybody into loving or even liking Donald Trump – I'm just pointing out the facts that this is all a part of the narrative.

I've watched celebrities who have met him, getting interviewed and being asked stupid questions like: "Does he really talk like that?" Talk like what? A New Yorker? Yeah, he does – he's from New York.

I live in the South, most yankees sound like that to me – especially the ones from New York. What do you mean "does he talk like that" he's not an alien – but that's how they treat him. They talk about him as if he's somehow weird or different or unnatural. The only thing unnatural about Trump is his tan – and even that's not the worst one I've ever seen.

This is the narrative of division. The running theme that is designed to undermine and divide. Designed to dictate and control.

Everything you do. Everything you say. Everything you think.

These are the reasons that I cannot condone the Democrats. These are the reasons that I cannot abide the Liberals. Because the only thing in life they want is to see me dancing like some puppet on a string.

Well I am not a puppet – and my strings have all been broken.

Chapter XX: Nickels and Dimes

One of the most frustrating, and frankly infuriating things about the entire concept of Socialism, is the blanket deception which it throws over anything and everything that it touches. It is so utterly astonishing, and it never ceases to amaze me how just so many people, from so many places, can so ignorantly and blindly buy into the lies of socialist rhetoric.

These people – these Governing bodies – seek only to subvert your freedoms and personal liberties.

They push and impose the most wicked and atrocious of economic policies – and will tell you with a smile on their face that it's all for your own good. And you believe them. You believe in their twisted words and hollow promises as they coil around you like a serpent, constricting every part of your life and forcing you to become wholly reliant upon them in the process.

"But the Government is just trying to step in and lend you a helping hand," they say. No, the Government is trying to make you dependent upon it in order to survive. In order to simply exist, and maintain any level of personal functionality.

I won't swear with my hand on the Bible when it comes to how every country functions inside of a socialized-healthcare environment, but I know for a fact that my friends living in states that offer State Socialized Healthcare packages, have to struggle and suffer through the most outrageous restrictions imaginable when it comes to being taken care of. Like my friend up in Pennsylvania – she's on their state officiated healthcare program, and it takes her weeks just to her general practitioner.

Local clinics, doctor's offices and general hospitals all require an outlandish waiting period just to be seen – and God forbid that she needs to see a specialist, because in order to do so she has to first visit with her family doctor so that she can be referred, get the referral bounced back to the insurance program – and then get an appointment to see whoever it is that she needs to, several months in advance.

And she has to go through this entire ordeal every single time with absolutely no guarantee of success with her visit. If whatever specialist she went to wasn't able to help her, they bounce her right back to the general practitioner to get another referral, and wait another few months to see whichever specialist the first one recommended.

Maybe you could argue that it's just "America doing it wrong," but I don't really think so.

I have several friends who are Canadian, and one of them very recently had to go through an incredibly difficult ordeal when his mother-in-law got into an accident and had her eyeball popped halfway out of the socket. The family waited in a practically abandoned emergency room for hours, before being told they had to travel over two hours away to another hospital – only for them to give her some medication and an eye-patch, and set an appointment some three-months later for her to finally be treated.

They didn't even stick this woman's eye back in her face.

In Canada alone there has been a recent study suggesting that some 17,000 Canadian citizens died last year just waiting to have their operation, their surgery, their procedure – sometimes even just waiting for a goddamn diagnosis. This same study also suggests that the number is probably much higher, and that it's been a well-known and growing issue for years.

Then of course you have the numerous cases of people being killed off in socialized countries simply because the cost of treating them lands on the government, and not the individual.

Cases like Evans, like Fixsler, like Gregory in England – or cases like McKitty, Bittersbee and Maraachli in Canada – if you bother to look into this issue and read about it, you'll find case after case where there families are torn apart on the order of state officials and court ordered mandates.

Some of these cases even saw U.S. doctors calling for a transfer from overseas because they believed there was still some hope when the socialized system no longer cared.

That, to me, is monstrous. It's deplorable and pathetic.

Yes I do have to pay money for my healthcare, but if I have to see my doctor I just go into the office and sit down. If I have to make an appointment to see a specialist, it's usually for the very next week – maybe two weeks at most if it's not an emergency.

But speaking about money and paying for healthcare, the same people that advocate for this kind of society often preach the promise of "free" healthcare under a socialized system, and scream words of condemnation against the institution and practices of medicine where you are required to pay out-of-pocket – and people actually believe it.

I hear the same jabs and snide remarks all the time – either from people in foreign countries attempting to boast of their "superior" medical practices – or from other Americans trying to hold up these same foreign countries as an example of why we should be changing to the socialized system.

Now to be completely fair, it is true that they do not walk into a doctor's office like you or I and hand over $125 just to be seen – but it is also true that they are taxed beyond reason and that their average cost of living has risen through the roof.

At the time of writing this, I am able to walk into a grocery store and purchase a cab bottom round steak – which is a humble cut of meat, yet still very filling and still very flavorful – for the modest sum of around $3.79 American.

This single cut alone may not feed a King or his family – but paired with a rustic baked potato and a little salad, it makes for more than a satisfying meal.

That same cut of meat, in a comparatively rural part of Canada, costs an average price of around $11.98.

A gallon of milk costs around $1.67, and in Canada it is approximately $6.30.

That is not "free" healthcare. You *are* paying for it, each and every time you make a purchase of any product in these countries – you are paying for it.

If you really wanted to push for a middle-ground on the issue, you might look at my own state of Georgia, which offers Indigent Care through the state trust fund. Individuals that are able to pay for medical services are still required to do so – while those who are financially unable are either treated at no cost, or have the overall cost of their treatments dramatically reduced to be more affordable.

Now don't get me wrong, it is true that American healthcare is expensive – and frankly, it's a lot more expensive than it really needs to be

– but I don't have to pay for it unless I am sick. I do not have to pay for a service unless I am actively making use of it.

And that's exactly what it is – it's a service, just like any other. That is the way it's supposed to work, and that is the way in which it should be working everywhere across the country.

Inflation is another major issue surrounding the socialist movement in America. It's a critical problem that has grown exponentially over the years and if not treated soon, it's going to cause a complete financial and economic collapse of the nation.

But how exactly does one get on top of it?

You often hear Capitalist criticizers insist that the idea of low-taxes and high income are the chief causes of inflation – and that in order to battle inflation we have to raise taxes, raise minimum wage, socialize the economy and generally mangle the financial stability of the nation.

This idea is completely absurd.

I just went to Google out of sheer curiosity and typed in "ways to fight inflation" and that search engine kicked back seven different search results all saying the same thing: You fight inflation by raising wages, raising taxes and reducing spending. Anything speaking to the contrary was pushed further down the list.

That is where we have gotten to in this country – where misinformation is promoted while intelligent thought is hidden away.

While it is true that having too much money circulating throughout the system will cause the value of our currency to depreciate over time – the balancing of an effective economy negates this problem by ensuring that not only are prices staying down due to consistent business – but citizens are also able to reserve money in their savings should the economy take a bad turn.

Raising taxes doesn't help to battle inflation – it causes poverty, reduces spending, and forces prices to rise. Raising the minimum wage doesn't help to battle inflation – because it causes unemployment, takes more money out of the economy, and also causes the prices to go up.

When prices go up, the value of the dollar goes down. That *is* inflation.

Let's say for the sake of example, that in your town there is a small local business – maybe a restaurant. That business is owned by Bob, and

Bob employs three workers to help effectively run his establishment. One in the back that cooks on the grill, and two servers out front waiting on customers.

Let's keep the number round for the sake of simplicity, so we'll say that Bob pays each employee $5.00 an hour – which is what I made when I first started working – and we'll also say that the restaurant is open from 10:00am until 10:00pm for a total of twelve hours a day.

That's $60 a day, and we'll say that Bob is fairly religious, so he isn't open on Sundays – which comes out to $360 a week – and rounding months down into four weeks, that's ultimately $1,440 a month.

For the sake of simplicity we can just assume that all of those extra days we're leaving off are due to family emergencies, sick days, violent weather or otherwise unforeseen events – and seeing as he's closed on Sundays, I'll also assume that he's closed for Christmas and Easter, so I'll go ahead and subtract two days from the yearly total.

With all of that in mind, if Bob runs his business every week of every month, that means that he's paying each of his employees approximately $17,160 a year. Since he's got three guys working for him, that comes out to around $51,480 total in payroll – not counting any kind of bonuses.

Fifty grand isn't exactly something that most people would sneeze at – and Bob does have other expenses that come with the territory of running a business. Electrical bills, heating and air condition, plumbing, utilities – not to mention buying the produce that he sells. The beef, the lettuce, etc.

Of course Bob off-sets the cost of hiring employees and dealing with maintenance upkeep by managing his business and marketing it to the public. He keeps his prices fair and his standards of quality high in order to help assure repeat customers and a continued stream of revenue.

Once everything is said and done, Bob probably doesn't actually make that much money in profits – but he makes enough to keep a roof over his head and feed his family.

As for his workers, while yes it is true that seventeen grand isn't really a lot of money – most people working minimum wage jobs aren't living alone, and that extra level of income goes a very long way in helping with household finances. Plus, realistically, Bob is probably paying his fry cook a bit more – probably around $7.50 – and the servers are almost certainly making tips, which if you've ever worked in a restaurant you know that's where the real money is anyway.

But back to the point of the example: When taxes go up, and minimum wages get increased – Bob suddenly has a very tough decision to make.

On the one hand, he can either raise the prices of his goods to try and keep even with the changing economy – but his customers, who are also paying increased taxes, probably won't be able to justify eating at his restaurant when the $8.50 burger meal has now gone up to $12.00. After all, even if minimum wages were increased – if a person is making just over the new minimum threshold, they're not getting any more money than they already had – and so ultimately they're in the same financial position as they were before.

Now on the other hand, what he could do is decide to let one or two of his employees go, or perhaps reduce his hours of operation, or both to try and cover the cost – but then his business will likely take a sharp dive in quality – and while the prices may still be affordable, his customers no longer want to buy whatever he's offering.

If nobody is buying food, Bob goes out of business.

Raising the minimum wage does the exact same thing. The current discussion being had is about raising minimum wages to an astounding $15.00 an hour – which in the case of Bob having three employees to pay out – turns that 51,480 annual expense into a whopping $154,440.

I don't know about you, but Bob ain't got that kind of money.

So he has to cut two of his staff in order to pay a single person what he was paying all three. The same result ensues. Bob is not properly managing his business because he's spending too much time trying to make up for the loss of manpower – the quality of his services goes down, his prices are also probably going up – and ultimately Bob is forced to shut down his restaurant, rendering a total of four people unemployed in your local area.

Four more people that aren't earning money and pumping it back into the economy. Four more people that might need government aid and end up on unemployment, putting more pressure on the Welfare system and causing taxes to go even higher.

This line of thinking doesn't work. This economic practice is disastrous, it's childish to think that it's effective – it's like saying that if you've suddenly run out of money, simply "printing more" will somehow solve the problem – and it's exactly why small businesses are folding across the nation.

If you really want to talk about the horrors of inflation, then let me tell you a story: In 1938, my nanny was born on a dark and stormy night at the family farm some miles outside of Pamplin, Virginia. Ben Anson, my namesake, rode on a horse and buggy through the rain and the mud to fetch the doctor in town, and bring him back to the house. He delivered my nanny, and they paid him $15 dollars and breakfast for his trouble.

Now let's see, a single dollar in 1938 comes out to a little under $21 dollars today. $15 comes out to approximately $311 today.

When was the last time anybody saw a baby being delivered for three hundred bucks and a side of bacon?

I'd wager it hasn't been any time in recent memory. Not from an actual doctor anyway.

So what exactly do you do to fix the problem? Certainly nothing Biden or the Democrats are doing. Just look at prices in the grocery store.

I could not believe a recent CNN headline that I read which stated that "Biden's harsh economy is actually better than you think." I don't know who they're trying to convince – me or themselves.

Now I've come back to finish up my final edits on this chapter, almost a whole year later, and that steak I mentioned you could buy for around $3.79? That same cut is now on sale in the same spot, at the same store, for $7.68.

That's just over double the price in a single year.

I used to go to the Krystal over in Byron – it's somewhat like a White Castle for the folks that don't know – and every now and then I'd order their 12 Krystal Combo, which came with 12 cheeseburger sliders, two medium drinks and two medium fries – all of that for about $17.26. I hadn't been in a good long while, so I went the other night and that same meal now costs nearly $27.00 on the dime. I asked how much it would be if they left off the cheese, and they said it would be around $20 bucks. That's a *seven* dollar difference over fucking cheese.

I told them to kiss my ass and left.

If you really want to battle inflation, then you stop crippling the population with stupid financial policies and overbearing taxes so that people can actually make a decent living. The more money they earn, the more money they will spend – and the more money they spend means that prices start going down. When prices start going down then even more people will be able to afford the things they want to buy – which means that even more people will be actively helping the economy.

If you really want to battle inflation then you'll stop actively handicapping the economy by over regulating the private and industrial sectors and stifling competition within the marketplace.

All of these countries that have three telephone services, three internet providers, three TV stations, three airlines, three computer companies – their economies are in the toilet because there isn't any *competition*. America isn't doing much better, and if you asked me, it's high time to start getting a little stricter with things like monopoly laws.

It isn't rocket science.

When I was growing up, my local area had a Media Play, a Circuit City and a Best Buy. Once Media Play and Circuit City went out of business – and Best Buy became the de facto "tech" and computer store – it became the laziest, most awful, sloppy, low-quality store that you could imagine. Half of its employees don't seem to know what they have in stock – the other half doesn't seem to care – and most of the time they'll just tell you to order whatever you're looking for online anyway.

Their prices went up because they had nobody to compete with, and their quality of services went through the floor.

Not only should this discussion not be happening, but it shouldn't even be a partisan issue. During the Great Depression, Republicans voted to raise taxes in an effort to offset the country's economic crisis – and it didn't work. Republicans learned that this doesn't work – it never works – so why can't the Democrats?

The only way to battle inflation and stabilize the economy is to open up the market. Take your boot off the necks of private citizens and allow people the chance to breathe and earn money for themselves.

The government earns infinitely more sustainable revenue through the symbiotic relationship of public consumers and sales taxes than they do by forcing people into destitution.

If you really wanted to find more creative solutions to the problems of today, then you'd target businesses that are actively spitting in the face of American principles, and penalize them if they're benefiting from the various tax incentives of being an American based company, while moving the majority of their business and jobs overseas.

You'd create fines that penalize major media corporations for verifiably falsifying information to the general public. They'd maintain their "freedom of the press" by having the active choice to run whatever bogus story they wanted to – but they'd have to do it with the clear understanding that if it's provably false, they'll be making a big fat payout to the United States treasury.

That's how you acrew more revenue and help tamper down on some of the problems within society, without strangulating the majority of your population.

I'm certainly not claiming to have the answers for everything. I am not a genius or mystic and I do not know the infinite mysteries of the world – but I do know that *this*, this right here, this situation that we're dealing with – it doesn't work.

Look at Romania, look at Cuba and Venezuela, look at Russia, look at China – it's all the same. If you don't want to look that far then turn your head west and look at California. This system doesn't work.

America's economic structure is designed on and around the principles of Free-Market Capitalism and Free Enterprise Investments. Low taxes, low cost of living, high income and increased individual expenditure on goods and services are just a few of the things which afford this country its ability to maintain a stable economy, and affords the average family their ability to maintain a comfortable living. To keep money saved in case of emergencies – and to have money to spend on the things they want to spend it on.

When you do not tamper with the system – the system actually functions.

What we have now, however, is a troublesome case of riding the fence. One foot in and one foot out of the proverbial door. We are openly taxed for Medicare and still expected to buy health insurance or pay out-of-pocket at every doctors visit. Our cost of living is increasing and our expenses are getting worse – yet our income remains low, and is almost immediately swallowed by high taxes to the point that we cannot make ends meet.

One of the very first things Biden did as President, was to kill the Keystone XL Pipeline, costing thousands of workers their jobs and "forcing" oil barons to go from selling oil at $30 a barrel to $130 a barrel. Over taxed, underpaid, prices up and no money saved. Policies like these are designed only for one purpose – to crush the middle-class. Abolishing the middle-class creates a two-class society – Rich and Poor. When all you have is rich and poor, you have the poor depending on the rich and the rich getting richer off the poor.

Socialism – which is what the crowds are calling for – is a system designed specifically for taking your money and giving it to the people already in power – not to the people who need it.

Our money is taxed from us at the Federal level for a multitude of socialized programs such as Medicare, as I said, and Medicaid. We're taxed for CHIP and the ACA. We're taxed for our Social Security and for Welfare. Thanks to Obamacare we're taxed if we don't have private insurance, or otherwise don't make use of it – even if we can't make use of it because we don't qualify.

We're taxed for a bevy of educational programs – almost all of which simply lines the pockets of the Teachers Unions and does nothing for our schools – as our current state of education can attest to – and most of that tax money gets funneled back into the hands of politicians who are also sitting on the boards and committees of those various unions and organizations – taking their paycheck from our tax dollar and getting their little extra cut on the side.

Then of course you also have any number of individual State Socialized Programs which you can be taxed for, regardless of whether or not you consent or agree with where your hard earned money is going.

As Christopher Lunsford wrote in his recent hit song Rich Men North of Richmond: "Taxes ought not to pay for your bags of Fudge Rounds" - but they do.

Our tax dollars help to fund programs like SNAP which can be used to buy junk food instead of items that they really need – again putting more money not just into the hands of these companies that market and manufacture those goods – but also the politicians that stand shoulder to shoulder with the various Corporate Presidents and CEOs on the golf course.

Don't even get me started if you win the lottery in the United States.

I'll give this much to other countries – I know for a fact that if you win something like the lottery in New Zealand that you get to keep the full amount of money. I could be wrong but I think the same rule applies for Australia and Canada – but here in the States? You're taxed on lottery winnings. Again, both by State and Federal income.

Same thing for game show winnings.

I can't speak for other states in the U.S. but here in Georgia, if you've ever been in a restaurant or bar that had a jukebox or pool table? The owner is taxed on those machines under the Coin Operated Amusement Machine law. Not only are they paying licensing fees to have them in their building – but just about anything you might slip a coin or dollar bill into in the state of Georgia is considered gambling – so the Georgia Lottery Corporation comes to take a cut.

Unless those machines break down of course, then the repairs are your responsibility. I don't know if the percentages have changed over the years, but a lady I knew who used to run a bar – may she rest in peace – she told me that every month a man from the lottery came in and took 50% of whatever she made on her jukebox.

She only stopped paying on the pool table because eventually she had somebody rip the coin mechanism out of it.

Our tax dollars can go to specialized clinics and facilities that offer medical procedures that we may not agree with due to any number of religious or ethical reasons, but it doesn't matter. Several Government Officials have been ousted for having personal connections to Planned Parenthood – one whose name I forget got caught on camera gloating over how much money she was raking in.

No, I'll say it again. It doesn't matter. Not for us.

We are just the grapes being squeezed for all that we're worth – and being told to be happy about it.

And that's the great lie of Socialism.

The truth of the matter is that socialized cost, and socialized spending, does not equate to socialized profit.

Let me ask you a question: How many times has the United States Government "bailed out" a Private Sector business with tax-payer dollars?

The recent COVID-19 debacle has seen companies like Pfizer, Biontech, Moderna and Sinovac gross a net income of some approximated 90 billion dollars off the vaccine research – 30 billion of which was paid for by tax-payer money.

There is no more Free Enterprise to be found. It's simply privatized profit at socialized cost. They socialize the investment of funding and then privatize the return of that funding.

If the system were truly socialized – we should be getting our 30 billion back, as well as a percentage of all future profits from these companies for the rest of our lives.

Now that may seem, at least on the outset, to be a very small sum of money in return – especially on an individual by individual basis – but not if that procedure were followed with all tax-payer bailouts.

These are just the numbers backing Big Pharma, but what about the airlines? American, Delta and United? How about the big three auto companies, General Motors, Chrysler and Ford? How about the numerous Banks and Energy companies? These loans were paid back to the U.S. treasury – but it was our money used in the deal.

Our money which is taxed from us before we even receive our paychecks, as well as after depositing those checks in the bank and again when we draw on these checks for Social Security and in some cases even Retirement.

Hell we're even taxed on what the Government gives us for unemployment.

My mother worked an online class out of Amarillo, Texas, and she had to pay Texas State Income taxes because that's where the money was earned – and also pay Georgia State Income taxes, because that's where she's a resident – and then still has to pay Federal income taxes on top of it.

That's getting taxed three times on a single fucking paycheck.

By all rights, those loans and bailouts should be paid back to the taxpayers who were harvested like cattle to fund them in the first place – not back to the Government in a slush fund, but to us. 90 billion here, a few hundred billion there – add all of these expenditures up and before you know it, you have trillions of dollars in taxpayer money that isn't returning to the taxpayer. Why?

Because it is socialized spending, and privatized profit.

This system does not work. It is not designed to work. It is only intended to cripple and to maim – which is exactly what it's doing.

It's Marxism 101 – and it is wrong.

Socialists do not care if it's wrong. Liberals do not care if it's damaging. The overwhelming majority of voices on the Left cry out for the dissolution of Capitalism, and condemn the very notion of Free Market investiture. They rail against the wickedness and greed of Capitalist societies – and in some rare cases they aren't entirely wrong.

Capitalism is the single most effective form of economic-structure ever created by man – but it isn't perfect. Nothing is perfect.

Capitalism, much like freedom, is a very fragile thing – a thing which can be corrupted and taken advantage of by anybody with so much as a modicum of greed and ambition. Two traits which most human beings possess in spades.

No, the people crying out against the "evils" of Capitalism, are actually crying out against the evils of Materialism – and more specifically Consumerism – two concepts and issues which have less to do with pure economics, and more to do with the culture of our society.

I know that it's an issue of Consumerism, because 99.9% of "protesters" lashing out against the "wickedness" of Capitalist society, are all wearing the products of said-Capitalist society.

From their Nike sneakers and Rag & Bone jeans, to their Hanes t-shirts and Adidas hoodies that almost certainly were bought at Hot Topic or American Eagle – all the way down to their cheap Walmart makeup and gaudy jewelry that probably came from Spencer's Gifts. These people are walking billboards for Capitalism.

Consumerism is what allows Capitalism to get out of hand. It is the incessant need to buy more, and more, and more – regardless of the rights and wrongs involved.

Why can some corporations get away with jacking up their prices to unreasonable levels that nobody can truly afford? Consumerism – people will still buy the product.

Why can some corporations move overseas and manufacture their goods while utilizing child labor? Consumerism – people will still buy it regardless of how it's made.

Consumerism – especially the rampant Consumerism we have in the West today – is the sole reason that so many companies and corporations are able to get away with the things that they do. If you truly wanted to help make a difference in some company applying dirty business practices, or supplying its customers with poor-quality goods – you'd stop buying from them.

That's why it's called a "free market." You are free, to go to *another* market.

If I see an actor grandstanding on stage and abusing their celebrity social status to make an ignorant statement and sway the general public, I'm not going to support them by purchasing tickets to their movies. If a musician does the same thing, I'm not going to buy their albums.

If I see some YouTuber making videos about painting miniatures or something, and then randomly in the middle of their video go off on a politically fueled tirade, I'm not going to give them "views" by watching their content.

That is called taking a stance, and having principles.

If you truly cared about Apple using child labor to build its products, and wanted to make an active difference in the world, then you wouldn't be sitting on your ass with the latest version of the iPhone, scrolling through Twitter feeds and swiping on dating apps.

If you truly viewed Elon Musk as some kind of "Filthy Capitalist Oligarch" and wanted to put him in his place, then you wouldn't be cruising down the street in your brand new Tesla or giving him extra money by utilizing his social-media platforms.

If you truly felt outraged that video game companies such as Blizzard Entertainment, who are known to systematically abuse their employees and continuously gouge their customers with inferior quality products – then you wouldn't keep playing their games, renewing your subscriptions and buying every new Collector's Edition that they release.

That is called hypocrisy.

If you truly wanted change, then you would first look inside of your own socio-political atmosphere and get the ball rolling. If there're some 258 million-plus legal adults living inside of the United States, and half of them, around 129 million suddenly up and stopped buying a product or supporting a business – that business is going to *change*.

But these people don't really want change. They don't actually want to lose access to the things that they have – because that would be uncomfortable.

I once saw a young man shouting down Capitalist society, and when asked why he would be willing to wear the products of said-society – he claimed that he wasn't. When he was asked how he would continue to wear all of the brands and all of the bling if and when Capitalism would be shut down – he said that he'd "just go buy them."

He was so arrogant, so cocky – and had absolutely no idea what he was talking about.

A lot of Lefties want to tax the rich in order to generate more revenue – to be honest I wouldn't necessarily disagree with the idea of higher taxes for millionaires and mega-corporations – but the problem is that nobody wants to do it responsibly.

You can't just tax somebody "because they have money" that's idiotic, absurd and short sighted.

If you really wanted to get more money out of the wealthiest elites, you'd first need to create new tax brackets – not increase taxes across the board or single out one party at the very top.

You also need to widen the margins of "financial grey areas" between the brackets, because there are a lot of people out there that get hurt by accidentally earning an extra hundred dollars than they were expecting. You go over that line by just a few bucks and suddenly you're getting greased by the IRS like you're a top-earner in the next bracket up.

That's a pretty huge deal when you're talking about the difference between 12 and 22%.

Anything and everything could be done if there were reason and thought behind it

But these people don't want to stop and plan anything out. They don't want to be reasonable – they don't want to be responsible – they only want everything right now and in shades of extreme.

They aren't really going to tax the rich, because the rich are the ones pulling their strings. They aren't really going to try and push for change within major corporations, because they're already owned by all the corporations due to their own greed and avaricious nature.

Liberals don't think for themselves. They're incapable of critical thought – all they are are ants, marching to the orders of whoever tells what to do next – following along in their perfect little line, even when they walk into the water and drown.

These scrambling masses that are pushing for Socialism are only doing so because they are blind and ignorant. They are sheep being herded by the shepherds that genuinely do want to sit on top of the pile and watch everyone and everything else writhe on the ground beneath them.

That is why every time you talk to an immigrant from Cuba, an immigrant from Venezuela, an immigrant from pretty much anywhere in Eastern Europe – they will say the same thing. That they cannot believe that America is calling for Communism.

These people know exactly what happens in Socialist countries – they've seen the horrors first hand, or at the very least felt the lasting effects of it in their lives. Most of them have come here in order to get away from the devastation and chaos brought on by this ideological nightmare.

To escape this outlandish plague called Socialism that eats up and spits out everything that it touches.

I just hope their efforts weren't in vain.

Chapter XXI: Corruption of Justice

I'm going to be perfectly honest here, and just go ahead and say that I really don't know where I should begin with this subject or how exactly I should try to lay out what it is that I want to say.

I don't know if I should attempt to convey a lot of statistical information, or lean more heavily into my honest feelings and observations – it's difficult – because this issue that I want to talk about has gotten so drastically out of hand in the world we currently live in.

The issue on my mind is the death of justice.

It's an omnipresent concern which hampers every day life to an extreme degree, and I have no idea where or how to even begin talking about it. How does a person go about talking over such a broad, vast and extensive – and sometimes even abstract subject – such as "justice?"

I suppose that, first and foremost, in order to talk about justice – a person has to be able to admit to themselves that true justice does not actually exist. What is just and righteous to one person does not necessarily mean that it is just or righteous to another. It is a thing – a concept – which has to be agreed upon by society at large in order to be incorporated and effectuated throughout any given civilization.

Throughout history of course we have seen many different iterations on the concept – many different trains of thought surrounding the various theories of justice as a concept. The theory of Divine Justice, the theory of Natural Law – theories of the Social Contract – theories of a more Utilitarian approach.

The theories and ideas behind "justice" are as great and many as there are people on this planet – but the one constant to a concept such as justice is that it must be concrete in order to be effective.

This agreed upon set of standards is the basic foundation for any form of law and order – but for law and order to be effective, it has to mean something. You can't just say "we're going to have X, Y and Z" and then expect X, Y and Z to take care of themselves – you have to maintain it.

Like so many things I have written about over the course of this book – justice is a living and breathing thing that demands constant attention. It requires maintenance and upkeep. It requires commitment – not just from the people who are tasked with upholding the law – but also by the societies which have put those laws into place.

What we so often see today is the complete and utter breakdown of those laws and the deterioration of their effectiveness within society, as the current culture bends and sways with the changing of opinions and whims.

The "Free World" is a place in which the principles and ideals surrounding the Freedom of Speech exist as a form of civil rights and personal liberty – but contradictory laws such as "Hate Speech" have been put in place which effectively counteracts the ability for individuals to have their voices freely heard.

I think we can all agree that if someone is screaming "I'm going to kill you, you cock sucking faggot!" while they are aggressively brandishing a knife – that is hate speech and the attempt to harm or cause harm is quite evident through the context of this person's actions. The problem is that it often gets conflated with incredibly mundane things such as sitting in your car and singing along with the music.

Songs like Straight Outta Compton, which have lyrics such as: "Straight outta Compton, another crazy ass nigga. More punks I smoke, yo, my rep gets bigger. I'm a bad motherfucker and you know this. But the pussy ass niggas don't show this"

Now, that is not a song that I wrote – but it is a song which exists – does that make me a hateful person to repeat the lines of this song? I would say no – but many people would say yes. In fact, many people would go another step further and suggest that I am a racist for simply "thinking" the words that are being said within the context of this song.

You might say to yourself "Well that's absurd, it's a song – you cannot possibly conflate the idea of a person repeating its lyrics with a person engaging in hate speech" but you'd be wrong. I'd agree with you – but quite a lot of people would not – and even more disturbingly, quite a lot of laws would not.

Back in 2018 there were over 3,300 people arrested and criminally charged in the United Kingdom for violating "hate speech" laws while posting online to social media. One case that I will point out – being the case of Chelsea Russel – is when a nineteen year old girl in Liverpool posted the lyrics from a rap song to her Instagram account which contained a racial slur.

Nobody needs a "good reason" to post the lyrics of a song online – but in her case, Chelsea posted this snippet specifically to pay tribute to a thirteen year old boy whom she knew who had died in a car accident.

Thankfully in Russel's case, I do believe her conviction was able to be overturned through the court of appeals – but the point stands that it never should have happened in the first place – not to mention the question of how many other similar convictions have there been which weren't overturned in court?

Just to put this in perspective mind you, in the same year of 2018 only 400 some-odd people were arrested in Russia for posting to their social media profiles. When Russia has a more lenient policy surrounding the topic of "Free Speech" than you do – something has gone terribly wrong.

In our world – the "free" world – the Western world, many of the most fundamental laws which we have grown to accept as "the norm" were created through the application of time, attention, and dedication to the understanding of those laws and the ways in which they would impact the general public. The problem is that many of them have either become outdated, or simply been painted over.

A huge smattering of new laws have been created over the course of the past few decades and most of them were not built with the same level of care or consideration as the ones which came before them – resulting in a huge, confusing mess of a legal system that has become ridiculously overly complicated and completely ineffective.

I'll walk you through a couple of examples.

Let's look at the Anti-Discrimination Laws for instance: Anti-Discrimination Laws exist to prevent anyone from discriminating against another person on the basis of their race, sex, orientation, disability or mental illness.

These laws have not been very well thought out.

First and foremost, in order to discuss the issues of "discrimination" we have to understand what discrimination means – and what discrimination means is the ability to judge based on the recognition and understanding of a person, object or behavior as it appears to you.

Modern society would dictate to you that discrimination under any circumstances is wrong and cannot be tolerated. The problem with that logic is that discrimination is not "wrong," it's normal.

In fact not only is discrimination perfectly normal – it's a virtual necessity of life.

If you are a parent and you have ever needed go out for the evening in order to attend some kind of late-night function for work or answer an emergency call – or even just take a night for yourself and the spouse to get a little quality time together – you've probably had to find some kind of babysitter to watch your children.

Not everybody has the luxury of close friends or family to watch their kids, so you may have to put your faith in a total stranger by either asking the neighbors or, assuming you've had enough advanced notice, placing an advert in the hopes that somebody will apply for the job.

Now let's say you have two potential prospects for the person you are going to trust with the safety of both your children and your home. You can either choose the homeless looking man with a teardrop tattoo who looks like he's just recently gotten out of prison – or you can choose the perky, bouncy high school cheerleader who looks like she's on her way to winning "Prom Queen" this year.

Which one of these two people are you realistically going to pick? The prom queen might spend the whole evening talking on the phone to Bradley or Jennifer while the kids watch movies – but the other guy has a much higher chance of robbing, raping and killing your kids.

That is discrimination – you have just discriminated against this man based on his appearance – but it's perfectly normal, because assuming that you're not literally insane, there's no way in hell you would ever choose him over the girl.

It's also not just a case of discriminating based on appearances. Numerous studies and statistics have shown that homosexual men are far more likely to engage in predatory acts of child molestation than heterosexual men – but that men in general are also far more likely to engage in the act of child molestation than women. In fact with specific regards to male vs female and engaging in the act of molestation – the ratio is approximately 80% male to 20% female.

Which, by the way, is exactly why when you are looking at the ratio of men and women actively working as professional babysitters – roughly 97% are women and only 3% are men.

This isn't to say that every man you know is going to rape your child. It isn't to say that only the gay men you know are going to rape your children – and it is certainly not to say that women are somehow "incapable" of doing it at all – but I am pointing out the general law of averages. These statistics are real, whether you like them or not – and based on these statistics alone you have several fundamental reasons to discriminate based on both sex and sexual orientation in regards to your children.

The safety of your family is not something that most people want to gamble with.

But all of this of course is just sex and orientation – what about disabilities and mental disorders? I think these sort of answers themselves to be honest. If I'm going to look for someone to watch my kids, I need to know that they are physically able to go up and down stairs or rush outside in case of a fire, a burglary, or even just one of the little tykes slipping out the front door.

You might be the sweetest, kindest, more humble and respectable person in the world – but I'm probably not going to hire you to watch over my kids if you're a paraplegic person stuck in a wheelchair.

I'm also not going to trust you to watch over my children if you're some kind of sociopath or psychopath. I'm not going to hire a person who is schizophrenic or has multiple personality disorder – because these are my children and I need to be able to trust completely in the mental stability of whoever it is that I'm allowing to watch over them.

If you're the kind of person who is so disconnected from reality that you can't even figure out your own pronouns – I'm not going to hire you – I'm not going to take that gamble.

This is why discrimination isn't a "bad" thing. People have to be able to discriminate between things in life in order to make an informed decision.

If you don't like the human element of my example, then let's just look at the grocery store. Have you chosen between two different watermelons or cantaloupes? Maybe one bunch of bananas over the other? That's discrimination. When you're thumping the melon or checking its rind – when you're picking the greener bananas over the spotted ones because you know they'll last longer – you are discriminating. You are making an active choice between this thing or that thing, based solely on what you perceive to have a higher quality, or higher value.

You wouldn't hire a man with no arms to come and move your furniture.

But let's talk about how laws can overlap one another and turn life into one big mess. Let's say that you are a private business owner in America – you are granted the constitutional right to refuse service to any customer, for any reason. Anti-Discrimination laws contradict this however by adding the caveat that no service may be refused on any grounds of discrimination.

Well, this gets kind of tricky now doesn't it? If you run a bar and you're serving alcohol but a pregnant woman walks in and demands a drink –

what do you do? If you refuse her service because she is pregnant, you're discriminating against her based on a medical condition – but if you give her the drink, you are now aiding and abetting in the act of fetal abuse – which of course is against the law.

If you don't serve her the drink, you'll be at a probable risk of losing your liquor license, paying a hefty fine – not to mention the lawsuits – and possibly even lose your entire business.

If you do serve her and that woman loses her baby because of it – depending on what State you're in and how hard that Judge throws the book at you – you may be charged with a homicide conviction.

That is a great big rock and a very hard place for someone to find themselves in. There is absolutely no reason on earth that small businesses which serve their local communities should ever be placed into those kinds of positions by the American legal system – but they are – and it happens a lot more than you might think.

If you're a Christian and you're running a bakery, but a gay couple walks in and asks for a "wedding" cake – you have the legal right to refuse them based on your religious beliefs. Except that by refusing them you are now discriminating against them based on their sexual orientation – but if you're forced by law to make the cake, then you yourself have just been discriminated against based on your religion.

In fact this exact scenario played out in the early 2010s I believe, and the court did rule against the bakery – though ultimately I think it was able to be overturned in the Supreme Court – but that overturning would not have taken place for several years after the initial trial.

The point being that it all gets very, very, messy – and in reality it doesn't "need" to be messy.

Anti-Discrimination laws are wrong on a fundamental level because not only is their creation driven by emotions – but also because they are incredibly shortsighted in practice. Laws such as these restrict the freedoms and liberties of the people suffering under them, far more than they offer freedoms and liberties for the people they're intended to represent.

If you want to run a restaurant called "Bubba Ray's BBQ (no Negros or Queers)" you should have the full legal right to run your business – just as much as I have the full legal right not to endorse your business with my patronage. I've said it before and I'll say it again – America is built on the idea of a Free Market – that means that if you don't like something, you are free to attend a different market.

A private business owner should be allowed to offer or deny service to anyone at any time based solely upon his own discretion. So long as his business is privately owned and operated – meaning that it has not gone public in any way – it should be his choice.

If you don't want to give him business, then speak with your money and don't – but utilizing badly designed laws to harass businesses had ought to be illegal in itself.

While I would never deny my theoretical services to someone based on their race or nationality, let me tell you right now that if I owned my own business, I would absolutely refuse my services on my own discretion, should I see any legitimate reasons to do so. If I were an artist and somebody came to me looking for a "pro-gay" drawing, painting – a cake – I'd refuse it. I am Catholic and I don't support that kind of lifestyle or political ideology.

If I were selling food and drinks – serving alcohol – and a pregnant woman came in asking for a double-shot of whiskey, I'd tell her to take her tail somewhere else in a heartbeat. If some guy that I'd seen on the local news for raping children had just gotten out of jail and came in looking for food – I wouldn't serve him. I'd tell him to get the fuck out of my diner and never come back.

Enacting laws which prohibit a person's free agency over themselves and their actions, does not make them legal, righteous or just.

There is no power on this earth which may compel me to provide a service that I do not intend to. You cannot force me to do something just because you want me to – at that point you are holding a "legal gun" against someone's head and threatening to pull the trigger if they do not do what you want.

That is not "justice." It is the antithesis of justice – it is reprehensible and wrong. Forcing people to capitulate to your whims on the basis of nothing is the reason that our laws are falling apart.

The American justice system is a laughingstock. The justice system of Western civilizations as a whole is currently viewed as a laughingstock. So many of our fundamental laws keep being overlapped by newer and often emotionally driven additions, to the point that it has become unstable.

Like painting a fence, you need to scrape away the old paint before applying a new coat – otherwise the paint is going to peel. You're going to be left with nothing more than an ugly botched mess. You can't just slap a new coat on top of it and call it a success, it doesn't work that way.

We have so many laws in place right now that half of the time when a person defends themselves from an attack, the attacker is able to charge the defender with assault and win the trial. Cases flooding in from all over states such as California, New York, Pennsylvania and elsewhere of home-invaders being shot – but not killed – and the people who held off the invaders were charged with criminal activity. Where people are attacked in broad daylight and defend themselves – only to be arrested as if they had committed a crime.

If someone comes running towards you with a knife, or backs you into an ally – or confronts you and the people around you on a bus or train – you have the full legal right to use deadly force. You shouldn't need to piss yourself hoping that he'll change his mind. You shouldn't need to ask him to wait and double check with every other person involved to see if they, too, feel threatened. You shouldn't need to hope and pray for some kind of miracle to happen and make the problem go away.

If someone comes onto your property and is attempting to steal from you, to damage your property, to threaten you or your family with violence – you have the full legal right to kill them. You shouldn't need to wait for them to break down your door. You shouldn't need to make sure they are facing you when you shoot. You shouldn't need to make sure they won't fall backwards onto the porch.

In other words – you shouldn't need to jump through fucking hoops when your your life is on the line.

Different States have different laws of course. Some have "Stand Your Ground" laws, some have "Castle" laws – but most of them still manage to fuck it up in one way or the other.

I don't care if the scumbag is running back to his vehicle – I'm gonna shoot that son of a bitch while he's running. For all I know he could be out of his mind on drugs, and might try ramming his car into my living room.

For all I know he might be rushing out there to grab a bigger gun and come back. I'm not going to take that risk – and I shouldn't be prosecuted, or be at risk of being prosecuted – because I defended myself and my property from a criminal.

Now if I hopped into my truck and chased him down the road I think we can all agree that that's taking things just a little too far – but as long as he's on my property – I don't give a damn.

You have people out there trying to do their jobs – trying to be good employees – getting fired left and right because of criminals coming into the stores and they actually do something about it. You have business owners getting arrested because of assholes coming into their gas stations waving a gun around, and then the clerk shoots him as he runs out to the parking lot to try and make a getaway.

Those clerks are heroes, not criminals – they shouldn't be treated like ones.

I remember the story of a man out in the Midwest somewhere who owned a farm and let an old friend of his come and stay with him in exchange for work. The farmer trusted him – he was his friend – and when the farmer walked away for something, the man raped his daughter. This wasn't some seventeen year old "farm girl" who was flirting around the haystacks – this was a small child, I think around twelve or eleven – and when the farmer came back to the barn after hearing her scream, he shot the man who was on top of her.

The police arrested the farmer and charged him with murder.

My own friend up in Pennsylvania had her uncle taken away and locked in prison for years because a one-time "friend" tried to rape his son. The first altercation, my friend's uncle didn't do anything drastic. He threw him out of the house and called the cops – but the man came back a few days later, with a gun. He broke into their home, started screaming that he was going to kill them – screaming that "The boy is mine! He wants to be with me!" So the uncle killed him – shot him to save his family from a predator.

They locked him away for over a decade for protecting his family – inside of his own home – from a would-be murderer and rapist.

That is the state of our legal system.

A person should never be dissuaded from doing the right thing because he's in fear of the law.

That is not "justice", it is failure.

It is a failure on the part of the legal system not only because it impedes a citizen's right to self preservation and community service – but also because it actively deters a sense of faith and trust in that system.

There is a reason that the majority of people right now do not trust the law – because the laws that are currently in place have made it very clear that they are not trustworthy. I would not trust the current justice system to have my back and keep me safe any more than I would trust a boat full of holes to keep me from sinking into the river.

And considering that more and more you hear from cousin-countries such as Canada where the Prime Minister actually said: "You can't use a gun for self-protection in Canada. It's not a right that you have." I think that it is no small wonder that the people – the general public – are beginning to lose faith in the law.

Just look at the gun banning laws that Democrats keep trying to get signed in. Every single one of them punishes law-abiding citizens and does absolutely nothing to restrict gun access to criminals. If you're a convicted felon, you cannot legally own a firearm – but if you're a convicted felon who is intent on committing a crime – you do not give a shit about breaking the law. The only people who are affected by this are the ones who have their guns taken away – or their access to guns reduced – because they are in fact obeying the law.

Somebody once said to me "Well, that's up there in Canada – but they don't have an influence on what happens down here." Really? They don't have an influence on what happens down here?

In Canada, citizens do have the legal right to own a handgun – but in order to have that gun in your home, you have to keep the gun unloaded with the ammunition stored separately from the firearm.

Maintain a trigger lock on the firearm itself – and house the firearm inside of a gun cabinet or safe.

The ammunition for the firearm must also be stored in a secured and locked container.

So let's run through this real quick: The gun is in your house, but it is unloaded, behind a locked door and has a secondary lock on the weapon itself. The ammunition for that firearm is locked away in a separate container, safe or cabinet.

That means that if somebody breaks into your home, wants to kill you, rape your wife and steal your children – you have to first: Roll out of bed, find the key to your gun safe or remember the combination. Find the key to the trigger lock on your weapon to remove it. Make your way to a second gun safe and fiddle with the key or combination to unlock it. Retrieve the ammunition and then load your weapon. All of this under a very high-stress and time sensitive situation.

And even then, after all of that – because Canada has no Castle Doctrine laws – you will probably be charged with "assaulting" the invader because you could have "retreated" from the home.

Those laws and regulations I just cited to you are already setting roots in several different states, with varying degrees of stringency. There are also bills being put before Congress which aim to apply gun storage laws on the Federal level.

Now don't get me wrong, I am all in favor of responsible gun ownership – especially if you have children – but introducing laws which essentially renders the main purpose of a firearm "moot" is not the sort of thing that is enacted in the best interest of the people.

It is a law that specifically seeks to take power away from the individual – and that is exactly what the people writing these laws intend to do.

Most of these laws have been enacted or are attempting to be enacted, in response to the rampant gun problem that is sweeping the country. Gun violence in the United States is at an all-time high with various mass-shootings taking place each year. The problem is that enacting tighter restrictions on gun laws are not going to reduce violent crime – at least not by any substantial margin.

A lot of people often cite the United Kingdom for the great strides they have made in the prevention of gun related violence – or most cases of criminal violence – and will often hold them up as an example of why the United States should be more restrictive when it comes to access to firearms.

These same people seem to forget however, that the entirety of the U.K. can almost be fitted three times into the state of Texas alone – and that a total of ten European countries can fit inside of Texas with extra room to spare. In fact the United Kingdom can fit inside of the continental United States just over forty times in terms of landmass – and the United States itself is home to over 333 million people, compared to the United Kingdom's population of just under 70 million.

So no, I don't think that little game plays out quite the way most people seem to think it would.

The problem with America's gun violence – or crime violence in general for that matter – is that the culture of this country is one which actively discourages a sense of discipline. Which discourages an education surrounding the power and responsibility that goes along with something like a firearm.

Like riding a motorcycle, you have to respect the power of that machine between your legs – because it will kill you in a heartbeat if you become complacent.

As our nation endures more and more attacks on the structure of family and the concept of fatherhood – crime continues to rise. We didn't used to see this much gun violence in the 30s, the 40s, the 50s.

It's not that there weren't less guns. It's not like guns used to be "harder" to get a hold of.

It's the culture that has changed, and whether you like it or not, the simple fact is that as a love of God and Christian values were removed from the public systems, and the teachings and ideas of goodwill were taken out of schools – while the media we consumed became more graphic, violent and incendiary – things began to change. People began to change.

I cannot give you a completed timeline of everything that has happened, in the perfect order that it's happened – but the general way in which we used to go about things started shifting.

News became less about relevance and more about sensationalism. Huge swathes of the population were getting whipped up into bouts of public frenzy. Tensions across the country began to rise. Drug consumption started spiraling out of control. General crime across the nation spiked

– and so many laws within the United States were created solely for the purpose of protecting criminals.

That is why violence has become such a problem in America.

Liberals have been pushing for softer and softer stances on crime in this country for generations. Public executions such as hangings – which actively deter potential criminals from committing crimes – were abolished in the 1930s. While the Death Penalty does still exist, it has been rolled back and reduced by so many states that more often than not "Death Row" is a very harsh sounding name for permanent residence. Over time, more and more emphasis has been placed on adding additional years to a criminal's sentence – to that point that most of the worst offenders in our country face multiple-life sentences – totaling up to unprecedented numbers.

That is why our prison system is famously overburdened. American prisons were over capacity with convicts back when I was a boy – and that was thirty years ago. When a man has raped and murdered his way across the country, sentencing him to "39 life sentences plus 1,710 years without parole" does not equate justice. It equates to another inmate getting to live out the remainder of his life rent free on the taxpayers dime.

It's ridiculous – it's asinine – and it's the core reason that so many criminals are able to keep going free.

After decades of "Progressives" showing leniency towards crime, and prisons becoming overloaded with inmates – the issues of trying to address criminal reform started being pushed as a way to relieve some of the pressure on the prison system. Of course this doesn't deal with the actual problem of keeping convicted felons alive – but Republicans eventually attempted to find some form of bipartisan compromise.

Several attempts failed, until in 2018 the "First Step Act" passed Congress and came into law.

First Step included several amendments to numerous prior acts and becomes very involved with its use of "legalese" but the general concept is that it ensured reduced prison sentences for criminals on the majority of possible charges – with some reductions being so outrageous as to go from a life sentence down to only 25 years, even with prior convictions of the same crime.

It was a stupid thing for Republicans to do. Softer stances on crime do not diminish criminal activity – it encourages it.

This is not the sort of thing which helps to unburden the prison system in our country. This is the sort of thing which adds to the growing amount of policies and laws which support criminals at the expense of private citizens.

In 2020 California passed the California Racial Justice Act which allowed any and all convicted felons currently serving time to challenge their conviction and sentencing on the grounds of racial prejudice. The law is so open-ended, that the incarcerated prisoner doesn't even have to prove that he himself was the victim of discrimination – but that any member of his own ethnicity had ever been the victim of discrimination. That it all it takes for a felon in California to challenge his sentencing.

All throughout COVID and into 2023, numerous cities in California enacted some variation of the "Zero Bail" policy – which effectively eliminates the need for bails or bonds within the legal system for all but the most violent criminal offenses. This policy has led to police stations becoming a literal revolving door of criminals committing acts of theft or robbery – getting arrested – and being released with a citation within hours.

Numerous reports, police records and video evidence have confirmed that many criminals have been subject to repeat arrests for continuing to engage in criminal activity – including one man that I saw who was arrested a whopping seventeen times in a single day.

In February of this year, Senator Kennedy grilled the director of the Bureau of Prisons, Colette Peters, over the recidivism rates associated with criminal release under the First Step Act.

Peters acknowledged that in the six years since First Step was enacted, over 30,000 prisoners have been released – but in spite of being the director of the BOP she had absolutely no idea how many of them returned to crime and went back into the system.

For context on this issue, there are over 40,000 people working at the Bureau of Prisons, and according to the director herself – not a single person has any clue as to the number of repeat offenders that were released under the conditions of this law.

That is horrifying.

The sheer ineptitude on display in this nation is staggering – but this is what happens when you take a soft stance on the issues of justice. When you concern yourself more with political correctness and keeping up appearances than you do on matters of virtue and integrity.

More to the point – this is what happens when you willfully attempt to undermine the law.

In 2021 the Senate Judiciary Committee had to address the issue of Rachel Rollins, the Presidential nominee for U.S. Attorney of the District of Massachusetts. Prior to her nomination by Biden, Rollins served as the District Attorney for Suffolk County and the city of Boston.

During the senate hearing, Senator Cruz produced an article written by Rollins in which she candidly outlines not only her motivations for office – but also her express intentions of how she would approach the law, should she be instated.

In her article on policy, Rollins states: "Charges on the list of 15 should be declined or dismissed pre-arraignment without conditions. The presumption is the charges that fall into this category should always be denied, even when attached to another charge."

That is not only an astoundingly broad stance to take – but it is also an astounding display of self entitlement.

What this woman has said is essentially, that she is not the prosecutor – but in fact the legislature. That she considers her office to hold more authority than the duly elected legislators which actively voted on the criminal code within the State of Massachusetts.

Now obviously I am not a resident of Massachusetts, I have mentioned many times that I reside in Georgia – so I am in no way intimately familiar with all of their state and local laws – but as a fellow resident of the United States, there are a few common themes throughout our legal system which typically resonates with just about everybody.

Let's go over the full list of 15 laws which Rollins declined to prosecute.

1: Trespassing.

Well, right off the bat that seems like a pretty terrible idea not to charge anyone for trespassing on private property. According to Rollins a person can just come onto your land or right into your home and it shouldn't be considered an issue.

2: Shoplifting, including offenses that are essentially shoplifting, but charged as larceny.

That sounds about right. No need to punish someone for theft – I've already mentioned how well that's working out in California. It seems like a great idea to me to encourage thievery. Why not?

3: Larceny under $250.

Well there you have it – theft of personal property – so long as it's under $250 it's fine, it's no big deal. That was only my great grandfather's watch – a precious family heirloom – or maybe it was part of the rent or grocery bill. No, it's perfectly acceptable to just rob somebody of their possessions.

4: Disorderly conduct.

Public drunkenness, indecent exposure, threatening or aggressive behavior – I mean who hasn't been guilty of at least one of these – that all seems perfectly fine. No need to worry about how we behave in view of the public.

5: Disturbing the peace.

This one usually goes hand in hand with disorderly conduct but I suppose screaming vulgarities and aggressive behavior are technically different. I'd love to see the look on someone's face when they walk out to find some stranger shitting and pissing on their front lawn while calling them a "cunt." I bet it would make for quite a story.

6: Receiving stolen property.

Oh, so back to theft and larceny – this one easily could swing into small-time organization and racketeering since it's perfectly legal to not only steal from the public, but also to hand off those stolen goods to someone else. Makes perfect sense to me.

7: Minor driving offenses, including operating with a suspended or revoked license.

Why even bother having a driver's license at this point? Don't get me wrong, I can sympathize with this one to a certain degree – there are plenty of people who are perfectly capable drivers that have lost their licenses either because they misplaced them or forgot to have them renewed who probably should get some kind of leniency – but this specifically points to people that have had their licenses suspended or outright revoked. That means those individuals did something to warrant the loss of their license.

8: Breaking and entering, where it is into a vacant property or is for the purpose of sleeping or seeking refuge from the cold and there is no actual damage to property.

So this one... this one I have very mixed feelings about. The first half is about breaking and entering into a vacant and or presumably abandoned property – I can understand that. Homelessness is at an all-time high in this country, and even sometimes when a person isn't homeless, they might get stuck somewhere for whatever reason and need to seek shelter. I can't really condemn the idea of slipping into an old abandoned barn or building.

The problem comes from the second half of this, which says "or" for the purpose of sleeping or seeking refuge. That implies that any form of breaking and entering is acceptable, even into none-vacant properties. Imagine a world in which it was considered to be perfectly acceptable for someone to just break into your home and take a nap on your couch. What if you're a woman living alone? What if you have children in the house? The potential for horrific acts of harm are staggering. I cannot believe that someone actually wrote this.

9: Wanton or malicious destruction of property.

Well I couldn't believe that someone wrote the above – but apparently you can just show up somewhere with a baseball bat and start swinging and it's perfectly acceptable. I'd also note that there's no monetary value attached to this one – so stealing more than $250 worth of personal property is illegal – but you can outright destroy as much property as you want, regardless of the overall cost. You cannot steal someone's car – but you can absolutely blow it up. Got it.

10: Threats (excluding domestic violence).

This one sent me for such a loop when I first read it. Now obviously every state has different laws and different definitions of those laws. Georgia state law is perfectly clear on this issue. But according to Rollins, this sounds like her stance is that it is unacceptable – inexcusable even, for a man to threaten to beat his wife – but he can march right across the street and threaten to beat his neighbor's wife and that's not an issue. This makes absolutely no sense whatsoever. It's insanity.

11: Minors in possession of alcohol.

I can sort of understand this one, I mean catching teenagers drinking under age you really ought to just call their parents and give them a slap on the wrist. I've already made my stance pretty clear in another chapter that the drinking age should be 18 – so I suppose there isn't anything too outlandish here.

12: Drug possession.

That seems fairly...vague. It seems irresponsibly vague – almost intentionally vague. Drug possession could be anything from marijuana to methamphetamine. You can't just say "drug possession" and leave it at that – unless there's another version of this documentation, I can't believe that I'm reading this.

13: Drug possession with intent to distribute.

Fentanyl. The only thing I have to say about that is Fentanyl. How shortsighted do you have to be in order to suggest the distribution of "drugs" should not be considered a crime.

14: Resisting arrest where the only charge is resisting arrest.

I think I understand the logic behind this one – you see a lot of illegal arrests taking place today and so she's trying to say that if you know that you're innocent you can resist arrest by the officer – but that seems like it's opening the doors to a lot of very serious problems which can occur during an altercation. Again, I think I understand it and frankly I might even be inclined to agree with it – but this seems irresponsibly written and poorly thought out.

15: Resisting arrest if the other charges include only charges that fall under the list of charges for which prosecution is declined.

Oh well I guess this is sort of a cover-all for the above. You are free to resist arrest by an officer, so long as he is attempting to arrest you for drug possession, the intent to distribute, possession of stolen property, breaking and entering, disorderly conduct, destruction of public and private property and making threats – along with everything else.

I feel like I am starting to sense a pattern here. Remember that at the top of this article on her policy, Rollins states with crystal clarity that these charges should *always* be denied. That means trespassing on your land, breaking and entering into your home, larceny of your possessions and malicious destruction of your property are all perfectly legal as far as she is concerned.

And as if this list wasn't bad enough already, you also have to take into account the 'ripple-effect' that is caused by these kinds of decisions. By not prosecuting these criminals based on their actions, countless individuals end up walking the streets without an existing criminal record – which means that when these people commit additional crimes in the future, prosecutors will be unable to utilize any prior convictions in order to render a just sentence – because thanks to Rollins those convictions would have never taken place.

This is the failure of justice. People with policies and ideals like these are the reason that so many states across this country are plummeting into chaos.

I'd very much like something to be understood here – miss Rollins is not some outlier or pariah – she is one of many that have wormed their way into positions of power on the backs of radicalized voters who distort the democratic process in order to shoehorn in increasingly dangerous and irresponsible individuals who are likewise committed to the continued push for further radicalization.

She is very much the product of the party which seeks to undermine democracy. The party which has repeatedly attempted to dissolve the Electoral College. The party that has enacted laws which allow convicted felons the right to vote – the party who seeks to remove the requirements of identification in order to vote – and who actively flood the streets of our nation with illegal immigrants, and leverages them in order to bloat the ballots while calling it "democracy."

This entire system is a joke.

If I could have it my way, I'd say hang them all. You're going to sell drugs to kids? You're going to break into someone's home and threaten their family? You're going to destroy half the city because you feel like you're entitled to it? I wouldn't throw your carcass in jail – I'd have you shot.

That would cut down on the prisoner crisis.

Murderers, rapists, pedophiles – let their executions be public so that everyone can see what happened to them. If you weren't going to execute the pedophiles and rapists, I'd say castrate them like animals and brand them across the face so the whole world will know who they are – will know what they are.

Some people will say that that's barbaric – I would say that it's justice – but I'd also say that it's emotional.

Emotions often get the better of us, and imagine if we did that to men who were innocent? If you wanted true justice in the world – true fairness in the law – then any person who falsely accuses another should be sentenced to the same penalty as the accused. That would be fairness and equality – and it would force people to think twice before making false allegations.

Of course to do that you would have to master the art of investigation, and getting to the bottom of the truth – which is something we seem to be falling down on an awful lot late.

It doesn't really matter either way, because nobody asked for my opinion – but these soft stances on crime aren't working.

Regardless, the system of laws – whether State or Federal – are not the only reasons that people have begun to lose their faith in our institutions of justice.

Law enforcement in this country – and the Western world at large – has become a thing of mockery and ridicule at best, to outright disdain at worst.

Before getting too deep into this next issue I would like to make it perfectly clear that I believe in a healthy respect for the law, as well as in a healthy respect for the "Boys in Blue" who uphold that law and put themselves in harm's way on a daily basis to keep our communities safe.

I also believe that there is too much hatred being aimed towards the police in general, and that half of the problems which people experience while dealing with law enforcement are typically their own goddamn fault by acting like a bunch of jackasses.

That being said, I also feel as though there are simply far too many laws and regulations in place today for the police to be as effective as they should be – and that the world would be a much better place if we could get back to the days wherein people were able to handle their own problems without having to call on "Johnny Law" all the time to come and deal with them.

It used to be when two neighbors got into an argument and it spilled over into a scuffle – they'd duke it out and either end up sitting down and grabbing a beer while they bled all over each other, or they went back to their respective homes and stayed pissed off. Nowadays you can't have any kind of altercation – verbal or otherwise – without someone escalating the situation by calling the cops.

It might be the spouse, it might be the men themselves once the fight is over – it might even be a nosy neighbor sticking her beak where it doesn't belong.

The nation has become "law happy" despite how much they seem to hate it. Any time a person has the chance to press a charge or file a lawsuit – they usually take it.

And considering the way that a lot of cops are sort of "handicapped" today with their body-cams and excessive backup – usually what happens is that a very small and trivial incident gets blown massively out of proportion, and the police are forced to do something instead of being able to just walk away.

I feel bad for them, I do.

I think that this "legal culture" which we have cultivated in America can be traced back to cases like that lady who sued Starbucks for putting "too much ice" in her iced coffee – or further back when several people sued McDonalds for offering super-sized french fries, because they "made them fat." McDonalds didn't make anyone fat – McDonalds didn't force anyone to buy the largest size fries – but it's just sort of this attitude that we've built, where individuals don't seem to have any real sense of personal accountability.

That everything has to be battled out in court and taken to some extreme – always involving the law where it doesn't need to be involved.

Police officers are supposed to be out there catching the bad guys and throwing them in jail – not running down drivers because they didn't buckle their seat-belt, or dealing with Tim and Earl because one of them got pissed off that the other one put up a bunch of plastic pink flamingos in his yard.

With all of that being said however – and with all due respect still afforded to the officer who uphold the law – the police themselves are not entirely blameless in this issue of ongoing legal friction.

I think a great deal of the animosity and mistrust that is being garnered towards the police in general, is simply because of their image alone. The days of a cop looking like a "nice guy" have gone, and most of the time whenever I see an officer in the city – or even just a county sheriff sitting on the side of a dirt road – they're wearing those tactical vests with all of their equipment attached to it.

They don't look like police officers – they look like soldiers – like some kind of paramilitary or militia unit instead of local peace keepers. And I fully understand that considering the times we live in, times when people will just walk up alongside a cop car and shoot them – there's a very real necessity to help ensure the safety of our officers.

But understanding that necessity, doesn't make the image look any less "bad" in terms of optics. Long gone are the days when cops looked like the guys from Police Academy. Nowadays, most officers don't look friendly or approachable. They look imposing and intimidating – and again, I completely understand why – but it doesn't make the average person necessarily feel at ease when they're around.

And to be perfectly honest, I'm not entirely sure where this new sort of "image" has come from – because while yes I can understand it to an extent here in America – they look the exact same way in other countries that do not have such rampant gun problems. While I'm sure they do not wear their tactical vests all of the time – I've seen plenty of videos and photographs of police officers in Canada, in England, in France, in Germany – going about their daily business while fully geared up.

It's very much out of place, and I wouldn't say that it's a terribly "reassuring" image of the law.

It comes off looking both authoritarian and oppressive.

Even the red and blue lights on modern police vehicles are oppressive. They're so extremely bright – brighter than they have any reasonable right to be – it's disorienting. It makes people panic and tense up because it's blinding. The radios on the vests blaring static from dispatch transmissions while an officer is trying to talk to you is very frazzling and anxiety inducing. It's a visual and audial assault on the senses.

So what exactly changed?

Obviously this should go without saying, but America has no singular uniform for police. Every State, every county, every city – each of them are responsible for their own gear and equipment and so on – but it is very "striking" in a way that you can see this so often and in so many places. This cannot simply be the "Culture of America" when other nations are doing it too – so I have to wonder as to why there has been such a noticeable... shift in tone, I suppose, to the presentation of law enforcement.

My uncle Billy served over forty years in the Prince Edward County Sheriff's Department up in Virginia, and he looked every bit the way – at least in my mind – that a Sheriff's Deputy is supposed to.

Black boots, striped pants, dark brown shirt with a neck tie and his hat. He carried a heavy belt around his waist that had a billy stick, a pair of handcuffs and his standard issue service revolver – I think a Colt, though I'm not sure what model. I know it fired six shots and I'm fairly certain it was chambered for a .38 Special.

He didn't have a taser on his belt. He wasn't packing a Glock 22, and didn't have two extra guns strapped to his ankle and his knee. He didn't have body armor underneath his clothes, or a tactical vest over top carrying radios, flashlights, body-cams, pepper sprays and what all have you.

He was just... a Deputy. I think he had a pump action shotgun in either the trunk or the backseat of his car, but that was it. Essentially, he looked like Andy Griffith – just with a round hat and darker uniform.

What happened to those days? I guess life happened I suppose – but if this is the way that life is going, then I think that we've really managed to run off the rails.

You know he only ever fired that gun five times in forty two years? In the line of service, I mean. Five times – all of them warning shots and nothing more.

Lord, how I miss those days...

But he did talk to me about some things every now and again. I didn't get the chance to know him half as well as I'd have liked – but I did love him and he loved me – and he would talk to me. He'd tell me funny stories about the weird or wild things that he saw on the job.

Like this one story, he was called out to a farm over a domestic dispute between a husband and his wife. The wife drove off and the husband tried to hang himself from a tree with a tractor chain – so uncle Billy and another deputy had to run over and hold him up so that he wouldn't die. Somebody found a little wooden step ladder to put under the guys feet – but when he stood on it, the ladder broke and the man started swinging again – knocked Billy over, and the other officer had to grab the guy's legs to hoist him up to keep the pressure off of his neck long enough for Billy to get back up and climb the tree.

I shouldn't laugh at it, but can you just imagine these county sheriff's falling over each other on a muddy Virginia hill, trying to get this man down? The way he spoke about it sounded like something from the Keystone Cops.

Another story he told me was this time he and his partner, Branch, went out to a farmhouse somewhere – again over some kind of domestic disturbance – and they found a big crowd of people all shouting and hollering. The guy they actually came to pick up though – Billy said he was the nicest, most polite man that he'd ever had to deal with. It was the other people causing a problem.

In the end, Uncle Billy told me that him and Branch got swarmed by the crowd and had to "whoop a few of 'em." He said by the time they were done, they took seven of the worst offenders and piled all of them in the back of the squad car – while the one guy they actually came for had to sit up front between him and his partner all the way back to Farmville.

You just can't make these things up – the image alone is just so human. I could see it so perfectly from the moment he described it, and even now. I don't think that anybody involved got too harsh of a punishment in the end – mostly they just got brought back to the jailhouse to cool off – but it's so funny to picture them sitting back there, probably groaning at each other while the other guy sat up front.

Not all of my uncle's stories were funny though. He didn't just tell me about the "fun things" that he'd seen – he'd also tell me about some of the bad things that he'd seen – and how not all of it came from outside of the uniform.

He told me this one story about a high-speed chase that ran across I don't remember how many counties. I think he said at least six. This guy was running from small town to small town – Billy and Branch were sitting on the side of the road when he came flying past them. They popped their lights and took off after him – them and several other sheriff's from the various counties that he'd been through.

Billy laughed a lot when he told me that story. He said it got pretty boring out there, and that this was the most excitement they'd had in a long time. At one point, as the story goes, Billy was hanging halfway out the window and yelling at Branch to "Get up on him!" They were just loving it.

He said that he thought that chase was going to take them all the way up to Richmond – but somewhere along those highways a Virginia State Patrol rammed the guy off the road. He flipped the car several times off into the ditch, and that's when the tone of the story took a bit of a turn. Billy said he got out of his car and he watched that patrolman shove the barrel of his gun right down that man's throat on the side of the road – he said the look in that officer's eyes never left him. Billy told me, he said: "I thought for sure that he was gonna kill that boy."

He didn't talk too much about the story after that – he just got sort of quiet and thoughtful.

He warned me a lot about some of the problems in the world, and how some officers of the law could themselves be "problematic."

Prison Guards, County Sheriffs, Game Wardens, City Police, State Patrol, U.S. Marshals and Federal Agents of every branch – each one of these and then some are all related by the same consistent truth. They're all subject to being human – and humans are always subject to corruption.

It doesn't matter one iota what you do in life, whether you're a priest, a cop, a fireman, a judge – it doesn't matter. People are capable of being corrupt.

Now while I do personally feel – naive as this may be for such a cynic and a pragmatist – I do truly believe that the majority of people who get involved in law enforcement are doing so out of a desire to protect and serve.

That does not mean however that I am not fully aware of the vast and extensive corruption which is present within the law.

It is an unfortunate truth, that a lot of people do go into law enforcement for the wrong reasons. Either for money, for power – or for ambition.

Badges and ambition are a terrible combination.

It doesn't matter which state, which county, which city – it doesn't even matter which country – so long as there are people who are afforded a sense of power, then you will find someone who is willing to abuse that power for personal gain.

I've seen cops harass locals here in Georgia. I've seen Sheriff's stick their fingers into every pie. I've seen the effects of negligence on the part of law enforcement. It's terrible – and while I myself have personally never experienced a "bad cop" as of yet – I have certainly had encounters and experiences with them which were less than stellar.

And I don't necessarily have to go looking online for examples of police brutality – though you can find endless hours worth of footage documenting abuses of power or complete ineptitude on behalf of officers – but I don't have to go looking for examples of this, because I live in an example of this.

Imagine the shock and horror I felt – the shame that I felt – when in 2017 my little neck of the Georgia backwoods made international news. Imagine the feelings I felt when my friends up in Canada called me to ask about the "Special Investigator" right here in Crawford County, who forced a local resident to saw the head off of his own dog – in the man's own front yard – under the threat of arrest.

I was mortified and disgusted. I couldn't believe that a sick son of a bitch like that was working here in my county – in my home area – it was completely repulsive.

As much respect as I have for officers of the law – I have a lot more respect for my own conscience. If ever got pulled over on some bullshit stop and unjustly harassed by the police trying to plant something in my car, or get me on something I didn't do – I'm not going to just roll over and take it because you're wearing some kind of uniform.

And I'll tell you right now – if some wannabe "big man" came to my house, killed my dog, and ordered me to mutilate it? I'd rip that badge right off of his puffed out chest and pin it through his fucking eye.

You might say that makes me troublesome. That it makes me an outlaw, a renegade or a conspirator of crime. You might even say that it sounds as though I can do whatever I want – that I considered myself to be above the law.

Well I do not consider myself above the law – but the law can not be allowed to be above itself.

A man exists in this world with only one genuine possession in life – and that is his own conscience. All of these rules, all of these laws, all of these social expectations – they are nothing. They're ideals and fantasies which are little more than a constructed fabrication that we have all agreed to believe in.

And I do believe in them – for the most part at least – but I do not believe in abandoning my conscience on the basis of something that, should it decide to fluctuate, essentially becomes meaningless.

Those badges that you all seem so proud of, while you're strutting around like peacocks as if they somehow magically make you special – are not supposed to be a symbol of power and authority.

They are supposed to be a symbol of hope.

They are supposed to let people know that no matter what's going on, you are there to help them. That is your job. That is why you swore an oath – to serve and protect – you have a duty and an obligation to uphold that oath, and by God, as far as I am concerned if you are unwilling to adhere to your sworn services then you ought to be put up against a wall and shot.

Every one of you scumbags who beat down pregnant women and force them onto their bellies in broad daylight. Every one of you who shove a gun into a car full of children and shoots the family dog. Yeah, I've seen you motherfuckers – I know what you are. You're nothing but maggots who think you treat us like Ruby Ridge.

Well you won't tread on me.

I don't care what uniform you're wearing – I don't care how many stripes or pins you've stuck to it – those things do not make you any more or less of a human than the rest of us.

As far as I'm concerned you're just wearing a different set of clothes than I am.

And just as much as I wouldn't take abuse from any other man – I'm not going to take any kind of abuse from you. It doesn't make a single bit of difference to me what sort of outfit you're wearing – I'd lay you flat on your ass.

People are sick and tired of law enforcement officers taking advantage of their station, and abusing their arbitrary senses of power. What's worse is when the county offices and station houses know about the abuses taking place, and actively try to cover them up.

You are not supposed to show loyalty to your badge – you're supposed to be showing it to the people.

I don't care how much they cuss you, kick you, bite you, spit on your – that's your fucking job. That's the oath that you swore – and if you can't hack it then get the hell out of the way and get somebody else in there who can.

All over America people are calling to "defund" the police. We don't need to defund the police – but we desperately need police reform. They say our officers need to have additional training – more specialized training – but that isn't true either. Our officers don't need to undergo any "new" training, they need to be taught the old training. The basic rules that evidently they don't seem to be given anymore.

I see so many of you scumbags out there embarrassing yourselves – embarrassing the nation – by acting like a bunch of fucking school children. Like you can just ride roughshod over anybody that you feel like, and make up charges on the spot to get your way.

That's the sort of thing that gets all of the other cops – all of the good cops swept up under the rug with you, and lumped together with the rest of your filth.

The big thing today is to say we need more transparency – transparency this and transparency that – well I don't want any fucking transparency. I want to get back to having trust again.

The problem with things like transparency is that it doesn't breed trust – it breeds paranoia. When you can see absolutely everything that somebody is doing but you're still angry, you start to question if what you're seeing is real – if they didn't get around it somehow – it only ever escalates your expectations.

I want to be able to have a sense of trust – and in order to do that, you have to earn it back.

That's the only way that we can get out of this mess, and return to something resembling "normal."

With all of that said, however, the issues of criminal laws and law enforcement are only two pieces of this puzzle. There is still of course the third and greatest influence in the corruption of justice yet to come – and that is the issue of the Judicial System itself.

In this nation, the gold standard has always been the concept of "Innocent until proven Guilty," but in the modern day, any persons accused of committing a crime are now automatically considered to be "Guilty until proven Innocent," and more often than not, even after they're proven innocent.

Then again, being "proven" innocent is often up for matters of extreme debate, given how often the courts seem to allow political motivations and personal opinions interfere with proceedings.

The Judicial System in this country is a farce. It is a bloated, swollen, overly complicated and tangled mess of ineffective procedures, limitless bureaucracy and public grandstanding.

In short, it is a broken glass.

It is a thing which no longer serves its purpose – and instead only exists as a potential hazard to the lives of the American people.

Every U.S. state has their own local system of courts, and ignoring specialized courts or sub-courts or whatever you really care to call them – typically the order is broken down into three main categories.

State Trial Court, Court of Appeals and a Superior Court. Should all three of these fail on any given case, then assuming you have the money you can get kicked up to the Federal level and seek out the District Courts, the U.S. Court of Appeals and finally – ultimately – the United States Supreme Court.

I don't honestly know if having one unified system would be better or worse for the average person – but I do know that what we have is a confusing mess, with each court having its own procedures, stipulations and prerequisites for hearing – and typically the higher levels are barred off by nothing more than a monetary threshold.

Considering that most of the population is dirt poor and getting poorer by the day – that doesn't make the prospect of having your cases heard by a "higher" authority very likely.

And the Supreme Court? The crown jewel of the judicial system? It's a complete joke. It might even be the longest running joke in the history of this country. A judicial body that is more often than not bent and swayed at the whims of political bias – and has historically been used to try and further political ambitions.

It is a thing which exists to rule on only the most critical and pressing cases in the country – except that it cannot do those things until first a case has been brought to its attention.

Let's just say for the sake of argument that "murder" wasn't illegal. That people were running around killing each other left and right without any form of consequence. The Supreme Court is the court which would rule murder as illegal – except that they can't, until somebody – or some party – jumps through every hoop on every level of the system to get the question of murder sat on their desk.

That is when they could rule a decision on the issue.

That system of hoops is an obstacle course which often takes months if not outright years to get through. First you have to get a trial, set a date, have your hearing, receive your verdict or have the case dismissed – then do it again in appeals – and again in superior, and so on and so forth until you make it all the way to the top.

By the time you finally get there – how many people have been murdered? How many countless thousands have you spent in legal fees? And even then, they may take their sweet time in rendering a verdict – or they might not render a verdict at all.

They are an entity – a body of council – that pretty much just sits there doing nothing for most of the time and earning very substantial paychecks for doing it.

I do not hate the Supreme Court, as much as it may sound like it – I only recognize that they are flawed. They are a veritable Sword of Damocles hanging over the heads of the nation. They could, in theory, be given an issue and render a fair, unbiased and constitutionally grounded ruling upon that issue – or they could just as easily ignore the constitution and ignore the concepts of bipartisanship and make a ruling which completely flips the country upside down – such as what they did with Roe v. Wade in 1973. A ruling which, even that famous of "Lefty" Ginsburg herself admitted was "bad law."

Of course in 2022, that ruling was overturned – but even in the overturning of it, it sort of reaffirms the point that this "highest court in the land" isn't necessarily concrete, and nor are the rules that it supposedly follows. Even the number of Justices appointed to the court isn't set in stone and the judicial seats have fluctuated wildly over the years.

In short, it's just a mess.

But I'm not writing this to talk about the Supreme Court, and I'm not writing this to talk about the Appeals Court or the District Courts – I'm writing this to talk about American courts in general, and the way that they have been turned into a fiasco.

I can't sit here and write about every single court case that has ever come down the pipe in American history. I can't sit here and go into the untold depth of every case that I will talk about – because otherwise I'd never be able to leave.

What I can do, is point out the flaws of our system – at least as they appear to me – in the hopes of concluding my observation that "justice" has become less of an ideology, and more of a whim.

It's been several months now since I last touched this chapter – and coming back for my final cleanup in 2024 I think that it's proven to be a bit of an ironic blessing that I had not yet concluded my thoughts on the subject.

Originally, I was going to write a lengthy section about the way in which court trials have changed in their presentation to the public. About how the modern "courtroom drama" has become less centered around public information, and more around public entertainment.

About how political narratives and public opinion have taken the place of genuine legal scrutiny – and about how the non-bias of courtroom officials seems to be an idea of the past.

I was going to talk about the Rodney King trial, and go in depth about how yes – the man did commit a crime – but that the sheer brutality which he faced at the hands of the police would reverberate across the nation for decades. About how in spite of video evidence, those officers were acquitted of their crimes – and that only two of them were found guilty, once they were dragged to a different court on a different set of charges.

I was going to talk about the lasting effects of what happened to King, and of what happened in the wake of his trial. About how the failure of the law would leave the nation with unsteady ground for generations to follow.

I was going to cover the topic of the O. J. Simpson trial, and go into great detail about the motive, the murder weapon, the physical and forensic evidence, the infamous car-chase, the courtroom showmanship and acting – and how the trial itself dragged on for just under nine months to render a "not guilty" verdict against a man who very obviously committed the murder – simply because he was black and he was a celebrity.

I was going to talk about the effects that the horrible Rodney King incident had on the trial – even to the point that several jurors themselves admitted that they voted to acquit because of what happened to King – with one famously stating "we take care of our own" and another throwing up a Black Panther salute for the camera.

I was going to talk about how racism, emotional bias and public perceptions trumped hard evidence and common sense.

I was going to talk about the horrendous Casey Anthony trial, and go into great detail about how a mother murdered her own child and got away with it. About how she told police that she had left her girl in the hands of a caretaker, but the house had been abandoned for over 140 days. About how she took police on a wild goose-chase with one lie after another, and another, and another – until ultimately the body of that little girl had been found – decomposed and wrapped up in a trash bag.

I was going to talk about how in spite of all the evidence – in spite of the repeated lies and changing stories. In spite of the inquiries about chloroform which had been logged in her computer's search history and the chloroform found in her car – the smell of decomposition in her car and her backyard – and even strands of the little girl's hair found in her trunk.

I was going to talk about the fact that Casey Anthony showed no signs of remorse – or even emotion – for most of the trial. The fact that the night before the girl's body had been found, Casey was caught on film laughing, dancing, drinking and how she was generally just "partying the night away."

I was going to talk about the fact that psychoanalysts have pretty much universally pinned her as the classic Narcissistic-Sociopath, and that the eyes of the law closed shut when they faced a woman whose legal defense offered up a "sob story" of domestic abuse to the public.

I was going to talk about Derek Chauvin and the George Floyd murder which rocked the nation in 2020. I was going to go in-depth on the incident and the trial – and how the resulting cataclysm of civil unrest in this country once again hearkened back to the tragedy of Rodney King and the riots of 1992.

I was going to talk in great detail about the arrest of Floyd, which if you watched the full unedited body-cam footage that was available to anybody who wanted to find it at the time of the incident – you would see that this man was high out of his mind. He was behaving erratically, being completely uncooperative with the officers, engaged in active resistance of his restraint and generally devolved into a state of anxiety and panic.

Even as the event first started he was uncooperative and one of the passengers in the car could be heard telling him to "stop resisting" when he repeatedly failed to comply with the officer's requests.

I was going to address the fact that Floyd began having a drug induced meltdown – stating that he "couldn't breath" even while he was standing upright and prior to resisting the officer's attempts to secure him inside of the police vehicle. I was going to talk about how he kicked and screamed and thrashed around the officer's until they were forced to pin him on the ground.

I was going to talk about the fact that – despite claiming that he couldn't breath – Floyd was clearly talking and shouting for an extended period of time, which meant that he could in fact breathe. I was going to talk about how the true failure of Chauvin and the arresting officers was not brutality – but negligence in the fact that once he was appropriately subdued, they should have gotten off of him.

I was going to talk about how the court adhered to a biased media narrative, and hung Chauvin out as a sacrificial lamb for the masses. How, according to his own police handbook – the restraining move that he used was the correct policy of his department – and how that little tidbit of evidence was denied entry into the case. I was going to talk about how the jury outright stated that they were afraid for their lives and safety if they didn't render a "guilty" verdict – which means that the jury was itself compromised.

I was going to go into great detail about how body-cam footage of the arrest was freely available for anyone to see – until Left-wing media platforms began removing the footage.

I was going to talk about the fact that George Floyd was held up as a "martyr" for justice, despite the fact that he was a man who pressed a loaded gun against the head of a pregnant woman and robbed her.

I was going to talk about how public figures – duly elected officials – told rioters to burn, loot and rampage through the streets. About how Liberals and Progressives – how Democrats – utilized this incident to cause a public disaster, and ultimately dictated the outcome of that trial. I was also going to mention how none of them have ever faced any consequences for their actions.

I was going to talk about a lot of things – but then Donald Trump's verdict came in for his "Hush Money" trial – and nothing else seemed quite as relevant anymore.

I've said before that I support Donald Trump – and I still do – but this is not about trying to make someone love Trump. This is not about telling people they have to like the man, or agree with him – or anything to do with Trump himself really.

This is about the corruption of justice.

Donald Trump is currently running as the Republican candidate for the upcoming 2024 Presidential Election. He is also simultaneously facing four major criminal cases – for four crimes that he did not commit.

The Hush Money case, the Classified Documents case, the Georgia Election Interference case and the Federal Election Interference case.

Each one of these criminal cases are heavily flawed and politically motivated. As the 2020 election came to a close, serious questions were raised about the integrity of the election – and as I mentioned in a previous chapter – you do not have to believe that it was tampered with in order to understand why people were suspicious.

Too many oddities, irregularities and general "red flags" took place on the night of the 2020 election – and so Trump, as the President, made several statements of uncertainty and several inquiries as to the validity of the process and results – something which his office allowed him the full right to do.

The allegations of interference in Georgia is the case that I can speak the most boldly about – given that I am myself a Georgia resident and I watched everything that happened that night, along with everything that happened in the weeks to follow – in real time.

The entire thing started when Trump made a phone call to Georgia's Secretary of State and asked the simple question: "Can't you find more votes?" A lot of people have tried to spin this as Trump suggesting that the Secretary of State should fake a bunch of ballots in order to win the state – but if you actually bother to listen to the phone call, he's very clearly asking about the integrity of the election.

I don't know how to clarify someone's "tone of voice" through the medium of text – but considering that additional votes for Trump were found out in a ditch a few weeks after the election – and the fact that Georgia is far from a Left-leaning state – I think that it was a very fair question to ask. He didn't want the man to tamper with the results – he wanted to know why the votes weren't there in the wake of exceedingly suspicious activity in Fulton County.

The District Attorney of Fulton County, Fani Willis, decided that she was going to make her career by attacking Trump for election interference and used this phone call as the basis for her investigation. Willis is a die-hard Democrat, who is also in a romantic relationship with the man that she herself appointed as the Special Prosecutor – and has been caught embezzling money from her office. She has fought tooth and nail to have his trial take place prior to the 2024 election and the entire thing reeks of politically motivated electoral assassination.

What will ultimately happen to the case? I don't know. I hope to have the book done before then.

The second case against Trump is of course the big one – the Federal Election Interference case – which is predicated on and around the events of January 6th and the riots at the Capitol Building. I've already addressed this incident in a previous chapter, so I won't go into too much detail here – but the idea is that Trump incited riots and staged an "insurrectionist coup" to try and overthrow the election and the government.

The man stood there and said "Peacefully protest and make your voices heard." Democrats tried to hang the chain on him saying "we have to fight like hell" it's a common turn of phrase. There's an entire video reel of over one hundred Democrats screaming "fight like hell!" It's a complete joke.

They said that Trump attempted to use then-Vice President Pence to overthrow the election by demanding that he throw out the results – but that's not what Trump did. Trump pointed out that the Vice President, as President of the Senate, should have the theoretical power to send the votes back to the states in order to be recertified. And considering all of the strange and shady things that took place during that election – all of the doubts over the validity and integrity of the election held by the American people – I think that it was a perfectly reasonable thing to ask. He never said to throw out the votes – he only wanted to have them re-certified without any of the strange irregularities taking place. That's all.

To argue that he wanted anything else is delusional insanity.

The third case, being the Classified Documents case, is so absurd that it isn't even funny. Trump held on to some official documentation after leaving the White House, which resulted in the FBI raid on his estate at Mar-a-Lago. The basis of this case is that Trump broke the Federal Records Act by failing to hand over classified documents to NARA – which I suppose is true – he did not hand them over.

The problem with this case is that several different Presidents have failed to hand over official documents in the past, including Trump's current political rival Joe Biden – who stashed several boxes full of official White House documents in his own garage both during and after his time as the active Vice President.

Biden would eventually be investigated by special counsel Robert Hur on the orders of Attorney General Garland – the man Biden appointed to office – over his retention of these documents. Through this investigation, Biden was found to have "willfully retained and disclosed classified materials after his vice presidency when he was a private citizen" and they still didn't charge him for anything.

As Hur so pointedly stated: "We have also considered that, at trial, Mr. Biden would likely present himself to a jury, as he did during our interview of him, as a sympathetic, well-meaning, elderly man with a poor memory."

Biden's own DOJ refused to press the issue concerning his willful retention of classified documents on the grounds that he is an old man that is riddled with dementia.

You don't have to think that Trump is not guilty, in fact as I said in this case, I believe he is guilty – but by charging one, and refusing to charge the other, that is wrong. It is effectively like showing up to a place where smoking is not allowed inside the building – seeing two guys smoking cigarettes – and only arresting one of them.

You cannot do that. You have to treat them equally.

Not treating them equally reads as blatant political bias.

But with all of that said, the case that I actually have to talk about is the Hush Money case – arguably the least important case that Trump is currently facing – and yet somehow has become one of the most important court trials in recorded history.

The District Attorney of Manhattan, Alvin Bragg ran on an election campaign built around the promise of going after Donald Trump in the most blatant and public display of political motivation that I have ever seen. He pledged that he was going to "take down" Trump no matter what – and now he's doing it.

The entire case is convoluted, baseless, speculative and ultimately it's a travesty. As one person put it – the "Hush Money" case is a Russian nesting doll – it is nothing more than layer upon layer, upon layer, with absolutely nothing of substance in the middle.

To make a very long story short, Trump had some form of physical relationship with the adult-film star Stormy Daniels back in the mid 2000s. Leading up to the 2016 election, Trump supposedly made payments to

Daniel's under a Non-Disclosure Agreement so that his former dalliances would not reflect badly on his public image.

The general idea is that by paying out "hush money" to Stormy Daniels – as well as some others – Trump effectively "interfered" with the election by covering up potentially harmful information from his constituents, which of course is completely absurd.

Non-Disclosure Agreements are not illegal.

Most forms of business or legal proceedings involve an NDA of some form or another. It's normal – it's a normal part of modern life. It isn't strange, it isn't weird – it isn't some kind of shady dealing – it's just a standard business practice.

Even Bill Clinton's own former FEC Chairman, Bradley Smith, has come forward to point out that "A businessman or candidate's intent to protect his public image before an election by settling a lawsuit or other potential legal claim, paying to have old divorce records sealed, settling up contested debts – none of which he has an obligation to pay before or after becoming a candidate – does not make these payments campaign expenditures. If it did, many more politicians than Trump would be in trouble."

Does that mean that anybody has ever bothered to stop and consider the larger ramifications of this trial? No, it doesn't. This simple truth has done absolutely nothing to deter political partisanship in the courtroom.

From the ground up, everything about this case has been a complete mockery.

Alvin Bragg's top prosecutor, Mathew Colangelo, has previously received payments directly from the Democratic National Committee. He served as the third-ranking official at Biden's justice department, and he joined Bragg's DA office in December of 2022, just three months before the investigation and indictment against Trump took place.

The Judge on the case, Juan Merchan, has been a life-long partisan Democrat. He's made multiple public endorsements and donations to the Biden campaign and administration, as well as Left-wing activist groups such as Code Blue. His daughter is a Democrat political activist and served as the president of Kamala Harris's 2020 digital campaign.

The trial itself took place in Manhattan, an extremely hostile political region – inside of an already hostile political state. The idea of being tried before a "jury of your peers" was not written into the Magna Carta to imply that you are supposed to be tried in a location where there is no chance of finding a neutral party.

Having the trial take place in the Bronx or in Queens would have made a lot more sense – because although Trump is not particularly popular anywhere in the state of New York – Manhattan was the least likely place to have a bipartisan jury.

Bragg built his case on the grounds of a misdemeanor charge for "falsifying business records." This charge however has a two year statute of limitations – and so Bragg made the argument that Trump falsified these records in order to cover up "a separate crime" by alleging that somehow these documents were directly responsible for a "Federal Felony." If and only if that were the case – the statute of limitations would be increased to five years by transforming this misdemeanor charge into a felony charge.

Of course, if you do the math – the case is built on the assumption that Trump committed this misdemeanor in 2016, and this is now eight years later in 2024 – so even with the extension added onto the statute of limitations these charges are invalid. Bragg then declared that COVID-19 somehow magically "paused" the statute of limitations in the state of New York – as well as asserted that any time spent outside of the state of New York, such as I don't know – being the President – also put a pause on the statute of limitations.

You have got to be joking.

It is true that under certain circumstances you can enforce a temporary suspension or "toll" to the statute of limitations – but those suspensions on the clock are usually only added when the accused person absconds from the state in order to flee prosecution. Not leave to do his job. Not casually stroll down to the airport to go on vacation – and certainly not because a bunch of people caught the flu.

Removing all of that from the equation for a moment, the real problem with this is that Bragg is a State Official – he's not Federal – he has absolutely zero jurisdiction to prosecute someone on a federal crime inside the state of New York. State prosecutors cannot under any circumstances prosecute somebody over federal charges.

It is completely mind blowing to me, that the same Biden Administration which is continually insisting that States do not have the right to enforce Federal law on the basis of Federalism – seems to have absolutely no issue with the Manhattan DA enforcing Federal Election Finance laws which have already been investigated and dismissed.

Bragg has essentially predicted his entire state misdemeanor case on a supposed federal charge that Trump himself has not been charged with.

Judge Merchan not only allowed Bragg to bring forth illegal charges outside of his jurisdiction – but he also allowed Bragg to make the suggestion that Trump had somehow already been convicted of some unspecified violation of election law – even though he hadn't.

How exactly did he do that? He did it through the "witnesses."

The prosecution brought forward Trump's former attorney, Michael Cohen – a convicted perjurer – who had already pled guilty to various "campaign crimes" in the hopes of cutting a plea-deal.

While typically prosecutors are not allowed to bring in a witness's history of criminal conduct, Bragg's team specifically targeted Cohen's history as a means to argue that his guilty plea of election finance violations – on Trump's behalf – somehow suggests that Trump is actually guilty of the crime, despite never being charged for a Federal election tampering.

The Judge then barred Trump from arguing his innocence, specifically because he was never charged by the Federal authorities. Merchan reasoned that Trump's non-prosecution is "irrelevant" because Federal authorities may have "dropped the case for reasons having nothing to do with whether or not Trump was guilty."

If that is indeed the line of thinking – how can you then also allow Cohen's plea to be considered in the election's case? How can you allow David Pecker's non-prosecution and conciliation agreement? It's not even a "double-standard," it simply makes no sense. It's an arbitrary application of the rules.

At the end of the day what actually matters is that Trump was never tried on these Federal Election charges. He's never even been indicted on these charges.

Bragg made his case by bringing in former Trump associates who have plead guilty to various crimes – and then used their guilty pleas as an excuse to suggest that Trump himself was somehow guilty of the same criminal activity – thereby allowing the prosecution to arbitrarily extend the statute of limitations on an outdated misdemeanor, so that they can wrap that misdemeanor around a different crime that Trump was neither convicted of or charged with, and then turn that into a felony of New York state law.

The sheer mental gymnastics that one has to jump through in order to argue that this has any form of sound legal grounding is insane. This is tantamount to a child playing a game and then changing the rules whenever he starts losing in order to make sure that he wins.

It's ridiculous and absurd.

The prosecution not only refused to overtly state what exactly Trump was supposedly guilty of – but they also failed to disclose whatever information they were presumably basing this claim on to the defense – which is of course illegal.

Trump's defense team wanted to bring in Bradley Smith in order to properly explain Federal Election law – which is essentially the predicate that this entire case is built upon – and the Judge said "no." Merchan refused to allow him to testify without such severe restrictions on what he would and would not be allowed to say – that he essentially hamstrung any argument that Smith could possibly make.

This is the definition of a rigged trial.

Ultimately the complete none-existence of any form of factual evidence or "legal" legal proceedings resulted in a jury being instructed by Judge Merchan to formulate their verdict based on the most abstract and vague set of instructions I have ever seen.

Quote: "Although you must conclude unanimously that the defendant conspired to promote or prevent the election of any person to a public office by unlawful means, you need not be unanimous as to those unlawful means were."

The alleged "unlawful means" for the jurors to consider were:

1: Violations of federal campaign finance law.

2: Falsifying other business records, such as paperwork used to establish the bank account used to pay Stormy Daniels, bank records and tax forms.

3: Violation of city, state and federal tax laws, including by providing false or fraudulent information on tax returns, "even if it does not result in underpayment of taxes."

So the jury did not have to agree on what exactly he did – only that he could have done any one of these three things – and all of this is heavily predicated on the suggested narrative that Trump supposedly committed any number of these crimes, in order to commit a completely separate crime that he is not being charged with.

And the jury rendered a "guilty" verdict.

It reminds me of that old song "The Night the Lights Went Out in Georgia," when they sing "The Judge said guilty on a make-believe trial."

This wasn't just the definition of a rigged trial – this is the definition of a Kangaroo Court.

While I am sure that this is going to go to the Court of Appeals and then inevitably get kicked up to the Supreme Court – whatever happens next doesn't necessarily matter.

What matters is that this "trial" sets the tone and sets the precedent that it is "acceptable" for the chief political rival of a sitting President of the United States, to be brought up on criminal charges by allies of that President – no matter how spurious, fictitious, fraudulent or unfounded those charges might be – specifically in order to smear that rival with a "felony" charge so that the current Administration and the Liberal media can publicly condemn them.

You do not have to love Donald Trump – you do not have to like Trump – and you certainly do not have to agree with, or even support Trump, in order to recognize the severity of what has just taken place. To realize how catastrophically ruinous – how dangerous – this precedent truly is.

This is the sort of thing which throws back the veil on incipient tyranny, and publicly states that it is perfectly acceptable for any political entity holding power to attempt to jail their opponent.

It's the death of democracy.

This is the sort of thing which dictates all future political maneuvers in this country from this day forward. Nothing else in this nation is ever going to be the same in the wake of this verdict – regardless of what happens during the election – because history will always be there to remind us that this was allowed to happen.

When you are allowed to just arbitrarily ignore the law – to twist the rules into pretzel-like contortions in order to achieve your desired outcome – then there is no more law.

The law is not real – it is a concept – it is an idea that becomes tangible through a universal agreement of the rules. If you break those rules – if you ignore them, or throw them out the window – then the law doesn't mean anything. It's just a word, a turn of phrase. It becomes powerless and ceases to exist.

This is the ultimate desecration of our legal institutions.

It is the literal rape of Lady Justice.

It is the symbolic manifestation of forcing her down into the blackened churning mud and sodomizing her in full view of the public.

Is this truly where we have gotten to in America? Is this truly what our once great nation – full of liberty and pride – now considers to be *justice*?

If this is what we now call "justice" then I will have no part in it.

Chapter XXII: Hatred

I want to talk about something very serious right now. Something which seems to have wormed its way into the very center of modern life – something dark and hideous that is rapidly growing unchecked in the world.

That something is hatred.

Hatred is such a strong word. It is an ugly and harsh word which gets thrown around an awful lot in the modern day – but what does it actually mean?

As a boy, I would use it so casually and without any real thought. If there was a show on TV that I didn't like, or food on the table that I couldn't stand – I said that I "hated" it.

My Nanny used to get so cross with me, and tell me that I shouldn't say such things – but I didn't understand. I was just a child and her reaction didn't make any sense to me.

As a man however, I do understand it. I have learned what it means to hate – as well as to be hated – but even with that fundamental understanding, I find that there are still some aspects to this most distinctly human emotion which I cannot comprehend.

I understand the concept, the principle and the practice of hating something that hates you in return. Something that threatens you or your loved ones with harm – but to hate a thing that you're not connected to? That is something which I cannot understand.

I am a man who hates many things – but hatred for the sake of hatred – is not an issue that I have ever struggled with.

Hamas has just attacked Israel – and they have done this out of hatred. I am not Jewish, and nor am I the correct person to ask about the distinction between Jews and Caucasians – but I am fully capable of recognizing this attack as an act of evil.

An act of terror.

An act of hatred.

I have friends who are Jewish and I have friends who are Muslim. I myself am Catholic. I have friends who are Baptists and Methodist – I have friends who are Agnostic and even friends that do not believe in spirituality at all.

I have friends of every ethnicity – all coming from many different social and cultural backgrounds.

I cannot for the life of me understand the concept of hating – truly hating – anyone or anything for simply existing. I can dislike certain things, or disagree with certain things – but to "hate" something that has no bearing on my life in any way, shape or form, is absurd to me. It's incomprehensible.

Since the biblical days of Abraham and his sons: Ishmael and Isaac – Muslims have held a deep-seeded level of contempt for the Jews. A hatred that goes beyond religion and into their very culture itself.

I have two friends that came to America from Palestine, one from Gaza and the other from Hebron – and they have both spoken very openly what it was like for them growing up in that area of the world. What it was like in school – the things they were taught.

Here we might often teach children the basic principles of mathematics by using apples – you know what I'm talking about: "If Bobby has 1 apple, and Janie has 2 apples, how many apples do Bobby and Janie have?" That sort of thing.

Over there, children in schools are taught from a very young age to view Jewish people as inferior. As lesser. Both of my friends have corroborated this sentiment. They said that instead of using apples, children are taught the basics of math by using Jews. "If Ahmed kills 1 Jew, and Hasan kills 2 Jews, how many infidels have Ahmed and Hasan killed in the Glory of Allah?"

That is despicable.

I had heard something about those sorts of practices before but I never believed them until I got it straight from the horse's mouth.

That's why my friends love America – they love it because over here, they can get away from that kind of indoctrinated hatred. That ingrained sense of malice.

I want to be perfectly clear – I do not view all Muslims as some kind of hatemongers or terrorists – so many of them are just the most beautiful people that you could ever imagine. Going through the motions of life and trying their best to make it in the world, just like everyone else.

After all, it was G'afur G'ulom who during the second World War and the persecution of the Jews by Nazi Germany – and despite himself being Muslim – wrote a vivid and touching poem in which he stated to Adolf Hitler that: "If you want to kill the Jews, then you must kill me, for I am a Jew."

But still, there is a very real element of radical hostility and violence that permeates from somewhere deep inside of the religion and culture which cannot be ignored. Like a cancer, blackening the inside of the heart and mind with its secreted poison.

Have any of you watched the footage of the October 7th attack on Israel?

I have.

I watched the footage of that music festival being attacked. I watched the footage of that young girl's body being dragged naked through the streets. I watched the footage of that injured man getting his head cut off by a gardening tool while he was still alive.

I watched the footage of a father, desperately trying to get his family out of the upstairs window – only to be shot in the back and dragged back inside the house before he could also escape.

I watched the footage of that Israeli woman being wrenched out of one vehicle – the seat of her trousers soaked with blood from the anal raping that she endured – only to be pushed into another vehicle and taken away to experience God only knows what else.

I watched the footage of Muslim children beating a little Jewish boy with sticks, taunting him to cry out for his mother who was already dead.

I watched the footage of babies heads being decapitated and lined on top of fence-posts up and down the road.

I watched the footage of top leaders inside of Hamas viewing the chaos and carnage – before getting down on their knees and praising Allah for such a "glorious victory" over Israel.

I watched that footage. That footage which Hamas provided on their own – because they wanted it to be seen.

And you know what else I watched? I watched thousands upon thousands of so-called "Americans" take to the streets all across this nation and cheer for the bloodshed and carnage. Cheer for the persecution of the Jews. Cheer for the slaughtering of civilians – the raping of women – the beheading of babies.

This country which has suffered so much at the hands of Terrorism, rang out in rapturous glee at the sight of this disgusting display of barbarism.

It made me sick to my stomach. I'm still sick to my stomach.

I lost a friend in that raid. She was an American Jew and wanted to go home to get in touch with her "roots."

It took weeks to find out what happened to her – but they found her body in a little town outside of Tel Aviv. I don't know any more details than that – other than they killed her alongside her boyfriend.

Do you know what great crimes she committed? She liked listening to music and watching bad movies. She liked tasting new foods and reading books. She owned a one-eyed old cat and had a job making ice cream, which she loved – because she loved seeing the children smile when they ate it.

I'll never know what happened to her. I'll never know exactly what she went through. I can only hope that she died quickly, and that those butchers didn't carve her up, or worse...

The very thought of those "people" rushing out into American streets to celebrate this kind of brutality – that is a thing which makes me hate.

I've sat here in sheer disbelief and watched as not just ignorant masses of the "American" public rallied in celebration of the events taking place – but as members of Congress itself have joined in the squalor.

"People" like Rashida Tlaib and Alexandria Cortez who froth at the mouth with warmongering ideologies and seemingly take some kind of twisted and perverse pleasure in their venomous hatred of the Jewish people. Calling for a demilitarization of Israel prior to the Terrorist attacks – and condemning them for retaliation afterwards.

And this disgusting mindset isn't found just within the halls of the American government, but stretching out into NATO and the United Nations as they all seem determined to tell Israel that they have no right to defend themselves. That they must simply roll over like a dog to be whipped. They bark orders, demanding a ceasefire and zero retaliation.

I've heard accusation after accusation being thrown at Israel, proclaiming them to be an "Apartheid State" with absolutely no evidence to back up this claim. Is the situation in the Gaza Strip messy? Yes – yes it is – but it's not so messy that Israel doesn't boast over two million Islamic residents that hold full citizenship, complete with state benefits, active and flourishing businesses and all of the freedoms guaranteed to any other citizen of the country.

This strange obsession with dismantling Israel's "Iron Dome" and demilitarizing the nation is so catastrophically irrational, childishly irresponsible and blatantly antisemitic.

As Golda Meir once so eloquently put it: "If the Arabs put down their weapons today, there would be no more violence. If the Jews put down their weapons today, there would be no more Israel."

These people are fighting for their lives and the rest of the world – at least the rest of the world's Governments – have basically told them to "Fuck off and die."

Do you even understand what Hamas stands for? This isn't some splinter-cell or internal faction that broke off to attack Israel – this was a democratically elected organization that freely offered up a mission statement: "The Day of Judgment will not come about until Muslims fight Jews and kill them."

You can go read it for yourself, this is public information – go read the 1988 Covenant of Hamas – they tell you to your face *exactly* how they feel: "Israel will exist and will continue to exist until Islam will obliterate it, just as it obliterated others before it." This is what "Americans" are cheering for?

This is the genocidal terrorist regime that "Americans" are using to justify attacking Jewish students on college campuses – forming human walls to keep Jewish students from attending classes – and revoking security clearance for Jewish teachers across the country?

This makes me fucking sick.

This is a thing which makes me hate. This is a thing which makes me feel hatred in my heart.

I feel so much contempt towards the modern Liberal. I hate them for their radical nature – I hate them for their oppressive existence.

I hate them for being alive. I hate them for knowing that they exist – like spiders under stones – they're there, breeding and crawling and wriggling with so much vitriol and malice.

If you were to ask me, genuinely, what would I do if I had the power to do anything in the world? I'd have anyone and everyone that has voted Democrat within the last forty years put up against a wall and shot – that's what I would do, and that terrifies me.

It terrifies me because that is not how a good man should feel. It's not how a good Christian should feel – how a good American should feel – but it is how I feel.

It is how I feel because it is how I have been made to feel. I have been made to feel this way because I have lived the majority of my conscious life feeling as if my back were against the wall.

Feeling as if there were no way out except forward.

And I know for a fact that I am not alone in that regard. I know for a fact that there are millions of people like me that are buckling under the weight of this antagonism and condemnation.

It's gotten so bad that, short of having any prior knowledge of a person beforehand – if you were to tell me that X, Y or Z was a Liberal – I automatically feel my stomach twist into knots just thinking about them. My instinctual gut-reaction is to despise them for being affiliated with this corrupted way of thinking. To revile them for their ideologies – and frankly to hate them simply for existing.

This level of hate that we see in the world today – it is not some hellish nightmare from a far-off land – it is here, it is everywhere.

When you indoctrinate half of the country into thinking that anyone they disagree with is a fascist – is a Nazi – that level of extremism becomes ingrained into the hearts and minds of the people that you yourself are demonizing.

They're never going to forget that.

I am never going to forget that – and it scares me.

It scares me because we are becoming a nation that teaches its children to count their numbers by hatred. We are becoming a nation where civil discourse has died.

The very nature of our modern lives is one of ingrained spite, bitterness and distrust. It scares me to think of what is going to happen next – of where this current road is going.

All it takes is one final straw to break the camel's back – and all hell breaks loose.

All it takes is for one person to say "enough is enough" and before you know it, there's another civil war on our hands. I don't want to see this nation torn apart by conflict. I don't want to see the bodies and the bloodshed spilling out into the streets of this country – but if things do not begin to change then that is where we're heading.

The only thing we're going to see is more destruction, more chaos, more devastation, more death.

That is all that hatred provides... and I hate it for it.

- dedicated to the memory of Alexandria -

Chapter XXIII: Storm Clouds

With each passing day, I wake up and look around myself at the world we have created. A world that is standing upon the razor's edge of a knife, teetering on the brink of global conflict. It is a planet which exists in a near constant state of fear, hatred and division. It is a thing of chaos – hell bent on total and absolute destruction.

It is my personal fear that we are plunging headlong into a third *World War*.

My entire life, it seems, has been shaped by war. That looming threat of *Terror* which has been ever-present in the East for just about as long as I can remember. The haunting images of burning bodies and blood-soaked sand that still awakes me in the dead of night, even all these years later.

It frightens me.

I am not a conspiracy theorist by nature. I do not walk around my house wearing a tin-foil hat and keeping a watchful eye for the "Little Green Men" to come down and abduct me or make crop-circles. I do not flinch away from my dollar bills, fearing that some illusive and shadowy organization has planted microscopic cameras and microphones into them in order to monitor my every action. I do not believe that half of our current political leaders are actually body doubles wearing rubber masks – and I'm certainly not an idiot who believes the Earth is actually flat.

What I am, however, a man who has a mind – a free-thinking brain, with two eyes and two ears and the cognitive ability to stop and look at what is going on around me and formulate a cohesive thought.

I truly believe, in my heart and in my soul, that it is no simple coincidence that Russia's invasion of the Ukraine, China's bellicose presence at Taiwan and the Hamas attack on Israel have so perfectly coincided with the crumbling state of America's domestic situation.

That the people who have wormed their way into prominent positions of power throughout every level of government in this country, are actively trying to destroy our nation and plunge the United States into an open civil conflict.

Democrats, Liberals, Socialists, Communists – whichever you care to call them – have openly demonstrated their *contempt* for America, both verbally and actively.

Their policies have crippled our economy to the point that they have sent this country into a recession, and all but dissolved the middle-class family. They have turned our southern border into a pipeline for illegal immigrants, cartels and terrorists, which flood into our cities bringing crime and drugs along with them. They have flagrantly abused every privilege and power afforded to their offices, stepping over the Constitution and weaponizing the Justice System for political sway.

They have sown the seeds of dissension, driving a wedge into the heart of this country by pitting the populace against one another with divisionist rhetoric and identity-based politics. They have fully-integrated themselves into our school systems and places of higher education, where they blatantly abuse and indoctrinate our children into aligning with their perverted ideology – and they have taken near-total control over almost all forms of mainstream media, where they have constructed a narrative that publicly denounces and demonizes *any* opposition to their agenda.

Numerous and prominent Left-wing political leaders and representatives such as Cortez, Omar, Tlaib, along with the rest of "The Squad" and other such figures in their wheelhouse, have openly derided the concept of Democracy and publicly condemned the practices of Capitalism.

Several-times Presidential Nomination Candidate Bernie Sanders has himself gone on record, stating that he believes the horrific effects that Communism has had on countries like Cuba and Venezuela, where the people have so little food that they have to line up for government supplied rations: "is a good thing".

Former U.S. President Barack Obama, along with the aforementioned members of "The Squad" and others on the Democrat side of the political aisle, have publicly and *frequently* denounced the teachings and practices of Christianity and Judaism, as well as the fundamental principles of Judeo-Christian Ethics – which are the cornerstone of our nation – in favor of a far more Pro-Radical Islamic sentiment and view.

Not an American, but still our neighbor, Canadian Prime Minister Justin Trudeau – a man whom these aforementioned political figures align with and have touted as an admirable and inspirational proponent of social justice in the world – has stated plainly that he thinks the way in which China's Dictator Xi Jinping handles his country is admirable. In fact, don't take it from me – take it from the man himself: "There's a level of admiration I actually have for China. Their basic dictatorship is actually allowing them to turn their economy around on a dime."

Then again, I suppose considering that since the Canadian government felt that it has the right to threaten to revoke Dr. Jordan Peterson's medical license unless he returned to Canada and underwent "Social Re-Education Training", it would make sense that Socialist paragons like Trudeau would admire the basic dictatorship of China, a country which captures and "re-educates" Uyghurs in their Xinjiang region.

As a matter of fact, just in the last few days Left-wing idol and poster-child Hillary Clinton suggested that Republicans needed "reprogramming".

Oh and I bet she'd do it, too.

These people – and the people who voted for them. The people *like* them – are the reason that we're in the state we are today.

In 2008, Barack Obama won the Presidential Election and took Office the following year, along with then Vice President Joe Biden, on a campaign built around the principle of bringing "*change*" to this country – and he *did*.

The Obama Administration was the first in American history to *routinely* tout the virtues of socialist ideological propaganda. To *openly* rebuke the founding principles of our nation's Constitution. To repeatedly attack the rights and practices of Jewish and Christian institutions.

To introduce divisional concepts such as equity over equality, systemic racism and intersectionality into the social zeitgeist – and to *willfully* disrupt the national system of checks and balances by increasing an emphasis on centralized, top-down governmental control, and the active abuse of executive powers through the wielding of unilateral authority.

He created a multitude of grossly overreaching new social welfare programs. Spent billions of taxpayer dollars on private sector industries.

Mocked and disregarded the previous administration's carefully laid out exit strategy from Afghanistan. Pushed a terrible and horrendous government _mandated_ healthcare system onto the public. Doubled-down on Federal rule and the reduction of independent States Rights. Spearheaded the efforts of Governmental-overreach by spying on the American people. Continuously attacked and suppressed American farmers and the agricultural circuit. Enacted a series of complicated new corporate tax incentives that only benefited the top 1% of financial earners – and forced the middle-class citizen to foot the bill for all of it.

In 2009 Obama was handed a Nobel Peace Prize for doing absolutely nothing, and then proceeded to sanction more "precision" drone strikes during his first year in office than Bush carried out during his entire administration – culminating in the indiscriminate death of thousands of civilians – including a Doctors Without Borders field hospital that had already established a well documented GPS location.

In 2011 Obama dragged the United States into the Arab Spring and the unnecessary Libya conflict without any form of authorization or adherence to the War Powers Act – claiming that the use of "kinetic-warfare" superseded the need for Congressional approval.

In 2012 Obama and his then-Secretary of State, Hilary Clinton, allowed the American Embassy to be attacked in Benghazi – and despite proven and documented knowledge of the impending terrorist assault – he gave _explicit_ orders for U.S. military assets and personnel to "stand down" and allow the embassy to fall.

Again in 2012, Obama drew his infamous "red line" in the sand and allowed Syria to cross it, essentially giving them full permission to openly utilize chemical weapons against civilians during its civil war and gave rise to terrorist organizations such as Al Nusra. His hollow threat not only allowed Russia the opportunity to sweep into Syria and look like the "good guys" for supposedly handling and overseeing the "dismantling" of Assad's chemical weapons – it also lost the United States a great deal of credibility in the eyes of the world stage.

In 2013 Obama backed the Egyptian military dictator Abdel el-Sisi and ensured further destabilization of the region by continuing to involve the United States in an ongoing series of regime-changes across the Middle

East, which would ultimately lead to the growing support of various organized Islamic terrorist groups throughout the region.

In 2014 Obama lifted the economic sanctions on Iran, allowing them to rebuild their nuclear weapons stockpile and begin to effectively regrow as one of the region's leading terrorist sponsors – utilizing their Hezbollah proxy and offering American-backed financial aid to support as-Assad in Syria, Hamas in Palestine, and numerous other terrorist groups throughout Bahrain, Lebanon, Yemen and the like.

Again in 2014, Obama allowed Putin's Russia to march unchecked into Ukraine and annex the Crimea – a decisive military conquest which Obama all but sanctioned when he showed the world that the United States was unwilling to "make good" on their promises or follow through with their threats.

The list goes on.

Barack Obama has been held up as some kind of hallmark of Liberal Progressivism, and touted as a true "tour de force" when it came to American statecraft. They said that Obama's economy was the "greatest economy" that the world has ever seen – and that all Americans were able to live through an unprecedented "Era of Hope" because of the efforts of this, one, man.

It's a complete lie.

I do not necessarily blame Barack Obama for inheriting the Great Recession that America faced in the wake of a near-decade long war and *serious* financial mismanagement by Wall Street and the bank systems – but his shortsighted and ineffectual policies did nothing but ultimately mangle the economy into a twisted, broken mess. I know – because I lived through it..

I watched as each month my mother's paycheck afforded fewer and fewer groceries. I watched as the gas prices soared to at-the-time record highs. I watched as fewer and fewer businesses were hiring because despite his insistence that he created the "lowest unemployment in history," unemployment skyrocketed. You cannot say that unemployment is going down when just about every state – even politically aligned states like California – were experiencing record high rates of unemployment at the time. It doesn't work that way.

The reality is that Obama was a terrible President who either indirectly or sometimes outright actively supported the rise of global terrorism. He completely dismantled the tapestry of American life through a combination of sheer ignorance, incompetence and often malicious intent – and his actions saw fit to thrust the country into chaos by shaping the United States into the dysfunctional political hotbed of division that it is today.

Joe Biden, who was Obama's Vice President, came into office on the back of the notoriously *questionable* 2020 election – and immediately set about the task of undoing everything that Donald Trump had set in place.

In 2021, Biden began waging a war against the Immigration System and threw open the American border, spending billions of taxpayer dollars on ineffectual policies and flooding the country with illegal immigrants in numbers spanning *to-date* an approximated 6.9 million. This issue is not relegated to the Border States or the West Coast – as my own state of Georgia is currently home to over 400,000 illegal immigrants who are actively tanking the state's economy.

Again in 2021, Biden actively illegitimized twenty years of blood, sweat and tears when he ordered American military forces to withdraw from Afghanistan and surrendered the country back into the hands of the Taliban. The botched withdrawal itself echoed the infamous *Fall of Saigon* in 1975, with thousands of Afghan civilians desperately clinging to the sides of U.S. aircraft leaving the runway.

Also in 2021 Biden's crucial role in the orchestration of the national COVID-19 lock downs, as well as his open contempt for the American public, became so pronounced and unhinged that he went so far as to utilize his executive power to force unproven and poorly tested injections onto the populace under the threat of unemployment if they did not comply – and further threatened to mandate special "tags" or other forms of personal identification in order for the average citizen to even be allowed basic access to highway and interstate travel – effectively threatening to take the American people hostage in their own country.

In 2022 Biden mirrored the inaction of Barack Obama by standing down and allowing Valdimir Putin to fully invade the Ukraine. Unlike Obama however, Biden then proceeded to send billions of dollars worth of weapons, artillery, armaments and munitions – as well as general aid funding – into the war while claiming total "neutrality." To date, Biden has spent over 44 billion dollars on a war that we're *supposedly* not involved in.

Again 2022 Biden's horrendous mismanagement of the economy, coupled with his active opposition toward the American people and his complete inability to quell the threat of Russia – led to the U.S. economy's backslide into open recession – with rapidly spiraling prices in store, and gas prices in my area alone reaching over $5 a gallon – forcing the nation to sign emergency tax cuts on the State and Federal level.

In 2023, Biden turned a blind eye to the plights of Israel in the wake of the terrorist attack by the Palestine-based organization, Hamas, in which they infiltrated and butchered over 1600 Israeli men, women and children using American military equipment such as the U.S. M4, Mk18 and M27 – most of which were part of the 7 billion worth of equipment left behind during the flight from Afghanistan – making him directly responsible for every single death sustained by Israel during the attack.

In 2024, Biden has now blatantly weaponized the American Justice System by effectively leveraging it against his key political rival – essentially damning the United States to a future dictatorial tyranny if nothing is going to be done about it.

I have sat here for most of my life, trying to keep my peace – trying my best to keep my head down – and I simply cannot do it any more.

I am not foolhardy enough to think that there is no such thing as corruption inside of the Republican party – or naive enough to think that politicians in general actually care about me, as a person, as an individual – but I have never seen the sort of rampant corruption and outright contempt for mankind as what is on display in the modern Democrat party.

These are the people who have funneled billions of taxpayer dollars into aggressive foreign powers that have used our own funding against our allies. The people who have not only endorsed the rise of domestic terrorism inside of this country, but have actively released known terrorists back into the world at large.

For God's sake, Canada paid over ten million dollars to a member of Al-Qaeda who murdered U.S. troops – and Biden literally just handed over a black-market arms dealer who was *so* notorious, that his name was actually

"The Merchant of Death," and he gave this man *back* into the hands of Russia.

There is absolutely nothing you can do to convince me that these people – and more specifically the people *voting* for these people – are not fully aware of exactly what they're doing.

Whether we are talking about sheriffs and judges, to mayors and governors, or assemblymen and senators – all the way up to the office of the President itself – I have seen *nothing* in my lifetime short of pure unadulterated *malice* on the part of Liberals and Progressivists.

This ideology... it's incompatible with the United States of America. Frankly, it is incompatible with the *world*.

I have watched as this twisted and perverse way of thinking has rooted itself into the very cornerstones of my country.

I do not trust you.

I *cannot* trust you – because you have shown yourself to be untrustworthy.

Everything you do – everything you touch – it rots away like a disease.

There is an illness at work here which eats away and erodes the very flagstones of my country – and threatens to eradicate every facet of American life.

It is called *Socialism*.

It is nothing short of Communism, repackaged and re-branded for the modern day. It is a malignant and cancerous blight – filled to the brim with black pus and corrosive bile which seeps into the very heart of a nation and destroys it from the inside out.

We have seen this outcome – not in theory, but in practice – time and time again. The great Communist Manifesto of Marxism outlines a very clear and consistent method of attack.

To win the people: you must control the narrative – and we have watched the mainstream media become utterly consumed by Left-wing political bias.

To win the people: you must abolish religion – and the religious persecutions of Christianity and Judaism are at an all-time high.

To win the people: you must break the home – and in record numbers we see families torn apart, and an unprecedented level of disdain for the traditional father figure in the American household.

To win the people: you must control the young – and we have seen the world of academia become dominated by radical Left-wing ideologists and liberal progressivism.

Every single strategy and tactic in the Communist playbook can be seen on full display, and is publicly at work here in America as well as the West at large. A single, overshadowing and all-powerful governing body which controls the country, removes personal freedoms and *forces* the population to become dependent on it is exactly what the Socialists want – and that's exactly what we already have.

Lady Liberty has been forced into the mud and raped – her principles violated and her image dismantled for all to see.

There is no instance in my mind where any man of sound reason could *ever* listen to these views and ideals and find them sane – and yet clearly there is come enticing infatuation which has given this agenda its rise to power.

Society has turned a blind eye towards the systematic deconstruction of ethics and morality. They have brushed aside the mass weaponization of the American justice system. They have looked away from the countless scores of aborted young and closed their eyes to the desecration of the human body.

If we wish to have a Democracy, then the poison of Socialism cannot be allowed to run within our walls.

Fyodor Dostoevsky warned us about the evils of Socialism some fifty years prior to the Russian Revolution. He watched in real-time as this ideological horror took its first steps into the world, and eventually spread across Europe like a wildfire.

In his famous novel, *Demons*, Fyodor gives a fairly clear and concise example of why mankind and "Socialism" are intrinsically incompatible with one another – quote: "Human nature is not taken into account; it is excluded, it's not supposed to exist...they believe that a social system that has come out of some mathematical brain is going to organize all humanity at once and make it just and sinless in an instant... That's why they so dislike the living process of life; they don't want a living soul...but what they want, though it smells of death and can be made of India-rubber is at least not alive, has no will, is servile, and won't revolt."

The core foundation of Socialism is a lie. It is not predicated on the well being of the masses – but on the well being of those in power who have successfully convinced the masses that they have their best interest at heart. That is why there can be no room for strong men in the socialist world – because strong men form strong opinions and are capable of speaking for themselves.

That is why there can be no God in the socialist world – because the existence of God itself dictates a higher authority than those who sit in power.

Dostoevsky outlines this issue as well in his last work *The Brothers Karamazov:* "For socialism is not merely the labor question, it is before all things the atheistic question, the question of the form taken by atheism today, the question of the Tower of Babel built without God, not to mount to Heaven from earth but to set up Heaven on earth."

Socialism – or rather its true name, Communism – is an ideology specifically designed to strip the people of everything they hold dear to their hearts and to crush them under the weight of intense scrutiny and excessive rule. It systematically cripples the masses by undermining every established aspect of human society and then collapses those societies by whatever means necessary, in order to rebuild them in its own ideological image.

That is why whenever you hear a raving Communist shouting down all the principles of Capitalism and denouncing every aspect of American life – they still aren't willing to leave the country. They aren't willing to leave because they do not *want* to leave – what they "want" is to *change* the country.

The issue for these people isn't simply a question of being in a place that does not align with their beliefs – it is a question of enforcing those beliefs onto everyone else. That's why they won't go.

They're conquerors and usurpers.

They're villains – and they're perfectly willing to do whatever it takes for them to win. Here in America they often claim to support the concept of "Democracy" so that they can come out looking like a team player – but then they'll actively abuse Democracy by attempting to subvert the systems of checks and balances. Pushing for legislation which lowers the voting age to sixteen in order to secure the uneducated vote – or pushing to remove voter identification requirements so that they can stack the vote with illegals.

These are not initiatives to protect democracy – these are initiatives to destroy it.

Every one of these actions are incredibly well thought out and calculated. They're strategical, surgical and efficient.

It was Khrushchev himself who once said: "We can't expect the American people to jump from Capitalism to Communism, but we can assist their elected leaders in giving them small doses of Socialism, until they awaken one day to find that they have Communism. We do not need to invade the United States, we will destroy you from within."

That is the prophetic state of my country – and we have ironically allowed it to become this way, because of freedom.

Our freedom of speech allows anyone the right to say whatever they want – at least in theory – and it denies the government any means of legitimately shutting down the radicalized factions that seek to destroy us.

Freedom of speech should not mean the freedom of falsehood. It should not mean the freedom of oppression – and it certainly should not mean the freedom of terror.

In short: *Freedom* should not imply the freedom to destroy itself – but unfortunately it often does.

Maybe *that's* truly what's wrong with America – that it is a nation which exists with a free license for self-destruction based on the grounds of its own founding principles – and the very nature of its own intrinsic virtues.

I truly believe in my heart of hearts – and in the pit of my very soul – that this "faction" for lack of a better term, is actively seeking to overthrow the country. It is attempting to supplant this once-great nation with a monstrous design of their own making.

They have completely crippled the economy and have utterly strangulated the middle-class. They have orchestrated a drug-crisis in order to keep the people complacent and subdued. They have thrown open our borders and rendered our cities into chaos. They have repeatedly attempted to dismantle our armed forces and to suppress the population so that the country cannot defend itself.

They have manufactured a sense of wide-scale division through the instigation of racial animosity and the rise of identity-based politics. They are openly indoctrinating the future generation with ideological brainwashing and emotional manipulation. They have completely embedded themselves into every level of mainstream-establishment media, and they use it to control the narrative – to set the tone and tell the people that somehow they are the "good guys" and that everyone else who does not comply with their ideology is evil.

For the love of God, this is the party who sat an "American President" up on stage against a blood-red background, so that he could give a Hitler-esque speech about how half of the country should be viewed as a "threat" and as the "enemy."

Every move that they make is a motion to divide and suppress. To cripple and to maim – I *genuinely* believe that this is an active effort in order to purposefully destabilize the United States, and to propel this nation into   a   second   Civil   War.

And if that is indeed the case, then this will not be a war of horses and wagons – this will not be a war of muskets and cannons. This will be a war of drones and planes – a war of tanks and bombs.

It will be a thing of pure destruction.

And it is also my belief, that should America begin to tear itself apart – the greater world at large will take the plunge – and a third World War will sweep across the planet. If the United States is not a player in the game – is not a piece on the board – then that is exactly what I believe will happen.

And I do believe it is by *design*.

I do not want to think that – I do not want to feel that – I do not want to live with the fear of that.

But that is what I *believe*.

I believe it, because you cannot do these things to people – you cannot keep the engine running full-open and expect it not to blow. The temperatures in this country are rising. The tensions in our nation are palpable. The harbored resentments towards each other are becoming visibly electric in the air.

I think that something is going to break – and I think it's going to happen very soon.

When it does, I fear that an irreversible tidal wave is going to wash across the world.

Dark clouds are gathering on the horizon, and I'm not entirely sure that we can weather this storm.

Acta est Fabula

Chapter XXIV: Ishmael

I feel so tired, so exhausted.

I'm almost thirty – but I feel so much older than I really am. I'm in so much pain.

Everything hurts.

My body hurts – my mind hurts.

I barely sleep.

Tolkien once wrote of his famous character, Bilbo, that he felt "thin." That he felt like butter being scraped over too much bread – and that's exactly how I feel. I feel thin, and hollow.

Like a tiny ounce of butter on the edge of a knife that has been scraped, and scraped and scraped across the bread, until I've been worn away to the point of nonexistence.

Chipped away, whittled down, picked apart – whatever you care to call it – there's almost nothing of me left now. I feel so empty inside. My hands are writing these words but the pen feels heavy – my arms feel heavy – even the air inside of my lungs feels heavy.

I'm tired. I'm so very tired.

Whenever anything starts to look up – whenever things finally start to go my way – it breaks. It always breaks – everything breaks – and I have been broken right along with them. I can feel the cold touches of reality dragging my spirit out to sea – forever washed away by the boiling tide of fate.

My mother is gone now.

An illness took her – ran through her like a knife – and now she's gone. In less than a month she was gone. My grandmother is ailing. I've no real money to my name – the estate is in chaos.

I see no end in sight.

I cannot see an end in sight. I'm looking – I swear to you that I'm looking – but I cannot see it. I've looked for it everywhere. I've looked all around myself but I cannot find my way. I do not see the road anymore – it's simply gone – vanished into the fog.

What else is left for me now?

I feel so very sick – a fever has gripped me – my sweat is pooling in the ink and I can barely read the pages anymore. Decembers never looked so bleak.

She's been sent home now – buried in the family cemetery on the day before Christmas Eve. I was too sick to go with her. I didn't even get to see her go to ground.

I will go to Virginia in February to tend to my mother's grave. I'll pick a stone for her – one that I think she'd like. I will weep, and I will mourn upon my hands and knees in the muddy snow – and I will place such tender kisses upon the soil above her head – because she is my mama and I love her.

Oh dear God, help me...

I have returned to Georgia now, and her affairs are set in order. It rained so much that my ragged boots are soaked clear-through. I did kneel down in the mud, and got on my hands and knees – and I did lay tender kisses onto the soil above her head. Heaven was weeping right alongside of me – but the coldness of the rain felt like nothing compared to the heat running down my face.

I do not know which was more difficult – seeing her grave for the very first time – or having to leave her when it was finally time to go. I feel like such a failure – like such a traitor – I should have saved her somehow, but I don't know what else I could have done. I should have done something, anything, anything at all – but I couldn't.

The hard truth is that this will probably be the last time that I will ever visit home. The last time that I ever walk the fields of my ancestors, and feel the Virginia wind in my hair – for all my lights are darkened now – and the fire in my heart is spent.

Everyone has told me that it will "get better" and that I'll "move on" in my own good time – I do not hate them for it, but I wish that they would stop. They tell me all the things that people tell you when you grieve – that they know how you're feeling and they know what you are going through – but they don't know. They don't know how I feel, and they don't know what I'm going through.

It's not their tears that are staining my pillow every night.

They do not know what I am feeling, because only I can know what I'm feeling and there's only one "me."

Perhaps a stronger man, or a harder man – a better man than myself – could simply take all this in stride. Maybe he could live again and carry on to better days – but I don't think I have it in me.

I wanted to be better, to be harder, stronger – but I'm not. I wanted to be John Wayne – but I'm not.

Everything I've ever had is now slipping through my fingers and I find my grip is failing – everything is failing. I'm tired of always failing. I thought I could turn my life around. I thought I could make things better for once. I thought I could finally build a future for myself – I thought I could make my mother proud – but I couldn't.

I couldn't do anything. I cannot do anything.

I thought that I could be John Wayne... but I could not.

Now instead I am as Ishmael – both orphaned and alone. Cast off into the endless churning seas of my despair. Here I drift in solitude, helplessly clinging to the ruined coffin of my own broken heart – ever watching, ever waiting – for a vision of The Rachel to come and save me from these troubled and sorrowful waters which have so enveloped my soul.

I am searching for her, but I know she is not there – and the saddest truth of all – is that I know that she never will be.

Chapter XXV: Goodnight

The day has been dreary and the rain has been nearly constant. It only broke just a short while ago, and now a heavy fog has settled in. I'd been sitting on the back porch, watching – looking out at what's left of my home – and wondering what exactly it is that I'm supposed to do.

Now that mama's gone, the estate is in tatters. She left no provisions – there is no real money, the mortgage is outrageous and I don't make enough to keep it on my own. She never talked with me about final plans. She never talked to me about what I should do in case of an emergency.

I wasn't even able to get a burial plot with a vacancy beside it – so I won't be able to lie next to her when my time comes.

This place isn't a good home – but it's mine. It's my home, and now I'm going to lose it.

So bleak is my heart that I have sat here in silence for the better part of an hour, with the barrel of a .38 pressed into my mouth – the dismaying prospect of my future circling around me like a bird of prey.

The acrid taste of gunmetal still lingers on my tongue.

It was cold – so very cold – colder than anything that I have ever felt before. I can still feel it on my teeth, on my gums – it was colder than ice – and it tasted like... "forever."

When I couldn't bring myself to pull the trigger I fired a round into the dirt as if in some vain and impotent way of venting my anger and frustration onto the earth itself. The smoking chamber and stench of gunpowder being my only recompense for the hollow emptiness I feel inside.

I know this may sound silly, considering everything that I've just said – but I do not think that I am suicidal.

I do not want to die – I just can't stand the idea of living out the rest of my life in this world that we have built. In this hell that we have created – and worse than that, to do it alone.

I have often dreamed or fantasized about running away. About getting in my truck, picking a random direction and just start driving – with nothing but the stars to shine my way.

Cutting all ties and severing all bonds – just to feel freedom in my heart.

I often feel envious of the people that do. The ones who just up and vanish into the darkness of night, building new lives for themselves in greener pastures on distant shores. The ones who go where nobody knows their name, and start again with a clean slate. A fresh canvas.

An increasingly daunting and difficult task in the modern world, where everyone is marked and tagged. Where everyone is cataloged into file cabinets and data banks, forever traceable like branded cattle.

Where freedom isn't free – and it's paid for in paper.

I wish that I could give it up and start again. To be a different man, and tell a different story – but I can't.

I can't escape the demons which hound me. I can't escape the ghosts which haunt me. I can't escape the world which plagues me – and I can't escape the anguished cries which wake me in the dead of night – or from the horrible realization that those devastated wails are coming from myself.

I cannot escape from the life that I live. I only give you my words as a humble offering from one human being to another – and hope that you hear them – that someone will consider their meaning.

It is time for a change.

It is time to stop treating human beings like animals. It is time to stop politicizing every aspect of life. It is time to stop targeting the weak and the vulnerable. It is time to stop cowering before corporations and masses. It is time to stop harvesting children for gain.

It is time to stop sowing the seeds of dissension. It is time to stop empowering the people of spite. It is time to stop accepting the overreach of the government. It is time to stop following the conventions of evil.

It is time to stop closing our doors to our neighbors. It is time to stop turning away from the world. It is time to stop punishing the right for the wrong. It is time to stop allowing the guilty to walk free.

It is time to stand up for our freedoms and our liberties. It is time to put an end to authoritarian regimes. It is time to start acting like Americans again, and remember that Democracy is easily exploited.

It is time to stand up and protect those that need protecting. It is time to stop listening to the lies and the rhetoric. It is time to stop crawling like dogs for our masters. It is time to dismantle this Socialist machine.

It is time to stop thinking that we have all the answers. It is time to accept that some things simply "are."

It is time to stop foolishly trying to play God, and it is time to respect that which we already have.

It is time to start paying attention to the people that need it. It is time to start making this a world worth leaving to our young.

If we cannot do these things here and now – then there is no future for our world – and there is no future for the history of mankind. There will only be destruction, there will only be devastation – and in the wake of all these things – there will only be nothing.

And that's what I'm most afraid of.

I suppose it has come to that moment, when now is the hour of our parting. Never before have I felt this way. My thoughts and my feelings stripped bare and laid naked before you.

My hands are trembling as I write these final words. My mind is racing and my vision is blurry. I can feel my blood rising, and the heat is causing pools of sweat to drop down from my furrowed brow and blot upon the page.

My blood, sweat and tears have been poured into this work. My veins have been opened – and the very essence of my soul has been given to you, for better or worse.

I don't know if this book is going to achieve anything. I don't know if all of these words will ever amount to much. If the effort I have spent will pay off.

I imagine that it doesn't really matter, because either way I'll have lost the house before this book has the chance to do anything.

I didn't write it to try and say that my view of the world is the only view worth having, or that my opinions are the only ones worth listening to. I didn't write this to try and say that I have all the answers, or that somehow I know everything that's ever going to happen.

I only wrote it to try and make my mama happy – and to say all the things that I've had playing on my mind.

Essentially, all I wanted to say is that this life – this life we've built for ourselves – it doesn't work. It does not *work*. It is not working – not for me, not for all the people I've spoken to, or all the people I've watched who are struggling day in and day out just to get by – it doesn't work.

I guess that's just about the jist of it... this life doesn't work.

As I said, I imagine the time has come to finally end this great labor of mine. I've talked so much and about so many things – but if I don't stop somewhere I'll never get it done.

So I suppose I'll leave you then, with one final plea –tThe last act of a desperate man who is begging on his hands and knees.

I want to live in a world where America still stands for Freedom and for Liberty.

I want to live in a world where politics remain the principal business of politicians – and radicalized ideas of virtue aren't forced upon the population at every given turn.

I want to live in a world where children are free to run and play, without being subject to the corrupt and perverse machinations of people in power.

I want to live in a world free of extremists and insurgents who seek to dismantle the fabric of life – and impose their subjugation upon others.

I want to live in a world where monuments are not toppled, faiths are not shattered and families are not broken at the whims of the government.

I want to live in a world where America is a country governed by those who wish to keep it – and not by those who wish to rule it.

I want to live in a world where men and women are not pawns, and the differences between race and creed are not twisted for the purposes of manufactured division.

I want to live in a world where history is written by those who have read it – and not by those that have never touched it, or bothered to learn from it.

I want some semblance of order returned to normality – and an end to the constant and daily struggle of Good vs Evil.

I want Justice to prevail over the wicked.

I want Reason to prevail over ignorance.

I want life to be a thing worth living.

I want love to be a thing worth having.
I want an end to all this madness.
I want... to see my mama again.
I want...
I want...
Hope.

FIN

I'd like to give thanks to the people who have helped and encouraged me throughout the past year and a half long process of creating this book. I do not know if it will accomplish anything of note, but your continued efforts and support have not gone unnoticed – and certainly will never go unappreciated.

Dr. Benesh, Robert Cadieux, Stephanie Farmer, Tony Grgas, Lucy Harrelson, Larry Jordan, Nicholas Kenny, Savannah Pennington, Randy Perry, Eric Piccione, Kelsi Rutti – not to mention Thom, Kieran, Dan, Amber and the others – and of course, my Nanny.

From the bottom of my heart, *thank you.*

I'd also like to add a very special thanks to the Pabst Brewing Company for all the PBR that has been cold and refreshing when I get home in the evenings, as well as the Brown-Forman Corporation for all the bottles of Jack Daniels and Old Forester that have kept me company through the endless long nights.

I would especially like to thank R. J. Reynolds Tobacco for making the finest cigarettes the world has ever known. I never would have made it through the first two chapters without my Camels.

Lastly I would like to thank my mother, to whom this book is dedicated – I will never forget you, your warmth or your smile. I wrote this book to make you proud, and it is my sincerest hope that if I have managed to accomplish anything, it is the keeping of my promise to you that I would see this through to the end. With any luck I'll be able to see you again soon. I love you mama.

Authored and illustrated by Benjamin S. D. Lockwood.
Photography by Benjamin S. D. Lockwood.
Editing, layout and formatting by Benjamin S. D. Lockwood.
Additional editorial assistance by Savannah E. Pennington.

www.ingramcontent.com/pod-product-compliance
Lightning Source LLC
Chambersburg PA
CBHW071357150726
48000CB00001B/58